CRITICS OF CONSCIOUSNESS

SARAH N. LAWALL

CRITICS OF

THE EXISTENTIAL

HARVARD UNIVERSITY PRESS

CONSCIOUSNESS

STRUCTURES OF LITERATURE

CAMBRIDGE, MASSACHUSETTS, 1968

TO RENÉ WELLEK

"Rien n'existe plus pour le critique que cette conscience qui n'est même plus d'autrui, qui est solitaire
et universelle. La première, peut-être la seule critique
qui soit, c'est la critique de la conscience."

—GEORGES POULET

PREFACE

The British or American reader will find it hard to reconcile his own views with those expressed by the critics of consciousness. These critics do not read literature as we read it, and their analysis does not seem useful to our manner of reading. We are trained to look upon each work as an object to be studied and appreciated for itself. Moreover, we are trained in certain analytical methods that are objective, easy to use, and invariably productive. Because this objective or "formal" tradition of criticism has allowed us to derive intellectual and aesthetic enjoyment from a work, we have little patience with any approach that cannot be measured in the same terms. We may resolve to open our minds, but we shall nevertheless be hostile toward what appears to be an irrational approach to literature.

The critics of consciousness proceed upon assumptions that do not coincide with our views of literature. They look upon literature as an act, not an object. They refuse to make distinctions between genres; they look for a single voice in a series of works by the same author; they will not consider each work as an autonomous whole. What is more, they seek latent patterns of themes and impulses inside literature, and do not discuss the symmetries and ambiguities of the formal text. These critics describe words as nodes of energy carrying a specific human voltage, so that words as such cannot be analyzed in our ordinary way. Such a criticism cannot be assessed in formal terms, as these terms are completely foreign to its approach. Therefore the reader who wants to understand these critics must no longer think of literature as an aesthetic object that can be judged "good" or "bad."

The reader must also be willing to accept the use of the adjective "existential" as applied to literary criticism. This term has been given so many separate meanings that it has come to mean nothing—or, if it does mean anything specific, it is usually taken to refer to a particular philosophy that developed in France throughout the 1940's, which can be traced to the philosophers Heidegger and Husserl. This historic existentialism is known for its emphasis on choice and for its attempt to define human liberty in a world that lacks values or a code of behavior. It is a humanistic or political existentialism, and its main figures, like Sartre and Simone de Beauvoir, emphasize political rather than "literary" perspectives. They refer their apparently "existential" literary criticism to preconceived humanistic values. This historic existentialism has little to do with the existential perspective on literature, which admits no attachments to any criteria outside the literary work itself.

The "existentialism" of the critics of consciousness is confined to the analysis of human consciousness in literature. Man's awareness of his existence, and his manner of expressing this awareness, is the material for a criticism that calls itself "existential," "ontological," "phenomenological," "genetic," "thematic," or a "criticism of consciousness." Because the critics themselves are not professional philosophers, they are willing to use any term that seems to describe their critical method at the moment. Georges Poulet was the first to describe this criticism as a "criticism of consciousness"; he then called it a "genetic criticism," and recently a "thematic criticism." But these descriptive terms are all linked by their common concern with existence. "Ontological," for example, usually implies a theory of being; "phenomenological" refers to man's total awareness of his environment; "genetic" indicates an attempt to re-experience in reading the very genesis or birth of a work from an author's experience to its structure in words (unlike the prevailing English definition of "genetic criticism" as a kind of biographical fallacy); "thematic" describes themes of perception that combine in patterns of consciousness; and "existential" and the "criticism of consciousness" are comprehensive terms covering any shade of an investigation into those human perceptions that combine as "literature."

Above all, the critics of consciousness look upon literature as the verbal transcription of a coherent human experience. Literature, for them, uses the writer's perceptions and skill only to conceive a new, purely literary figure: the incarnate "author" whose experience gradually takes form in the text. This "author's" act of consciousness is the "act of literature." The whole theory of literary consciousness refers to this definition of literature. For these critics, the text is not a formal object, a political tool, a biographical clue, an historical document, a psychological symptom, a sociological "myth," or a religious revelation. They believe that literature is a self-contained human expression, and they never call upon outside standards to justify their observations. Because they cling to their views as consistently as formal critics cling to theirs, they cannot be called "extraliterary" except in a very provincial definition of the term. For them, literature creates a coherent human experience in words, and is not a static verbal pattern. The structure of the literary text, they maintain, is built upon a pattern of impulses, so that the critic must analyze both the written text and the latent experience suggesting its words.

Such a critical approach is bound to diminish the significance of surface textual forms, for it considers these forms only a part of the total literary experience. The critics of consciousness want to observe the writer's perceiving mind, to discover the patterns of perception embodied in his work, and to understand how these patterns of perception coordinate with the formal patterns of the text. We must therefore not expect these critics to speak of the text as a technical object, or to pay much attention to technical competence. The criticism of consciousness is totally different from our own approach, and it requires from the reader a new understanding of literature and a different manner of reading.

A fellowship from the American Association of University Women allowed me to gather the initial material for this study in Paris from 1959 to 1960.

Amherst, Massachusetts   S.N.L.
January 1968

CONTENTS

CRITICS OF CONSCIOUSNESS

INTRODUCTION

The most prestigious place in modern criticism has for a long time been
assumed by a formal, objective approach based on the standards of
Symbolism and its technically minded disciples. These disciples pride
themselves on their craftsmanlike appraisal of a work of art and on a
professional stance which considers other disciplines irrelevant and im-
material. They approach the work as an aesthetic object with objectively
ascertainable forms, and their method has the advantage of being exclusively literary and producing unimpeachable aesthetic observations. Its
specialized emphasis is a welcome relief from the historical and philosophical attitudes that used to tie literature to a variety of extraliterary
beliefs. This same method, however, tends to assume that it is the only
approach to literature—at least, the only really "literary" one; and its

1

exclusive proprietorship is now being challenged by a new approach that defines literature as a metaphysical expression and a transcription of existence.

The historical lines are now drawn between "objective" criticism and a European movement that analyzes the consciousness manifest in literature. This criticism of consciousness adopts many perspectives from existentialism, but from an existentialism broadly understood and not tied to a narrow Sartrean definition. It is opposed to the objective tradition loosely defined as American New Criticism and to a French academic tradition that is highly historical and based on the work of Gustave Lanson. Any analysis that studies a work as an object, for forms, meanings, varying interpretations, and dictional peculiarities, runs directly counter to this new European attitude in which a work is not an object but an "act" or "experience." The criticism of consciousness looks to the works of philosophers like Kierkegaard and Husserl, Heidegger, Sartre, and Merleau-Ponty; it draws upon the literary tradition of anti-formalism embodied in baroque, Romantic, and surrealist literature and finds its illustrations in the works of writers like Rilke, Kafka, Claudel, Supervielle, Eluard, Perse, and Char. Not the only trend in a culture composed of so many international and intellectual movements, still it represents a dominant atmosphere in which, according to poet-critic Yves Bonnefoy, "the best French criticism would range itself against the analysis of meaning." [1]

This criticism of consciousness or criticism of experience has developed in complete opposition to the familiar analytical, logical-positivist attitude in England and America. It has different historical roots and responds to different intellectual needs. Arising out of existential speculation during and after World War II, it reflects the crumbling of prewar paper moralities and the desire for a newly vital philosophy of human experience. The individual roots of this existential philosophy are of course Husserl and Heidegger—perhaps Kierkegaard, Jaspers, and Kafka—the literary culmination is a desire to attribute new importance to words and human expression. The work of art as a combination of technical subtleties is no longer important; its existence is justified because it is the concentrated expression of all humanity.

In spite of its roots in existentialism, the criticism of consciousness is

1. Yves Bonnefoy, "Critics—English and French, and the Distance between Them," *Encounter*, July 1958, p. 43.

not to be confused with existential philosophy. The best-known figures of existentialism are not literary critics, nor do they inspire the contemporary literary analysts. Jean-Paul Sartre, Simone de Beauvoir, Albert Camus, Gabriel Marcel, and Maurice Merleau-Ponty share one other quality: they are not primarily concerned with literary theory. Even Sartre, whose early work in *L'Imaginaire* considers the same layers of existence studied by later literary critics, shifts in his later studies to a nonliterary frame of reference. The Sartre of *Baudelaire* writes about the social animal creating literature rather than about literature itself, and his influence on purely literary criticism is consequently much diminished. It would be misleading to find the roots of the criticism of consciousness in the nonliterary aspect of existential philosophy. The literary critics of consciousness are associated with the existential perspective, but they have their own provenance and owe as much to literary as to philosophical history.

The names that represent this criticism of consciousness in literature may not be familiar to English readers: Marcel Raymond, Albert Béguin, Georges Poulet, Jean-Pierre Richard, Jean Starobinski, Jean Rousset, and Maurice Blanchot. These writers share the existential view of literature as a mental act, and some are related by the ties of friendship as well. All but Maurice Blanchot are associated in some manner with Geneva and with each other. They have been called the new "Geneva School" [2] or, more recently, the "genetic" critics. The Geneva critics develop a personal, subjective criticism, closely related to the development of literary history after Romanticism. Their accents are moral and humanistic, and their method a kind of spiritual historicism based upon the existential evidence provided by literature. Blanchot's attitude is less historical and more impersonal; indeed he is primarily an "existential" critic, and his antecedents are to be sought in recent philosophical history. As "genetic" critics, all these men, including Blanchot, analyze the human consciousness in literature at its very focal point or genesis. As practical critics, they try to coexist with a creative consciousness at the moment when experience ceases to be mute and takes on the appearance of words and the structure of words.

The Geneva criticism stems from Marcel Raymond's *De Baudelaire*

2. Although this group recognizes and accepts the term "Geneva School," it should not be forgotten that the epithet was originally used to describe the Geneva linguistic scholars Charles Bally, Ferdinand de Saussure, and Albert Sechehaye.

au surréalisme and Albert Béguin's *L'Ame romantique et le rêve,* both of which direct criticism toward analysis of feeling and imagination rather than toward verbal precision. Both propose new horizons for literary speculation. Georges Poulet, in particular, recognizes the determining influence of Raymond and Béguin upon his own works and method; although he broadens their approach to include more technical and philosophical ideas. Associated with Poulet are Jean-Pierre Richard, Jean Starobinski, Jean Rousset, and in the United States Joseph Hillis Miller. The geographical connection with Geneva is no longer so strong, and Poulet himself, now teaching in Zürich, was born a Belgian. However, Raymond and Béguin were both born in Switzerland, pursued their studies at Geneva, and form part of the movement in French Switzerland to retain ties with French culture and literature. Starobinski and Rousset are presently on the faculty of the University of Geneva (from which Raymond has recently retired). Thus, the critics as a group do retain more ties with French Switzerland than with any other geographical center. In addition, these men recognize their own affiliations: [3] each is not only a distinct theorist in his own right, but demonstrates varying aspects of a centrally developing attitude toward literature as conscious experience.

Maurice Blanchot's attitude is rather special. He is, to be sure, a critic of consciousness, but of a negative consciousness. Although Blanchot's work deals with literature's continual revolution around an original point of consciousness, this point is an abstract, neutral, and colorless core. He is not concerned with a positive personal experience, but with nothingness and death. His vision erases all the meaningful human attachments of the Geneva view and focuses on something that can only be called the reverse of any positive subjective experience. In Blanchot, individual existence disappears. He proposes, as the only road to "literature," a conscious annihilation of meaningful experience. Literature, for Blanchot, is a consciousness unattached to any fixed subject or object, but it is also a consciousness that is perceived through shifting attachments.

The Geneva critics and Blanchot represent two poles of a contemporary existential or genetic attitude toward literary expression. Apart from

3. See J. Hillis Miller, "The Geneva School," *Critical Quarterly,* Winter 1966, pp. 305–321.

their separate importance, these critics share a collective responsibility for the development of this attitude. It is their common effort, then, which is significant for our purposes. Their separate works will be examined only in order to establish each author's distinct identity as a basis for comparison—and to compensate for the lack of material presently available in English sources. Throughout, the growth of an idea is most important, both for its own interest and as a provocative counterproposal to the prevailing English and American satisfaction with "objects" as literature.

In tracing the growth of an idea, the theoretical perspective requires a shift in emphasis from the usual literary-historical or even biographical assessment. Thus, a history of literary-critical works would probably dwell almost exclusively upon the importance of Raymond's *De Baudelaire au surréalisme,* and Béguin's *L'Ame romantique et le rêve,* to the detriment of both critics' attitudes as a whole. Raymond's book occupies a peculiar position as the opening wedge in a series of thematic, quasi-existential studies of modern literature after Symbolism; it opened horizons which numerous other critics were quick to explore. In time Raymond would go on to discuss baroque and Romantic aesthetics in more detail, beyond what he says in *De Baudelaire au surréalisme,* and to assume his full role in the development of the criticism of consciousness. Albert Béguin also takes on his full role in this criticism only when all his works are considered. To many, Béguin is merely the author of *L'Ame romantique et le rêve,* and this study of dream symbolism and of the similarities between the German Romantics and modern French literature appeals to comparatists, literary historians, and many who do not adopt the existential point of view. On the other hand, the book itself forms but a small part of Béguin's total work—even a part he later disavowed. Therefore any study of Béguin, whose role extends far past the doctoral thesis published in 1937, must assimilate the theoretical tendencies of *L'Ame romantique et le rêve* into a whole perspective. Such a perspective inevitably subordinates the separate historical importance of Béguin's most famous work. This historical subordination is a necessary part of an analysis illustrating the origins and growth of a modern French criticism of literary consciousness.

The criticism of consciousness is a criticism of the author's experience conveyed in a text, and of his active consciousness at the moment of creation. Poulet coins the term "critique de la conscience" in his preface to Richard's *Littérature et sensation* and shows that this consciousness takes many forms in literature. It is the consciousness of individual subjective perceptions, or of an all-encompassing general existence, and exists in a special mental region of "interior distance." In this inner space, the author meditates on the distance between words and objects, and between human thought and the expression it finally reaches. This consciousness is pure human perception, but its coloring may differ from subject to subject. The Geneva critics describe a human communion in the literary consciousness of reality; conversely, Blanchot describes a staunchly isolated consciousness in which "the mind is its own place" and recognizes only an all-encompassing, neutral, and impersonal existence.

The idea of literary consciousness leads to an analysis of the work as a mental universe, a self-contained world where human experience takes shape as literature. In addition, the text's "experience" may focus inward or outward. Literature for the Geneva critics is a difficult but possible representation of reality; for Blanchot, literature is an "impossible" but actual creation. The Geneva critics discover "authentic" or "profound" expression in baroque, Romantic, and modern literature. They are concerned with authors who seize reality in a new and virgin state, and who express it in authentic, unintellectualized forms of language. Blanchot, on the other hand, recognizes no such authentic expression of reality. He sees only the eternal isolation of subject and object in the mental "distance" that separates them. His "reality" comes as the impersonal, negative existence which is left when the author gradually withdraws all characteristics of positive life from his literary expression. Consciousness in the first instance is temporary but positive; it is terminal and negative in the second. Both Blanchot and the Geneva critics unite, however, in viewing "authentic expression" as a struggle carried on in the mind's interior spaces, and as a mental discipline which seeks to comprehend experience by framing it in language. This creation in mental space attempts to fuse human perceptions of subject and object, and is thus an "experience" of life and an "act" of consciousness. The criticism aimed at this consciousness sees literature as an act or genesis and analyzes it as a drama taking place in the mind.

In order to penetrate this conscious act, the reader must develop a systematically empathetic approach in which he tries to re-create the experience embodied in the text. He must subordinate his own subjective personality to a new subjective identity which is gradually created and revealed in the course of the book. Because the text had its genesis in the existential space of the mind, the reader is expected to place himself within the same confines and the same experience, and to accept as orienting indications the book's attitudes and expressions.

This empathetic reading is evidently not aimed at a formal analysis of the text. It views literature as an existential experience and act of cognition, and consequently attributes to the reader only the task of extracting the work's original creative experience. The reader cannot view the text "from outside," in an aesthetic, formal, or evaluative judgment, for he must attempt to coincide with its very being and identity. Such an identity is neither formal nor biographical: the "author" is a literary, created "existent" visible only in the evidence of the text.

The consciousness perceived in an empathetic reading need not fit into a familiar pseudo-biographical formula. Although the Geneva critics tend to personify literary identities, Blanchot maintains a predictably impersonal approach. The Geneva critics assume that there are real perceptions and communicable experience: their analyses draw upon the entire body of an author's work and treat separate texts as so many individual manifestations of the same developing personality. Because they define a work as the expression of an individual personality, their reading is openly personal. It is aimed at an available personal experience which symbolizes and communicates part of the human condition —which makes possible communion among men. Blanchot admits no such positive interpretation, for he sees all experience as eternally isolated from any communication with reality or with fellow men. The work for Blanchot is cut off from both author and reader, and exists only temporarily for either—for the author when he creates it and for the reader when he coexists with it in the dramatic interior "act" of reading. The "being" contained in Blanchot's work is not a revealed author but a textually-symbolized experience. As such, it represents the neutral existence of the universe, and is attainable in the recreation of a similarly depersonalized experience. Both Blanchot and the Geneva critics agree upon the reader's empathetic subordination to literary experience, but their interpretations differ according to pre-existing views of creation and perception. Each interpretation, however, upholds the main existential premise of an empathetic reading as opposed to an exterior judgment based on form.

The antianalytical approach of the criticism of consciousness appears in two complementary perspectives: a subjective, personal attitude for the Geneva critics, and a subjective, impersonal attitude for Maurice Blanchot. The Geneva perspective forms a definite historical pattern of discovery and related theories from Raymond to Poulet and J. Hillis Miller. Raymond and Béguin are the historical forerunners of this theory, but they show it emerging from traditional ways of thought rather than give a coherent philosophy of literary existentialism. It is with Georges Poulet that this perspective takes on its full philosophical significance and influences the work of Richard, Starobinski, Rousset, and Miller. Poulet and Blanchot are the two writers most famous in their own right: they form two coordinate, positive and negative poles of a criticism of consciousness, and both critics tend to end in a Cartesian withdrawal into the self as ultimate perception. Poulet manages to incorporate the earlier consciousness of reality into a whole vision whose texture depends on positive experience, while Blanchot has stripped away all ties with earth to emerge as an impersonal, pure, and neutral consciousness. Their combined attitudes, nevertheless, give form and structure to a contemporary view that is still developing—to a literary theory that may not yet have reached its final form. Each writer, moreover, conducts his own analysis of consciousness and pushes as far as he can his view of its literary potentialities. Together, they map out many of the possibilities for an investigation of literary consciousness.

Because this study concentrates upon those particular men who have developed the criticism of consciousness, it omits a number of important critics. Any survey of contemporary French criticism would have to consider Jean-Paul Sartre, Maurice Merleau-Ponty, Lucien Goldmann, Claude Lévi-Strauss, Charles Mauron, Roland Barthes, and a number of journalists and academic critics as well. Still more closely related to the critics of consciousness are Jean Wahl, Gaston Bachelard, André Malraux, Jacques Maritain, and Gaëtan Picon, whose studies often echo themes of the Geneva School. Indeed, most critics who explore themes of awareness are related to critics of the literary consciousness. However, the group studied here has one distinguishing characteristic: all its members devote themselves to literature and derive a *literary* theory from their analysis of consciousness.

The criterion of a purely "literary" interest distinguishes these critics from those who use literature merely as part of a larger frame of reference. Jean-Paul Sartre's early works (*L'Imagination, Esquisse d'une théorie des émotions, L'Imaginaire, Baudelaire,* and *Situations I, II, III*) are obviously important for any critical approach that is related to existentialism. However, Sartre (even before his political "engagement") is more concerned with a theory of knowledge than with "literary" criticism. Similarly, Barthes and Merleau-Ponty each explore philosophical theories that go beyond literary interests.

André Malraux is primarily interested in a human adventure appearing in various styles and shapes. Art is form, to Malraux, as well as being the embodiment of man's spirit. His emphasis on plastic and verbal form distinguishes him from a criticism that wishes to re-create verbal experience. When his criticism touches upon the human consciousness creating literature, or upon man's existence revealed through art, then he is closest to the humanistic existential analyses of our main group.

Malraux discusses literature as consciousness when he analyzes the way in which the formal text organizes visions of reality. In his preface to *Sanctuary* (1933), he suggests that Faulkner composes by means of intuited scenes and counter-positions, and that these are only later transformed into characters. This description of the way characters grow out of an author's vision suggests Malraux' own novels: for example, *La Condition humaine* and *L'Espoir*. Malraux repeatedly discovers such a connection between vision and written form. When he writes about Manès Sperber's . . . *qu'une larme dans l'océan* (1952), he describes the book's hidden organization of impulses and symbolic acts: "the crystallization born of the privileged encounter of creative forces, and through which facts, become meaning, unite in a coherence which is foreign to logic and belongs only to art."[4] In the preface to Louis Guilloux' *Le Sang noir* (1935), he proposes two visions of artistic genesis: in one vision the artist transmutes chaos and gives it a meaningful form; in the other, he imposes his personal stamp and significance on eternal

4. André Malraux, preface in Manès Sperber, . . . *qu'une larme dans l'océan* (Paris: Calmann-Lévy, 1952), p. x.

formlessness. D. H. Lawrence revels in this formless existence. Malraux' preface to *Lady Chatterley's Lover* describes Lawrence's fundamental desire for a pure sense of sensuous existence: "Lawrence wants to be neither happy nor great: he wants *to be*." [5] Lawrence's characters, like Faulkner's, follow the basic impulse of their myth. Malraux' description of this "myth" ("it appeals not to our reason but to our complicity," p. 11) echoes the idea of a literary structure connected by underlying impulses. The preface to *Les Liaisons dangereuses* (1939) also speaks of human myths and conceptions of self that interact in a novel and create each writer's special "tone." Malraux' criticism centers around the comparison and interpretation of stylistic elements and does not develop a method of interpretation. His essays on art, or his novels, are more famous than his literary theories. In his prefaces, however, he examines a series of attitudes organizing literature, and thus aligns himself with critics who find patterns of consciousness.

The Christian existential humanism of Jacques Maritain and Gabriel Marcel comes very close to the criticism of consciousness when it speaks of literature as "knowledge." The later career of Albert Béguin develops along parallel lines to explain literature as a knowledge of the divine universe. Maritain's studies, from *Situation de la poésie* (1938) to the Mellon lectures collected as *Creative Intuition in Art and Poetry* (1953), look upon poetry as a "spiritual exercise," or an experience that embodies and reflects the human condition. Strictly speaking, these genetic theories cannot be called pure literary criticism, mainly because they interpret creative experience in the light of Catholic doctrine.

Gaëtan Picon's humanistic viewpoint brings him close to any examination of human awareness in literature. Moreover, he is a theorist and a friend of Georges Poulet. Picon does not limit himself to literary criticism, however, and his criticism itself is quite eclectic. His personal method is humanistic before it is either formal or existential. In 1945 he calls this attitude a "new humanism," saying that "our fortunes are not those of a rejuvenated rationalism: they are those of a new humanism. Mythic humanism." [6] Although Picon is an aesthetician who discusses

---

5. Malraux, preface in D. H. Lawrence, *L'Amant de Lady Chatterley* (Paris: Gallimard, 1951), p. 8.

6. Gaëtan Picon, "Réponse à Julien Benda," *Confluences*, no. 6 (August 1945), p. 585.

style, he works within a large frame of reference and often seems to adopt the modern humanism of the critics of consciousness. Like Malraux, he tries to describe the organization of human impulses that he finds in an author and his work. He describes the general structure of a work rather than its verbal technique. In *André Malraux* (1945) he discusses human idealism in Malraux' novels and says that Malraux, Bernanos, and Giono, like others of this generation and like the Romantics, are so wrapped up in their own personalities that they have left a strong personal imprint on their works. He discusses the structure of Malraux' novels as a dialogue and leaves until the end a short and generalized commentary on Malraux' verbal technique.

Picon's prefaces to Balzac's novels resemble the essays on Balzac by Béguin and Poulet. His preface to *La Rabouilleuse* (1950) speaks of myths, of characters having a "confused appetite," and of a general sense of accepted tragedy that is reminiscent of Béguin's *Balzac visionnaire*. The preface to *Les Illusions perdues* (1958) defends the author's verbosity as "power and poetry" and develops a sense of creation and rebirth, of development in time, which recalls Poulet's study in *La Distance intérieure*. A sectional preface to the *Oeuvres complètes* of Baudelaire (1955) reiterates the familiar existential idea of creation as an act of the will, and of the artist as a creator separate from his biographical identity. In all these studies, Picon writes as a scholarly critic who is well acquainted with contemporary intellectual trends: above all, he manipulates those trends as he discusses various works.

Picon is a man of letters rather than a systematic literary critic. He has contributed to several encyclopedias, and written *Panoramas* of modern literature (1949) and contemporary ideas (1957), a volume of aesthetic philosophy (*L'Ecrivain et son ombre* [*introduction à une esthétique de la littérature*], 1953), numerous articles, and a recent collection of essays (*L'Usage de la lecture*, 1960).[7] All Picon's work reveals a synthetic, common-sense attitude that refuses to follow any one theory. It is in this sense that he differs from the critics studied here. While the critics of consciousness insist upon specific attitudes for literary anal-

7. Picon's essay on Maurice Blanchot ends by criticizing Blanchot for holding a negative and not a positive view of creation. See "L'Oeuvre critique de Maurice Blanchot," *Critique*, August–September 1956, pp. 675–694 and October 1956, pp. 836–854.

ysis, Picon's range is wider. He is a more eclectic reader whose actual involvement with literary theory remains that of a judicious, selective observer.

Jean Wahl's work is remarkably similar to the criticism of consciousness. Wahl may not have influenced literary criticism to the same extent as has Gaston Bachelard, who is often mentioned by existential critics, but his position more closely approximates the development of their beliefs. His *Études Kierkegaardiennes* (1938) mark a beginning stage of French interest in Kierkegaard, and his philosophical work henceforth assumes that the experience embodied in literature represents knowledge as well as does traditional Cartesian rationalism. Like Bachelard, Wahl uses literary references for philosophical ends. His courses in philosophy at the Sorbonne reflect this interest. In 1955, a course published as *Les Aspects qualitatifs du réel* refers to Valéry and to Claudel in order to illustrate the study of Husserl and Nicolai Hartmann. Wahl asserts that the contemporary existential movement has much to learn from the "existents" who create literature. More important, his own work leads the way in applying philosophy to literature; for he himself is a poet, a literary critic, and a non-Sartrean existential philosopher.

In *Poésie, pensée, perception* (1948), he demonstrates his ability to combine philosophical with literary theories of experience. Poetry is both a "spiritual exercise" (as it was for Jacques Maritain) and an experience which manipulates human perceptions. Foreshadowed here (although at almost the same time) is Poulet's manipulation of categories of time and space. Poetry, says Wahl, is "an exercise . . . which consists in manipulating time and space in mysterious fashion. Condensing and elongating time, the poet makes himself a time which is no longer everyday time . . . And the poet creates himself a space fully his, infinitely close, infinitely distant, this living space which is that of the work of art and which Rilke . . . could make us feel." [8] Poetic creation is an experience: "every work is an operation, an experience taking place" (p. 18). This analysis transcends verbal identification and becomes the comprehension of a whole state. "The poet names his state of consciousness, and this name is nothing else than the poem. The poem constitutes a great word . . . Naming himself, he has passed beyond

8. Jean Wahl, *Poésie pensée perception* (Paris: Calmann-Levy, 1948), pp. 17–18.

himself. He names something which can no longer be named" (p. 23).

Because Jean Wahl is a philosopher, he has not been considered at length in this study, which is restricted to those who make literature *per se* their main occupation. Gaston Bachelard, whose influence as a philosopher of literature is also great, has not been examined for the same reason. Bachelard, like Wahl, is mainly concerned with philosophical analysis, where "the image is in a continual dialectical struggle with the concept, and it is the image, the absolute and impersonal image, which bodies forth poetical intuition." [9] His influence upon literary criticism, and upon Poulet and Richard in particular, seems especially limited to his early works on the organization of manners of perception. These essays examine the four "intuitive" elements (earth, air, fire, and water) as they appear in various literary forms. Bachelard's criticism is also an early example of a self-effacing reading that attempts to strip away its own subjective traits in order to attain complete empathy with another's experience. Most influential, however, is his examination of an awareness in literature, and of the way a text organizes existential attitudes into themes and symbols revealing the author's experience.

Although Bachelard's early example influenced many critics (especially Georges Poulet and Jean-Pierre Richard), literary criticism may have exerted its own influence on his philosophical studies. In 1957, Bachelard shifts to an openly phenomenological analysis of literature. With the publication of *La Poétique de l'espace*, he remarks that (modifying his previous point of view) he is moving from a more "prudent" approach by intuited categories of experience to a direct attempt to capture the vital significance of images. Henceforth he studies the reverberation (*retentissement*) of this image in a reader's experience. Yet Bachelard's analysis of images still differs from that of the critics of consciousness. As a professional philosopher, he continues to reflect philosophical interests based upon the revelations of literature. The extrapolated significance of houses, drawers, nests, shells, corners, miniatures, immensities, and "the phenomenology of the round" (*La Poétique de l'espace*, 1957), and varying types of *cogito* in the dreams of *rêverie* and *rêve* (*La Poétique de la rêverie*, 1960), indicate that

9. Bonnefoy, "Critics—English and French," p. 43.

Bachelard's inquiry is philosophical and psychological rather than literary, or directed towards literature's inborn role as a manner of expression.

Bachelard's interest in patterns of human consciousness is strongly reflected in a contemporary "structural" analysis of human culture. Structuralism as a literary theory emerges in the 1960's, and hence follows the major works of our critics. The similarities between structuralism in its many forms and the criticism of consciousness are not to be denied—some readers may find an easy entry into structuralism's patterning of literature through the pre-verbal, latent structures hypothesized by the critics of consciousness. However, structuralism is at present a highly disparate study of the means by which man organizes his perceptions. It has neither the Geneva School's roots in literary history and criticism nor the unerring focus upon the author as literary being which is shared by the Geneva School and Maurice Blanchot. For the structuralists, literature is but one of many disciplines displaying a human "structure" behind its apparent form. Thus far, the preferred disciplines for structural analysis seem to be anthropology, sociology, psychology, and linguistics.

The first structuralists are probably linguists describing systems of language. Indeed, Josef Vachek claims for the Prague School the vision of interrelated function of language, and the terms "structuralist" and "functionalist." [10] This linguistic interest, however, is divided at present among at least three systems of analysis (Prague functionalism, Danish glossematics, and American descriptivism, p. 7) with differing stresses on the history and transformational forces in language. Although some attention has been paid to aesthetic language as such (for example, Jakobson on poetry), literature has no special value for the linguists except as it provides source material for the study of language. As philosophers of language, the linguists often sound like the theoretical critics of consciousness, but they do not emphasize literature for itself. In *La Phénoménologie de la perception*, Merleau-Ponty does speak of the necessary completion of thought by language, and of the manner in which structures of thought are finally determined by structures of language (the *parole originaire*). Even though Merleau-Ponty's "origi-

10. Josef Vachek, *The Linguistic School of Prague* (Bloomington: Indiana University Press, 1966), p. 6.

nating speech" is obviously close to Blanchot's reliance on language, or to the Geneva School's idea of an author incarnate in speech, his linguistic analysis remains philosophical—a given means of describing how man functions as a thinking, speaking being. It is not an analysis necessarily rooted in or related to literature. The scholars and philosophers of language are like the critics of consciousness in that they analyze patterns of language, and the way language is formed from latent structures, but as linguists they are first of all concerned with their own linguistic pursuits and not with problems of literature.

The other great province of contemporary structuralism lies in the social sciences—again with more or less frequent references to literature. Here the most influential studies are those of Claude Lévi-Strauss, whose study of tribal intersubjectivity and the structures of cultural consciousness have applications far beyond their apparent basis in anthropology. Lévi-Strauss is an analyst of consciousness, of a shifting "nebula" or pattern of consciousness emanating from a virtual source—a *foyer* never identifiable as such, but only as the interlocking planes and structures of consciousness which it emits.[11] In *Le Cru et le cuit* (1964), he proposes an open-end analysis of cultural structures, a musically-patterned analysis with no logical beginning or end, but only a series of thematic cross-sections ultimately interlocking to provide a larger structure. This larger structure is based in an impersonal "human mind," and is a somewhat Jungian concept which removes the individual statement of separate aesthetic works. "The human mind, unconcerned with the identity of its occasional bearers, reveals in that operation a more and more intelligible structure" (p. 21), and "when a myth is told, individual listeners receive a message which comes, strictly speaking, from nowhere" (p. 26). Music, he maintains, is the perfect structural form, for it is a meta-language in which (as for myths) the speaker can be omitted.[12] Lévi-Strauss's use of music, myths,

11. Claude Lévi-Strauss, *Le Cru et le cuit* (Paris: Plon, 1964), pp. 11, 13.

12. Some of Lévi-Strauss' dislike of subjects is reflected in the dictum that man, after analysis, is revealed by analogy as a totally determined being. "Since [the mind's] operational laws are not then fundamentally different from those it displays in its other function, it reveals its nature as a thing among things . . . if the human mind appears determined even in its myths, then *a fortiori* it must be determined everywhere" (*Le Cru et le cuit,* p. 18). This avoidance of individual subjectivity recalls Bachelard's early works and is directly opposed to a criticism that asserts the individual patterns of separate authors.

and "mythemes" indicates that he is discussing a larger, "virtual" work that goes beyond any one text. The work he analyzes is not a given "great" work with its own individual subjective organization, which is what the literary critics of consciousness explore. Instead, Lévi-Strauss tries to discover in several works the synchronic version of an "Ur-form": an hypothetical common myth whose separate appearances are only concrete variations of one utopic norm.

Other analysts adopt many points of view to discuss man as a social being operating within forms. Goldmann, following Lukacs in many respects, discusses the sociological framework of literature. He analyzes patterns of consciousness that organize the forms of the text, but (unlike the critics of consciousness) he refers this textual organization to a larger social structure enveloping each work. This social structure is further colored by Goldmann's Marxist interpretation of history, as in his study of Malraux in *Pour une Sociologie du roman*. Charles Mauron and Jacques Lacan pursue structures of psychology. Certain writers even propose diagrams to represent the "structures" of literature,[13] and yet another structuralist, André Martinet, criticizes any so-called "structural" approach that explains by using an objective "outer" pattern instead of describing an ineffable incarnate form.[14] In particular, these analysts stress a functional interrelationship of elements: they define their method as an analysis of active structures, from Lévi-Strauss' description of shifting patterns around a virtual core, to the linguists' discovery of functional patterns of language. The structuralists, as their name implies, are concerned with reaching behind the appearances of man's behavior (or better, analyzing what these appearances have in common) to get at the *manner* in which they work. Some theorists are trying to develop a structural "semiology" which would analyze, across the boundaries of language, art, or science, the means by which men make meaningful "signs." In general, the structural view of culture

13. For example, Jacques Ehrmann, "Structures of exchange in *Cinna*," *Yale French Studies*, October 1966, pp. 169–199.

14. André Martinet, "Structure et langage," *Revue internationale de philosophie*, no. 73–74. "It seems that most linguists hesitate between a realistic point of view in which structure must be sought in the object under study, and a concept that views structure as a construction set up by the seeker to explain facts" (p. 291). "What distinguishes this point of view from the realists' is not a different idea of the connections between object and structure, but another delimitation of the object" (p. 298).

is opposed to objective or historical analysis because it is a question of *how* rather than of *what,* and presents an inquiry into functions rather than into scattered historical truths.

Such an inquiry into systems, functions, and patterns of human impulses is indeed close to the systems of perception in literature proposed by the critics of consciousness. As Starobinski has shown in *L'Invention de la liberté,* there is no theoretical reason that these critics cannot adopt for their own ends structural analysis in other disciplines. Perhaps there will come a time when structural linguistics will be able to complement the Geneva critics' study of literature, which is weakest in its discussion of the role of literary language. At present, however, there is one basic difference between the critics of consciousness and the structuralists: only the former use literature as an end in itself, an imaginary universe created as a human structure but finally independent of other criteria. For these critics, literature is already a "true" expression because it is identical with itself, and not to be explained away in terms of other disciplines. They choose to see literature as the most important expression of humanity, an expression that reaches its purest form in a finite work distinguished by perfect language. If their definition of "perfect language" is seen in the order of authenticity rather than of traditional aesthetics, it nonetheless attributes to literature a certain existential perfection. For the critics of consciousness the language of a literary work is complete: it means only what it says in terms of its own system and does not hint at anything beyond the system latent in the work.

PART I | THE GENEVA SCHOOL

1

MARCEL RAYMOND

Marcel Raymond is the earliest of the Geneva writers, their most germinal thinker even if not their profoundest logician. Born in Geneva in 1897, he became Docteur ès Lettres of the University of Paris in 1927 with a thesis examining Ronsard's influence on French poetry from 1550 to 1585. After holding the chair of French literature at Bâle (in which he was succeeded by Albert Béguin), he returned to Geneva in 1936 and occupied until his retirement in 1963 the chair previously held by Thibaudet at the University. Raymond's work is tinged with a traditionalism not seen in his followers, even though they are heavily indebted to the antiformal, intuitive theories which he first began to express in 1933. These theories are not in themselves "existential," although they point the way to an empathetic reading of the text as a human expression.

Raymond combines traditional historicism with an "ontological" point of view. He stresses an intuitive manner of reading and shows a love for spiritually expressive literature rather than for displays of technical prowess. Most important, he believes that an anticlassical, baroque, and Romantic tradition runs throughout French literature and dominates modern aesthetics. This anticlassical theme expresses an historical taste rather than a philosophical system, and Raymond in general avoids critical doctrines. In most of his writings he discusses a vision he has found in the anticlassical tradition, a vision emerging in the Renaissance and again in modern times. His doctoral thesis on Ronsard is actually a truncated version of a projected work which was to set Ronsard's literary reputation off against the values of succeeding centuries.[1] Ronsard's rising favor in recent times illustrates a rebirth of anticlassical art and only subsequently a philosophy of literature. With his reputation rise and fall the fortunes of the baroque, Romantic, and modern attitude which is Raymond's first love and lasting preoccupation.

The first clear statement of Raymond's anticlassical theme comes in *De Baudelaire au surréalisme* (1933), which proposes an anticlassical "genius" as the dominant element in post-Baudelairean and contemporary poetry. Just as the Romantics had rediscovered Renaissance and baroque art after a prevailing emphasis on classicism, says Raymond, so the modern poets blend aspects of all three traditions in a continual development of one historical anticlassical motif. The basic elements in this modern neo-Romanticism are a quasi-mystical search for transcendental reality, experiments with forms to represent new modes of vision, and a general metaphysical introspection. Rousseau is the direct literary source for the "new Romanticism," of "Romanticism of profundity" as it comes to be called.

Raymond brings out the metaphysical depth or "profundity" of this new Romanticism in two studies which have had considerable influence on later Geneva writers: "Jean-Jacques Rousseau: Deux aspects de sa vie intérieure (intermittences et permanences du 'moi')" ("Jean-Jacques Rousseau: Two Aspects of His Inner Life [Intermittence and Permanence of the Self]" 1941–1942), and the preface to a critical edition of

1. Marcel Raymond, *L'Influence de Ronsard sur la poésie française, 1550–1585* (Paris: E. Droz, 1927), I, 1.

Rousseau's *Rêveries du promeneur solitaire* (1948).[2] Both essays bring
a contemporary philosophical terminology to the new Romanticism, so
that a reader quickly becomes accustomed to phrases such as "a direct
grasp," "the rhythm of stark life," "human time," "to seize being . . . in
its incoherence," "the *meaning* of things in this world," "to pronounce
efficacious words," and the statements that "things are petrified before
our glance" and "the frontiers disappear between subjective and objective feeling." Raymond constantly describes a new Romanticism
which comprehends philosophical and occult themes and which would
be defined as a "Romanticism of the soul" after a "Romanticism of the
heart." Baudelaire is the inheritor of this psychic tradition and the
precursor of its modern development. His poetry is "much more clearly
'psychic' than that of the first Romantics"; it speaks less to the "heart"
than to the "soul" or "profound self," and aims at "more obscure regions of the mind" beyond our normal perceptions.[3]

In 1942 the full historical dimensions of this anticlassical motif appear in an essay "Sur le Génie de la France" from *Génies de France*, a
collection of essays published during the war as part of an attempt to
revive the cultural pride of a defeated, humiliated France. In a time
when the Voltairean tradition of "clarity," "precision," and "rationalism"
no longer seemed to apply to modern experience, Raymond proposes
the Renaissance-baroque image as an equally valid type of "genius."
He opposes to Voltaire's terms the categories "assimilation of heterogeneous elements," a certain "equilibrium" of tension perpetually maintained between conflicting elements, and a general verbal abundance
which is not concerned with formal discipline and rules but expresses
an immediate "being" or "presence." Rabelais, Ronsard, d'Aubigné,
Hugo, Rousseau, Nerval and Baudelaire are exponents of this freer,
"baroque" French genius, which is not to be limited to the French pre-
classical period.[4] The anticlassical genius, as a whole, appears as a tradition originating in the Renaissance-baroque period, culminating in

2. Raymond is currently engaged on an edition of Rousseau for the *Pléiade* edi-
tions.
3. Raymond, *De Baudelaire au surréalisme* (Paris: Corti, 1957), p. 21. Unless
otherwise noted, I am using the enlarged edition of 1952 instead of the first edition
in 1933.
4. Raymond, *Baroque et Renaissance Poétique* (Paris: Corti, 1955), p. 63.

French Romanticism, and (in combination with existential philosophy) still influencing contemporary French literature. Raymond's evident tastes for a freer, openly subjective literature find ample scope in the study of this tradition, which he calls alternately a "Romanticism of profundity" and "literary baroque."

Perhaps Raymond prefers literary baroque to classicism because the former's "realism" is opposed to the latter's artificiality and submission to rules. Raymond's sympathies are definitely with the baroques, whose forthright grasp of reality he contrasts with classicism's gingerly embrace. Evidently, the critic has a personal definition of these terms. Reality here is no longer what is outside the human being, but is a combined experience in which objects and men have a reciprocating relationship. The kind of reality which the baroque artist grasps is an "integral" or whole realism, where objects acquire a "metaphysical dimension" without losing any of their concrete force. Exterior appearances are penetrated by what Raymond calls an "intense contemplation," or "patient attention and love." This realism is a new "fidelity to things" in that it wishes to get closer to them in order to seize their very "presences." [5] It is their total existence, an innate nature related to man's experience, which must be grasped by a style suited to such exploration.

The baroque attitude that tries to seize reality, to encompass and to comprehend it, entails a vigorous break with the restraints of conventional literary disciplines. It seeks a "direct grasp of the universe and of man, by man" (p. 34). Verbal abundance, so long a characteristic of baroque literature but decried as superfluous and inorganic, is necessary according to Raymond simply because it is a comprehensive procedure. It is the necessary mode of expression of a being who feels himself the center of a multiple universe and who is so strongly overwhelmed by this feeling that he tends to absorb and to spew out his impressions *in toto*. Standards of unity applied from the point of view of verbal exactitude, of precise and adequate description, are not valid here. What is important is the author's psychological insight and unique creative impulse, which alone give the work its unity and "reality." Art, from this point of view, is a "whole" expression, and the technical ele-

5. Raymond, *Génies de France* (*Cahiers du Rhône*, no. 4, May 1942, Neuchâtel: La Baconnière), p. 43.

ments used (imagery, recurrent themes, perhaps a quasi-architectural construction) are of importance only insofar as they are relevant to a central "animating creative process." Consequently, a reader's task is to become so intimate with the work that, under the guidance of a "central intuition," he is able to approach this same process and to appreciate the "necessity" of its various figures of speech.

Raymond has derived his empathetic reading from a particular baroque or anticlassical literary type. The tenets of this anticlassical approach, however, bear a strong similarity to the views of existential philosophy. Emphasis on vision, on a "whole realism" surpassing mere forms, and on "presences" created by the artist's conscious molding of his literary universe could reflect an existential outlook just as easily as a sympathetic attempt to coincide with the emotional expressiveness of baroque literature.

Raymond himself reinforces this parallelism. He states that his discovery of baroque art and expression was closely associated with his introduction to existential and phenomenological theories during a two-year stay at Leipzig as French lecturer.[6] The impetus given his studies in this period (1926–1928) was to provide the direct motivation for the metaphysical interpretations of *De Baudelaire au surréalisme,* but at the time it led rather to the critic's discovering new perspectives in earlier French literature.

Such influence appears to have come both from the example of other professors, and from discussions in his own classes. Raymond states that it was his knowledge of Hans Driesch which brought about his interest in phenomenological thought: "It was from him that I first learned that consciousness always has an object, that one is always conscious of something. Although I did not know it then, Driesch was presenting his students with the bases of existential phenomenology" (pp. 227–228). As French lecturer at the University, he noted the students' particular interest in Pascal and Rousseau—an interest which led to interpretations along the lines of German existential philosophy, and which introduced him to the work of Kierkegaard. "It was in reference to Pascal that I first heard the name of Kierkegaard, who was almost unknown in France" (pp. 233–234). During this period of lectureship, Raymond

6. Raymond, "Allemagne 1926–28," *Mercure de France,* no. 1098 (February 1955), pp. 224, 238–239.

came into contact with people who brought their own cultural philosophical experience to bear upon works which seemed comfortably familiar to him—and the works changed their appearance.

Raymond openly attributes to this period of lectureship in Germany his first awakening to existential thought. He is quick to point out, however, that his relationship with German thought is one of inspiration and not the continued specific interest maintained by Albert Béguin. "I received an influx of life from Germany, before returning to France and preparing a book on modern French poetry. It is quite certain that this book would not have been what it is if I had not known Germany, if I had not been induced to fuse poetry and metaphysics and to conceive the poetic experience intrepidly as a means of knowledge" (pp. 239–240). Raymond learned to reject rationalism for sympathy with unconscious forces. "I submerged myself in *irrationality*. Up to a point of considering the appearance of consciousness and of knowledge in a being as a fissure, a flaw, the only true failure. In Germany, I detached myself completely from something I will call, to simplify, *rationalism*" (p. 238). He mentions Dilthey and Gundolf in this connection, but constantly speaks of a personal discovery rather than any direct discipleship to foreign philosophical thought. Raymond concentrates upon a creative act which uses human perceptions, but he is likely to call this preoccupation either existential, ontological, or phenomenological, according to whichever term seems closest to the text at hand. He is never strict in his philosophical terminology; it is an approach which he has perceived, not a formula.

Raymond embodies a transitional approach which grows toward, but is not yet, the antistylistic and completely existential attitude of the later Geneva School. The new horizons opened to him by metaphysical awareness of the creative act are still combined with traditional, scholarly methods of interpretation. In this way he symbolizes a transitional point in the beginnings of the Geneva School. For him the study of literature still comprises two aspects: "on the one hand, the verbal study of a work of art (related to *Literaturwissenschaft*), and on the other hand, the perception of mind becoming incarnate in forms, or *Geistesgeschichte*" (p. 242). Although he does not reject the first, it is the second approach which expresses his own work best. *Geistesgeschichte* can unite Raymond's historical themes (the anticlassical tradition) with his idea of what is most important in art: the creative genius expressing humanity through literature. This "history" of "the perception of mind becoming incarnate in forms" is a good description of the movement of literary baroque which Raymond prolongs into Romantic and contemporary literature.

The authors studied in Raymond's *Geistesgeschichte* all appear in the refracted light of one central theory. All become aspects of creative genius; some closer, others farther from the ideal. Without actually rejecting those on the outskirts, Raymond obviously prefers a core of humanistic and visionary artists. The creative involvement of a sensitive, visionary human being, he believes, is represented especially by three figures: Agrippa d'Aubigné, Jean-Jacques Rousseau, and Victor Hugo.

D'Aubigné is an apt subject for Raymond's analysis because of his strongly evocative works, which express the passionate views of an individual who is also a Huguenot soldier during religious wars. As both individual and Huguenot, he is an active, violent being: "D'Aubigné's own passion, even for his time and milieu, is of a singular quality."[7] To Raymond, this passion is unique, but it is also representative: the profound expression of a man of his age. Because the poet dwelt upon his own passions, which were in turn formed by the pressures of the epoch, he is able to represent the contemporary humanity of his time. To succeeding generations of readers, his poetry overshadows and gives meaning to the drama of the period. "He is first of all himself, with force and violence . . ." and thus "concentrates and then displays such a large part of his contemporaries' obscure desires."[8] This quality of unique but representative expression is an attribute of genius, in Raymond's scheme. The creative genius is subject to the influences of his period and, by feeling them violently, "concentrates" them in himself. He also expresses his own personality when he writes: thus he communicates on an individual level the "obscure feelings" of his contemporaries. He expresses them in their universal aspect as well, for his genius is universal. In sharing his individual experience he is only speaking for his mute contemporaries. This idea of the representative artist is basic to a theory which prizes literature as an expression of humanity, and for which talent's highest

7. Raymond, *Génies de France*, p. 69.
8. Raymond, introduction in Agrippa d'Aubigné, *Oeuvres I* (Neuchâtel: Ides et Calendes, 1943), p. 19.

attribute is that "it is the genius who forever assumes the greatest humanity." [9]

If d'Aubigné serves as the representative genius, Rousseau is the archetype of the creative experience. Raymond speaks at one point of "an adventure, or a drama, in which a certain number of privileged beings have participated and still participate." [10] This adventure begins with Rousseau as the first figure in history who speaks of the intuitive experience of reality and the subsequent struggle to give it literary expression.

Raymond's earliest essay on Rousseau is the article entitled "Jean-Jacques Rousseau: Deux aspects de sa vie intérieure (intermittences et permanences du 'moi')." This essay studies Rousseau's personality; it analyzes particularly a continuing ebb and flow, or tension between opposing impulses, which Raymond identifies as the key elements in the author's self (*moi*). Here, as in all the author identifications given by Raymond and the Geneva writers, the *self* spoken of is purely literary. This personality has its roots in an historical and psychological being, but the only subject for critical analysis is the creator as he reveals himself in literature. There may be a connection between the historical and the literary figures, as there is for Rousseau, but it is Rousseau the embodied author who is uppermost and not Rousseau the historical person.

Raymond finds that Rousseau's literary self is constantly moving and changing in "an elementary movement of flux and reflux." [11] His method for analyzing this flux and reflux is not simply to catalogue states of optimism and of depression: in a technique which has unmistakable later importance for Georges Poulet, he extrapolates a series of revelatory words used by Rousseau himself. "Certain words recur . . . *intoxication, extravagance, rage, delirium, madness* . . . They all suggest . . . an eclipse of the normal self." The characteristic self exists in an alternation between two states: one of expansion, of reaching out towards other persons and beings, and one of persecution, of complete retirement into the self.

9. Raymond, *Génies de France*, p. 87.
10. Raymond, *De Baudelaire au surréalisme*, p. 13.
11. Raymond, "Jean-Jacques Rousseau: Deux aspects de sa vie intérieure," *Annales de la Société Jean-Jacques Rousseau*, 29 (1941–1942), 8. A revised version of this essay is given in *Jean-Jacques Rousseau: La Quête de soi et la rêverie* (Paris: Corti, 1962), as "Aspects de la vie intérieure: Renversements psychiques et permanence de l'être."

Such a person lives in a particular atmosphere created by his own traits, in an "interior world" which is literature. "In this interior world . . . various magnetic pulls . . . compose the substance of a being" (p. 25). At this point Raymond is transposing one of the phenomenological descriptions of self-knowledge for the purpose of describing a literary personality—this mental existence based upon pragmatic experience, but transformed into a new and totally literary *moi*. When Rousseau re-creates a feeling of reality in the familiar periwinkle episode, Raymond shows how the almost Proustian affective memory works to endow an object with spiritual transparency. "Memory does not bring forth merely the recollection or feeling of an object, but its absolute affective reson-ance: it frees a soul which is 'transparent' in its profundity" (p. 40). The term "resonance" (*résonance*), used to describe the object plus its meta-physical dimension, is one which will be taken up in other essays; it is synonymous with *retentissement*, a term taken from Eugène Minkowski and given approximately the same function in *La Poétique de l'espace* (1957) by the French philosopher-critic Gaston Bachelard. The exis-tential overtones of this term, and of the analysis in general, are fully understood by Raymond, who is quick to point out the affinities of the Romantic tradition with later philosophical thought: "One more step, and an existential intuition would open the way to a metaphysical or mystic experience" (p. 51).

The preface to Raymond's edition of Rousseau's *Rêveries du pro-meneur solitaire* (1948) continues to analyze Rousseau as a purely men-tal creation, a literary being who struggles to integrate his perceptions of reality. Rousseau's contradictory experience of reality appears as only the first step in a search for final unity. His "experience" is not, in fact, an accepted state of expansion and contraction, but an attempt to tran-scend contradictory elements and arrive at psychic fulfilment. Raymond comments that Rousseau's experiences are "arranged" towards this ful-filment, and such a climax is reached in his famous "June night." There, various contradictory emotions dissolve in a basic sense of existence. Both the elements of the universe and his own existence in relation to them seem re-created as new and integrated, not yet worn and differen-tiated by the passage of time. Through the parallel movements of water and the soul (Raymond's analysis is openly reminiscent of Bachelard's *L'Eau et les rêves*), Rousseau brings his struggling personality to a feeling of oneness with the universe. "The object is simultaneously the body of water . . . and the *self* which now exists only in the whole . . . Exterior (the movements of the water) and interior (the movements of the self) harmonize and are identified." [12] Rousseau has reached a larger, more harmonious self through being integrated (literarily) into the universe. His experience is the typical experience of Raymond's creative genius.

Raymond describes a similar experience for Victor Hugo, in a passage bordering on literary mysticism. Hugo, like Rousseau, has an intuitive experience of the whole universe, but the direction of this experience is reversed. The whole universe seems actually to press in on him. His creative experience is no longer individual, as it is with Rousseau, but is an almost involuntary involvement that reveals the connections of man with the universe.

To Raymond, Hugo is already remarkable for his assumption of humanity, for a stature which transcends that of a single man. His literary personality is not confined to the bounds of a narrow individualism, for "the poet Hugo transcends the man . . . it seems that the poet's power has not come entirely from himself, and that the forces concentrated in him come from some other region.[13] The somewhat mystical aspect of such a statement is not unintended, for Raymond finds at the base of both poetic and mystic experience a common desire for "sympathetic expansion." However, he distinguishes between the poetic and the mystic development as a development into words and a development out of them (p. 165).[14] Where the mystic wishes to lose himself in transcendental fusion, the poet tries to give the same experience a written expression. This quasi-mystical fusion of subject and object is a necessary element in the artistic experience. More than other men, the genius is conscious of a universal interpenetrability. We are all unconsciously

12. Raymond, preface in Rousseau, *Rêveries du promeneur solitaire* (ed. Raymond, Geneva: E. Droz, 1948), p. xxx.
13. Raymond, *Génies de France*, p. 174.
14. The relationship between mysticism and poetry was discussed by a number of writers during this period, and occupied among others Jean Wahl (*Poésie pensée perception*, Paris: Calmann-Levy, 1948, and a "Note" in "La Poésie comme exercice spirituel," *Fontaine*, 1942), Jacques and Raissa Maritain (*Situation de la poésie*, Paris: Desclée de Brouwer, 1938, and "La Poésie comme exercice spirituel," *Fontaine*, 1942), and Albert Béguin ("Poésie et mystique," *Présence*, 1933–1934, and "Poésie et occultisme," *Critique*, 1947).

related to the universe, "porous to the universe, constantly filled by it," but "it is the rather dreadful privilege of certain beings to feel the reality of these universal affinities" (p. 174). Hugo is one of these beings, and he "is almost never alone with himself, in himself. He is populated, over-populated, overrun" (p. 175). His creative genius is larger than life—his own life—because he assimilates forces outside himself to represent an essence of humanity. In emphasizing Hugo's sympathies, and attributing to them a mystical source, Raymond is inverting the usual nineteenth-century image of Hugo the Protean creator in order to justify his own concept of the genius as a representative human being.

Such an accent upon the subjective self, its feelings and mystical affinities, is typical of Romanticism. It is also typical of an intuitive criticism which tries to coincide with an author's experience. In studying the personality of each author, Raymond attempts to re-create the particular universe in which he existed: his feeling of self, expanding to embrace reality or shrinking to avoid it, and his feeling of existence in time and space, in a world of foreign objects which must be integrated into his over-all experience. This double creation, a re-creation of external objects into organized perceptions, requires a special faculty of memory. Memory now is inspiration, and as inspiration it creates a state, a psychic unity of vision. Raymond and his followers wish to analyze this vision, and their attitude has obviously very little to do with a rationalizing, stylistic approach. Literature, to them, is an act, a choice of vision, an experience: it is the expression of a becoming personality.

Raymond's most famous and influential book is *De Baudelaire au sur-réalisme,* subtitled "Essai sur le mouvement poétique contemporain" (1933). An innovation from two points of view, this book subordinates historical to intellectual affinities and speaks of modern poets in terms of metaphysical rather than verbal criteria. To eliminate the encyclopedic, factual emphasis of the Lanson school of historical criticism is one thing; to discuss poetry for its vision of reality is even more unusual for a work of French criticism at the time. Raymond arranges his book in such a way as to bring out what he calls "the major ambition of modern writers: to seize poetry in its essence." [15] His theme is that a certain baroque, Romantic, and now modern impulse seeks to form art into

15. Raymond, *De Baudelaire au surréalisme,* "Avant-propos."

"some kind of irregular means of metaphysical knowledge" (p. 11). Modern ambitions are leading toward a view of art in which existential perception is both the means and the end of creation, where "frontiers disappear between subjective and objective feeling" (p. 13). After Rousseau, Baudelaire stands as the greatest example of literary vision; it is with him that Raymond begins his discussion.

The "extraordinary complexity" of Baudelaire's soul makes him the source of the two traditions dominant in modern poetry: the tradition of the craftsman-artist and the tradition of the seer, or *voyant*. Mallarmé and Valéry represent the one, and Rimbaud and the surrealist experimenters speak for the other. Each separate tradition illustrates the values and risks inherent in its own approach. Each by itself is only a partial view, for the full artist must, like Baudelaire, integrate opposing tendencies to form an harmonious whole.

The aesthetics associated with the *voyant* tradition propose to transmit a subjective state, or to re-create the "expression of a soul." Baudelaire's soul is an "invisible universe, opening out its mystery everywhere," [16] and its activity is a "vaporization" of the self into transcendental reality. Subject and object are fused once more, for "all things are transparent and penetrable by the mind, in a unique milieu . . . in which objects live the same life as that of the self" (p. 193). To Raymond, Baudelaire's transcendental state is the basic human experience. The poet's task is to express it: to extract from reality a certain "hieroglyph" which will reveal the "eternal meaning of existence" (p. 213). By suspending his earthly, personal self, the poet is integrated into a transcendental reality, perceiving and re-creating the existence of a whole universe. This experience of the "au-delà" (the "beyond") is evidently a forerunner of Rimbaud's "disorder in all the senses," and of surrealist attempts to attain underlying reality through submerging the self in verbal flux or automatism. The tradition of the *voyant*, of the visionary aspect of literature, is directly in line with Raymond's anticlassical genre, and he is quick to claim it as a distinguishing element in modern literature. "Whatever its nature, a new idea of literature arises here—one which has not been clearly distinguished until our day—with the poetic sense becoming closely related to the mystic and prophetic sense." [17] This

16. Raymond, *Génies de France*, p. 191.
17. Raymond, *De Baudelaire au surréalisme*, p. 40.

literature and art is a kind of metaphysical realism, and represents an individual expression of the human condition.

Just as important as the *voyant* tradition is the craftsman-like approach which descends to Mallarmé and Valéry. The aim of these Symbolist craftsmen, according to Raymond, is to find an essence of meaning, to use only words which are ideas and thus purely efficacious. Mallarmé's language works by "suspending the normal activity of the self, and bewitching it, as if by an incantation" (p. 33). Words are ideal and purified, implements of a "suggestive magic," if only the poet is in sufficiently direct contact with their reality to use them properly.

As one might expect, the formal aspect of this tradition does not appeal to Raymond when he feels that it becomes technique and plays with allusions beyond the actual concrete force of words. At its logical conclusion, form alone invites "a continual postponement of the fact, or object, for the sake of the allusion" (pp. 33–34). In order to combat such over-methodization of experience, the critic proposes that the writer must keep close contact with reality, using only words which he can feel in direct connection with his experience. The work must be "inspired" as an expression of the writer's whole being, and not constructed from a public language which has no roots in the author's experience. Raymond places continual emphasis upon this literary integrity, which is far more important to him than any mere technical triumph. "What is necessary for man is integrity, the fullness of his nature and of Nature in general" (p. 44). His quarrel with the classical genre is not primarily with a system of forms, but with an unreal abstraction of human qualities, with a separation of man from his environment. The Mallarméan tradition is absorbed into Raymond's analysis of modern literature insofar as it uses words and discipline to achieve a particular emotive force —to "disturb souls." But it is clear that the Swiss critic deplores the tendency of this poetry to lean toward a classical genre that intellectualizes experience, and he regrets the fact that at times "subjective poetry changes into intellectual poetry" (p. 35).

Raymond's survey of modern poetry is mainly concerned with the adventure of a new consciousness of reality. Reality must be present in this literature or there will be no "whole being" whose self-consciousness also involves a consciousness of environment. The "adventure of the self" which Raymond follows throughout *De Baudelaire au sur-*

réalisme may be defined as each author's attempt to come to terms with reality. Valéry and Claudel, the great twentieth-century examples of this adventure, pose the same problem in differing terms.

Paul Valéry, usually seen as the archetype of modern classical discipline, is to Raymond a "mystic of the consciousness of self" (p. 154) whose spiritual drama consists in an inability to reconcile sensuous and intellectual tendencies. Valéry's great virtue is that he never loses sight of material reality—his poetry remains closer to his experience than does, for example, Mallarmé's. Much of the analysis in *Paul Valéry et la tentation de l'esprit* (1946) rests upon this sense of the density and impact of objects in Valéry's poetry, and upon the physical sensitivity of his images. However, Valéry falsifies material reality by his need to give it the structure and meaning of philosophical poetry. By using the restraints of formal discipline, Valéry hoped to arrive at some reconciliation of the creative and the perceiving self. In this he was unsuccessful: if the poet could "know himself" he could not "comprehend himself" or provide a rational basis for his being. He has nothing "authentically real as a basis inside himself" (p. 168), and Raymond can find no integration of the poet's experience into poetic utterance. Valéry's drama, then, remains unresolved.

Both Valéry and Claudel try to re-create their immediate experience as literature and to give it the status of an intuition of reality. If Valéry never reaches any authentic feeling of self, his failure can be attributed to an obstinate intellectuality that is lacking in Claudel. The latter sets out to re-create reality in a coherent and significant perspective. He is not interested in struggling with philosophical objectivity and interprets his experience in the light of a given world view. Convinced that he has a valid apprehension of reality (which is the same as Christian revelation), Claudel tries to possess his experience in a calculatedly "realistic" prosody whose long, cumbersome sentences reproduce the natural unfolding of an image in his mind. Raymond defends these lengthy sentences with the same argument that he uses to defend baroque expansion: their artificiality is calculated to parallel mental reality. Moreover, Claudel's sentences "tend to reproduce the movement of the first psychic crystallizations" (p. 183). Such a style is the exact opposite of Valéry's, who attempts to master his experience, and it is closer to Raymond's ideal of original experience making itself felt in literature.

After considering the two giants of the century, Claudel and Valéry, Raymond passes in review a number of poets and movements before reaching his conception of the "modern myth of poetry." The "unanimist" movement, and its "profound intuition of a real, irrational, and immediately felt universe" (p. 202) easily falls into Raymond's familiar anti-classical genius. Unanimist and Whitmanian poets "are all carnal beings, who think with their bodies and oblige their minds to adhere to reality instead of dissipating in dreams and infinity" (p. 213). The experimental poetry of revolt in Jarry, cubism, and Apollinaire is evidence of the change from a poetry "steeped in dreams" to a modernistic poetry with a new perspective on reality.

Dadaism and surrealism interest Raymond mainly as attempts to express the human condition, and as a terminal adventure in the development from Baudelaire to surrealism. Dadaist poetry is not creative, but it does express "the precariousness of the human condition, and the suffering of an isolated being who cannot resolve to accept his destiny" (p. 271). Surrealism builds upon Dadaism's negations and consequently has a more complex doctrine. It represents "Romanticism's most recent attempt to break with *things as they are* and to substitute others in full activity, in full genesis, whose moving contours are inscribed in filigree at the core of being" (p. 291). The surrealist creates relationships which are purely mental and purely human because they are generated in the unconscious mind. His aim is a "return to chaos" in a humanly-identified universe: "he does not stop at creating abstract relationships; he makes objects participate in one another, and identifies them mysteriously" (p. 286). Through leaving himself open to involuntary, spontaneous forms emerging from a subterranean existence, he satisfies a certain "interior and poetic sense, which perhaps fuses with the feeling of our profound life" (p. 287). It is Raymond's opinion that this assimilation of poetic and ontological feelings is the primary attitude of surrealism, and that never before in France had any school of poets consciously united "the problem of poetry with the crucial problem of being" (p. 297). Surrealism is then a "great investigation of man" which looks for its antirational discoveries to be used by poets.

The modern poetic myth stems from a metaphysical and social evangelism based on surrealist experiments. Modern poets try to capture and communicate the unconscious current of life. Pierre Jean Jouve's poetry is "a spiritual exercise, a possibility of perceiving the world, for an instant, in the lightning flash of revelation" (p. 323), and Jules Supervielle appears as the "poet of metempsychosis, of metamorphoses of being, of mysterious telepathies in which 'the same is other'" (p. 328). In Raymond's view the contemporary writer's new and extra-aesthetic function is to bewilder and dismay the reader until he enters into a truer understanding of his own nature. "The poet's task will be to upset man, to make him lose heart before his life and the universe, and to put him in permanent contact with irrationality" (p. 341). Such a role puts the poet far beyond the personal lyricism of Romantics or the introspective discourse of surrealists. Emphasis is upon transcendental feelings, but there is also an attempt to communicate.

It is through poetry's new evangelical role that Raymond is able to salvage craftsmanship and bring us back to the technical aspects of poetic creation. The will to communicate entails conscious use of a medium of expression and comprises a more sophisticated approach to composition than surrealist "automatic writing." Raymond is no apologist for facile composition and recognizes that a poet must explore—before he can employ—all the associations of his language. If the poet uses words, he must use them consciously; any gap between experience and expression is still a flaw, whether the original mistake be metaphysical or technical.

Raymond's epilogue to the re-edition of *De Baudelaire au surréalisme* in 1939 clarifies literature's dual role as both experience and creativity. Although much of his argument has pointed out that modern poetry is based in a quasi-mystic experience, he also stresses a creative attitude inherited from the Symbolists: the artist is a maker who deals in forms of language. For Raymond, the creative act is expression as well as perception, and the greatest poetry exists at a "maximum point of spiritual tension" [18] between these two impulses.

Raymond's aim has been to illuminate a side of human genius hitherto left in the shade of literary disfavor or left to the philosophers. His initial response has been to literature rather than to philosophy: although his stay in Leipzig clarified certain literary perspectives for him, the

18. Raymond, *Génies de France*, p. 232.

preface to his study of Ronsard shows that a preference for anticlassical tradition came before any philosophical formulation. This anticlassical tradition—which Raymond calls a *"ligne de force,"* or magnetic pull of similar impulses—can point to a long genealogy in literary history, but it also has relationships outside literature in the modern world. The concern with a sense of existence to be communicated in literature is obviously an "existential" preoccupation, and yet it is important to see the dividing lines which separate Raymond the literary critic from extra-literary theoreticians.

As Raymond himself points out, his experience in Leipzig did not make him a professional philosopher. Although his analysis leans towards metaphysical interpretations, he cannot be assimilated into the ranks of philosopher-critics such as Sartre, Wahl, and Bachelard. He may use psychological elements in his analyses, but it is not with the same sense of finality that Bachelard demonstrates in proposing a psyche of water imagery, fire imagery, and lately of the drawer, the nest, and the shell.[19] His interest in Bergson is that of an historian who sees parallels, but not dogma, in Bergson's sense of flux and intuited reality. If Raymond discerns at one point a common "leap towards things, a 'taking possession of the world,'" he does not deduce from it any eternal philosophical verity, but only "the curious convergence of diverse intellectual manifestations" at this epoch.[20] Raymond has none of the social or political evangelism of Jean-Paul Sartre; his analysis of Baudelaire speaks of the poet's assimilation of opposite tendencies and not of his shameful failure to face up to life. Nor does he adopt Sartre's vision of each man locked in a solipsistic castle, his being in constant jeopardy from the look of *autrui.* Such concerns are far afield from a rather academic, certainly literary sympathy with the text. Raymond is not sufficiently sectarian to associate himself with the so-called "Christian existentialism" of men like Gabriel Marcel, Jacques Maritain, or even Jean Wahl. In fact, the basic difference between Raymond and the many critics usually spoken of as existential is that the former brings outside references to bear upon the work of art, where the latter tend to bring out the literary work as proof of a system. Raymond and his followers are literary critics who

19. Gaston Bachelard, *La Poétique de l'espace* (Paris: Presses universitaires de France, 1957).
20. Raymond, *Génies de France,* p. 224.

wish to use certain existential perspectives, but not philosophers or social thinkers who find the human expressions in literature useful material for their separate ends.

Even the term "existential" is not one which has any exclusive significance for Raymond, who uses it interchangeably with "ontological" and "phenomenological" to mean simply an analysis of being. From *Paul Valéry et la tentation de l'esprit* (1946) to *Senancour, sensations et révélations* (1965), he explains his preoccupations as "ontological" and concerned with a sense of existence. "We are concerned with a kind of preoccupation which could be called ontological . . . a conflict of being and consciousness." [21] This ontology is general and not tied to phenomenology or any systematic analysis of perception. "Solitary, man questions himself before impenetrable reality. He responds to the silence of things by ideas, words, constructions of ideas and words." [22] Such general metaphysical curiosity is not as systematized as it will be in Jean-Pierre Richard, who turns it into a method of analysis rather than seeing it as the framework of a question. When Raymond speaks of "an original datum, a manner of apprehending man and the universe which is legible in each word," [23] he is proposing this vision as a new standard of structural unity. The author's metaphysical view is the basis for a hidden coherence in the text, and thus has a literary focus.

Raymond's existential or ontological thought consists of three main elements: the interrogation of personal existence, the perception of environment, and both attitudes united in a proposed, essentially human image of the creator. These elements are just as predominant in Raymond's literary preferences as in his theoretical speculations. The baroque-Romantic-surrealist tradition with which he sympathizes is based upon an immediate sensory intuition of existence, and thus finds its natural echo in the existential wish to represent the complete, unformulated perceptions of a whole being. In the existential and the neo-Romantic view, art is defined as a human expression. A collateral assumption

21. Raymond, *Paul Valéry et la tentation de l'esprit* (Neuchâtel: La Baconnière, 1946), p. 7 and cf. also Raymond, *Senancour, sensations et révélations* (Paris: Corti, 1965), pp. 12, 37.

22. Raymond, *Paul Valéry*, p. 88.

23. Raymond, introduction to *Anthologie de la nouvelle française* (Lausanne: La Guilde du Livre, 1952), p. 17.

is that great art is the profoundest, most basically human expression, and that its creator—the genius—is best able to represent humanity.

Raymond places constant emphasis on human interpretations and on human values. This openly humanistic view of art does not spring exclusively from existential speculation, nor is it completely explicable on the grounds of a taste for the baroque genius. There are several indications that contemporary history has had its effect in shaping the social and communicative aspect of art for this critic. Certain of his less well-known writings deal with ethical problems, and much of his work was done immediately before and during World War II. Raymond cooperated with Albert Béguin in the clandestine *Cahiers du Rhône,* which were created to keep alive French patriotism and cultural values during the occupation. The concept of a "French genius" was elaborated from such a point of view, and the essay on Lamartine begins with a reiteration of this aim: "Now that France, all overrun by foreigners, searches herself in humiliation and bitterness—doubtless also in hope—the time has come to recall what is highest and most human in her past." [24] The epilogue to *De Baudelaire au surréalisme* (1939) adds a postscript which meditates upon the moral climate present at the beginning of World War II: "Expectation and ripening of the catastrophe, all instants gliding like an inexorable hourglass towards these first days of September . . . No one knows, any more, what dark tasks are being prepared in blood and in steel." [25] It is quite clear that the shock of the war, which gave such impetus to the existential philosophies in the 1940's, quickened the sense of urgency with which Raymond (and Béguin after him) looked for persisting human values in the literature of the time. The crumbling of the old values and the search for a new foundation upon which to form a conception of the human being are common concerns in postwar philosophy and literature. A *chronique* by Raymond on Benjamin Crémieux, a specialist in Italian literature and intellectual history whom Raymond calls a "second Thibaudet," quotes Crémieux in 1941: "It is now evident that a gradually increasing number of men, in France, no longer believe in printed words, but in what they have seen, what they have felt, or in the testimony of a friend, a companion . . . Human

24. Raymond, *Génies de France,* p. 150.
25. Raymond, *De Baudelaire au surréalisme,* p. 358.

speech, with its accent and warmth, takes back its weight." [26] It is this emphasis upon "human speech," its "warmth" and "weight," that interests Raymond in his own analysis of literature.

By the late 1950's, Raymond is mainly concerned with a single author's spiritual identity. Gradually he focuses on the quality of an author's spiritual involvement and on the various steps in his metaphysical thought. Such a development brings Raymond closer to Albert Béguin, although Raymond maintains an historical perspective, scholarly appraisal, and a willingness to judge form, while Béguin tends to become the proselytizer of a new Catholic literature. These later periods of both critics are important in themselves, as personal extensions of their common interest in a surreal vision fusing subject and object. Such a development also points out the tendencies of this subjective and empathetic approach to become a personal metaphysical history aligning itself voluntarily with other spiritual biographies. However, it is the early work of both men which has the greatest influence upon the developing theory of literature in the Geneva School. By 1950 Raymond has already given the impetus for the school's metaphysical historicism, and his later works display the reciprocal influence of his disciples as well as his own personal development.

The first published evidence of Raymond's new interest in religious thought comes in an essay of 1961. "La Maladie et la guérison." The essay reflects a gradual mood of change, ranging from his first annoyed reaction to a "father-confessor" tone in Béguin,[27] to the more religious tones of his essays in the later 1950's, to the sense of loss evoked in poems for his dead wife (*Poèmes pour l'Absente, 1966*) and the change in perception noted in "La Maladie et la guérison." According to the preface of *Jean-Jacques Rousseau: la Quête de soi et la rêverie* (1962), it is a sense of weakness that has allowed him to recognize similar feelings in other writers—that has allowed him to include new sympathies in a subjective critical approach. In this preface he comments that it has been easier for him to analyze the "movements of Rousseau's being . . . following an experience where literature was only indirectly involved, the experience of my own weakness, coming from general human

26. Raymond, "Benjamin Crémieux," *Lettres,* March 1945, p. 79.
27. Raymond, introduction to "Quelques Lettres d'Albert Béguin," *Cahiers du Sud,* no. 360, April–May 1961, p. 208.

weakness . . . If this experience has let me sympathize more deeply with Rousseau, it has also let me see more clearly the fragile foundations of his 'Pelagianism.' " [28] Raymond's discovery is that Rousseau erred in separating self-love from selfishness, "l'amour de soi" from "l'amour-propre," and that this unnatural separation kept him from yielding to an overwhelming religious experience. "His too-watchful sense of self prevented him from forgetting himself . . . here is one of the limits of his religion, or rather one of its central points" (p. 8). It is Rousseau's connection with religious experience, "the always-fleeing image of a kind of mystic experience" (p. 12), that Raymond wishes to analyze—an admittedly partial concern, but " 'objectivity' has no meaning in a search of this kind, where there is a necessary personal involvement even if only in the choice of points of view" (p. 11). However much Raymond may wish to accent his change of vision, and his metaphysical discovery of Rousseau, it is the appraisal rather than the analysis which has changed. *Jean-Jacques Rousseau* is a collection of essays and lectures (1941–1962) whose common theme is the tension of opposite pulls in Rousseau—in fact, the same analysis of dualism which Raymond has always favored. Raymond's analysis follows the theme of self-knowledge in various aspects of Rousseau's works, a "problème de la connaissance de soi" (as he titles the last essay) which has concerned him from its earliest humanistic form to its latest appearance as a kind of mystic failure.

Two years after *Jean-Jacques Rousseau: la Quête de soi et la rêverie*, Raymond published another collection of essays and lectures dating from 1942 to 1963, entitled this time *Vérité et poésie* (*Truth and Poetry*). In the preface (dedicated to the memory of Albert Béguin) he denies that he is equating "truth" with "poetry," but feels that both are inextricably connected—that the poet experiences an ontological truth which he, as poet, is best able to convey. This poet "is called upon to know the experience of the human condition to its extreme." [29] His language is not the "institutionalized, conventionalized language" which "objectifies" the world, but a sacred connection, a "far-off echo of the Word," which gives

28. Raymond, *Jean-Jacques Rousseau: la Quête de soi et la rêverie* (Paris: Corti, 1962) p. 7.
29. Raymond, *Vérité et poésie* (Neuchâtel: La Baconnière, 1964), p. 9. (The title is consciously modeled on Goethe, *Dichtung und Wahrheit*.)

the poet a possible "contact with things, a possible approach to lost unity, or even a possible meeting with God" (p. 8). Such a view is a natural extension of the Romantic view of the poet as seer which Raymond evokes in *Génies de France* (at a time when he was linked closely with Béguin as both wrote to "keep alive a sense of human values" in time of war). The essays in *Vérité et poésie* tend to focus on single authors' spiritual dramas: "La conversion de Pascal," "Pierre Bayle et la conscience malheureuse," "La rêverie selon Rousseau et son conditionnement historique," "La carrière poétique de Rimbaud," "Situation de C.-F. Ramuz," and a study of Senancour. Raymond has not lost his interest in the historical relevance of an author's work, but this relevance is seen more and more in a religious perspective. In *Vérité et poésie* he comments that the modern writer, although usually possessing a "mystical atheism" for religion (p. 7), can nonetheless express divinity. Raymond does not seem to care for the "new novel's" manner of imitating life without commentary: "the true mythological fable (*affabulation*) has been degraded into the fable in novel form, and this in turn threatens to disappear before a novel with neither fable nor story, which would appear a simple imitation of life at all levels (a new mirror walking or at a standstill on the highway)" (p. 272).[30] The last essay in *Vérité et poésie*, "Culture ouverte et langage de la poésie" is addressed to a contemporary audience. Raymond tries to evoke an "open humanism" combining scientific knowledge and poetic experience, and to suggest a frame of mind which could accept all aspects of existence in the

---

30. Raymond's "mythological fable" reflects a contemporary use of the term "myth" in anthropological and psychological contexts. He shares with many writers (of whom the best example is Lévi-Strauss) the use of "myth" to describe a pattern of human consciousness. It is a "mythic or archaic consciousness . . . drowned in a cosmic totality" (*Vérité et poésie*, p. 270), or a primitive, "savage" thought in which a word shares the life of the object it names, and the speaker does not differentiate between the reality he sees and the one that he utters. Such a word is a living symbol, comments Raymond after Goethe (pp. 9, 272). The overtones of this description of symbolic (almost "structural") language undoubtedly persist in *affabulation*, a stringing together of incidents to organize a story and give it the larger meaning that Raymond requires.

Raymond's attitude toward the "new novel" seems a peculiar conservatism in favor of traditional plots, and against a freedom of vision that he himself helped to inaugurate. It could be argued that the "fusion of subject and object" has actually been attained in the "new novels," and that a coherent perspective or series of perspectives can very well be a latent "plot" more successfully absorbed into the work's mental universe.

name of one transcendent unity. The essay ends on a touching note of hope for this new humanism, a spiritual combination which must be possible, at some extreme, "if the world is not in pieces, if spirit is not broken, if unity exists" (p. 272).

For all its interest in showing Raymond's preoccupations over a series of years, *Vérité et poésie* remains a collection of separate essays and lectures of varying dates, and not the more ambitious study which the author has undertaken in *Senancour, sensations et révélations* (1965). In *Senancour* (dedicated to Georges Poulet), Raymond undertakes another "ontological" study of a single author as he did for Rousseau and Valéry. All the broad range of his scholarly training is used to relate Senancour to European Romanticism in art, music, literature, and philosophy. The main emphasis is not historical, however, nor biographical nor psychological: "it is first of all a question of ontology." [31] Raymond wishes to follow the spiritual career of a *génie manqué*, to point out the "striking authenticity of Senancour's experience" and "frightening isolation." Once again he finds a "dialectical pattern whose constants are opposed," a "basic movement of uncertainty, then of oscillation, finally of a sort of back and forth" (p. 13). Thus far the analysis follows the pattern of a familiar dualism, but Raymond's central theme is that Senancour heralds the introspective struggle of contemporary existential thought. "I will not hide my intention of stressing what is closest to us in him, and foreshadowed, more than a century and a half ago, the preoccupations of that future towards which he was turning in his last years." This close connection lies in the solitude in which Senancour and contemporary man try to find a meaning to their fate: "The climate of Senancour's last writings is that of the most complete solitude, the same as that in which his sensualist—and already almost 'existentialist'— *cogito* was being formulated against a background of absence and nothingness" (p. 241). Senancour's experience is relevant to contemporary thought, and Raymond follows the itinerary of a contemporary mind *avant la lettre*.

In Senancour "everything begins with a great refusal" (p. 35) of the past, an introspective "philosophy of the passive rather than the thinking being, of the self who feels and feels abandoned" (p. 37). Senancour's

31. Raymond, *Senancour, sensations et révélations*, p. 12.

extreme subjectivity leads him to feel "excessively" (p. 94), at once to search for truth inside himself and to realize the impossibility of fixing truth with any permanence. In trying to attain a durable sense of self, he only "opens his eyes to the internal changes of his own being . . . passing, without leaving his own personality, from one self to another" (p. 103). Senancour passes from pure humanism to a mystic humanism to a *"nocturnal* poetics, a universe of confusion where this *something possible* is revealed in ambiguity, between existence and nonexistence" (p. 195). He ends with a "laborious movement of hope," a kind of "reasonable theosophy" blended with "magical idealism, and illuminism" (p. 208). Such a blend tries to accentuate the reasonable possibilities for the existence of God as Senancour tries to convince himself that there is indeed divinity behind the final curtain of death.

Raymond's analysis in *Senancour* is a personal extension of his own criticism blended with the unmistakable influence of others in the Geneva School. His concern for the interrelationships of aesthetic form and the artist's ontology continues. If Senancour's range is limited, it nonetheless reflects his exact experience, for "his experience itself left him few possibilities" (p. 198). Toward the end, Senancour's "style has lost its vigor" and becomes wordily sententious (p. 240), so that both language and experience end by revealing the *génie manqué*. Along with this familiar blend of ontological and formal criticism, there are certain observations and even phrasings which show that Raymond has felt a reciprocal influence from the members of the Geneva School. Passing comments about the "center" or "circumference" of perception may be spontaneous, or a shared recollection from eighteenth-century imagery, or may reflect (for example, on page 95) the terminology of Georges Poulet (to whom *Senancour* is dedicated). When Raymond speaks of Senancour's "milieu propre" being "immensity, emptiness, the abyss" (p. 21), he speaks again as might Poulet. Raymond refers to Jean Starobinski several times (especially to the historical perspectives described in *L'Invention de la liberté,* p. 195), and a passage devoted to Senancour recalls phraseology used by Starobinski in *Jean-Jacques Rousseau, la transparence et l'obstacle.* "The obstacle to this movement of expansion, every boundary or limit, will henceforth be something to push aside, to avoid; what can be seen transparently will be manna in the desert" (p. 143). Another passage recalls Richard's description of the material substances encountered by poetic vision: "The firm consistency of separate objects, objects you bump into, whose walls and angles tangle or intersect, such is the obstacle's first aspect. Then comes the tight texture of matter, its weight, its opacity . . . Senancour speaks of the soul somewhat as of a soap-bubble" (p. 144). Richard, Poulet, and Starobinski have shared an increasing interest in the discovery and patterning of external reality, and it is only likely that such preoccupations would interest their friend and mentor, Marcel Raymond. In this later period Raymond takes the role of a senior member of the Geneva group. He is actively interested in the work of his colleagues, but has a particular attitude already developed and matured while the others are still engaged in framing their analytical perspectives.

Raymond's main influence upon the members of the Geneva School rests with his first book, *De Baudelaire au surréalisme,* and perhaps with his studies of Rousseau. It was the metaphysical historicism of this first book—its willingness to break the rules of accepted chronological perspectives—that set the example for a criticism based on the human qualities innate in a work. This early work of Raymond's is of course germinal, rather than definitive, for the attitudes of the school. He provides the basis for a theory, and a pivot upon which a sensitive traditional criticism can be seen turning toward contemporary manners of expression. Raymond's early analyses are often at this pivotal point and contain a peculiar ambiguity in which remnants of the traditional formal approach of the "explication de texte" mingle with a new (ontological or existential) manner of perception. At its least helpful, Raymond's analysis falls into an oversimple subjectivism: "The emotion which emerges from these lines proves that Ronsard knew these obsessions" [32] or an overabstract synthesis: "I therefore propose this temporary formula: in Racine, what is meaningful resolves into what is expressive, which in turn is based in what is poetic; just as a wave, after rising to make its sign and accomplish its gesture, is reabsorbed into a body of water." [33] Perhaps the most prevalent indication of this generalizing, humanizing approach to a text is the often-repeated phrase typical of the whole Geneva School, that "everything happens as if" ("tout se passe bien comme si").

32. Raymond, *Baroque et Renaissance Poétique,* p. 84.
33. Raymond, *Génies de France,* p. 118.

With this phrase, the work is treated as "everything," a whole: it automatically becomes a rather abstract general entity which is neither a collection of texts nor a biographical study, but the figure of a human attitude which would be perceptible in the work taken as a single expression. This approach ignores the separate existence of a literary work as an individual object, with correlating parts which can be seen in purely formal relationships. For example, the intrinsic nature of such an art form as a play, in which separate characters and scenes react upon one another, would be obscured in an approach which tends to fuse all elements into an over-all world view attributed to the author. Raymond's attitude is limited, in a certain fashion, to monolinear literary types.

"Everything happens" and there is no fixed object of study; the "explication de texte" must meet instead with a series of attitudes, a sense of existence which traverses various states. The critic's attention, instead of being focused upon the formal structure of the related states, is focused upon the sense of existence manifested through them. Such an attitude is accepted and chosen by the later Geneva School, and in particular by Georges Poulet. In general, however, Raymond possesses a wider and more aesthetic approach in which separate words and phrases continue to have intrinsic value.

The last segment of the phrase "as if" accents at once the technical disadvantage and the potential benefit of this extremely subjective approach. The interpretation is dependent upon the point of view—in fact, on the whim—of the critic. Even though he tries conscientiously to assemble significant evidence in the text, he is attempting to re-create a human experience and it will be extremely difficult for him to distinguish his own from it. Thus one critic may consistently see the same pattern in a number of authors—Raymond finds tension of opposites in most of his authors, and most recently a near mystic experience in Valéry, Rousseau, Senancour, and Fénelon.[34] Perhaps Raymond is merely recognizing some basic human character traits, particularly since this dualism is usually a fundamental philosophical problem "of being and consciousness." However, the study of a work as human expression can easily lead to the

34. Raymond, "Le Dialogue de Mme Guyon et de Fénelon," *Nouvelle Revue française*, May 1967, pp. 1052–1061. This essay is a chapter of a book to be published on Fénelon.

study of the common humanity in a work, and the risk is then of an analysis which is neither literary nor individual.

In spite of the evident risks of subjective criticism, Raymond may be indicating a new vantage point from which to approach the work of art. If it is true that the critic tends to neglect formal considerations for metaphysical ones, it is perhaps also true that he is reacting against an over-rigid, intellectualized approach which has claimed to solve too many literary problems upon the basis of a mechanical aesthetics. Literary expression in France has progressed through Dadaism, surrealism, two world wars, and existentialism: it has surpassed the formalizing criticism developed in the time of the Symbolists, and still taught in American schools, while literary historiography dominates the French. A newly applicable criticism is needed for a new literature. Just as Raymond the literary historian demonstrated the traces of an emotional, quasi-mystical second Romanticism in literature, so Raymond the literary critic wishes to see a modern criticism which will take into account the history of the last half-century, and the morally charged words being used in the present. He would speak in terms of the metaphysical values of words, because an author has by nature the highly developed ability to understand and use language. He would also include in literary history the quest for underlying reality which has been dominant since Baudelaire.

Raymond's contribution to the history of French literary theory is that he is the first to assert the close connection between metaphysics and modern literature. The literary criticism which he applies to existential questions combines naturally with a taste for the anticlassical, more freely expressive *ligne de force* leading through the baroque-Romantic-contemporary tradition. Such a literary genealogy illustrates a concept of French genius which now opposes, now surpasses, the static and technical concept attributed to classicism and neo-Symbolism. Raymond himself does not adopt a completely existential perspective. He remains free to deal with all literature and with any aspect which he chooses to emphasize: his attitude may perhaps lose the extreme internal consistency characterizing Béguin and Poulet, but it marks him the more liberally "literary" critic.

Albert Béguin and Georges Poulet, both of whom recognize the marked influence of *De Baudelaire au surréalisme* and other of Raymond's works, adopt more partial, extreme points of view dominated by their particular philosophical exigencies. The later critics draw from Raymond's theories especially the recognition of creative fusion between subject and object in an existentially perceptive act, the genius' unique yet representative expression of human existence (his "assumption of humanity"), the role of language as an expressive medium deriving authenticity from the writer's experience, and the belief in historical patterns of consciousness. Each member of the Geneva School will adapt these observations for his own use, but all recognize that Marcel Raymond's work provides the example and inspiration for a succeeding theory of literary consciousness.

2

ALBERT BÉGUIN

Albert Béguin has much in common with his early associate Raymond. Both men analyze literature as a spiritual adventure and both wish to reinterpret modern literature after Romanticism as a peculiar metaphysical development. Raymond has remained a more traditional academic critic, however, while Béguin moved out of academic circles and into a varied role as free-lance writer and critic, editor of *Esprit,* and herald of a new Catholic literature in modern times. His exploration of metaphysical dimensions in writing quickly turned into a personal quest for salvation through literature, so that he pushed to an extreme the mystic aspects of Raymond's neo-Romantic existential criticism. Béguin's approach escapes being just one more facet of Christian existentialism in that he never abandons the study of literature for philosophy. His early

49

works describe the Romantic soul's vision of reality, and his later ones emphasize the visionary reality of Catholic authors. Instead of forcing all literature into a traditional dogmatic mold, he has gradually restricted the number of his subjects while multiplying the avenues of interrogation. Because Béguin is a professional literary critic, he is not content to founder on simple assertion but uses his trained mind to measure a personal approach against formal, psychological, and philosophical standards.

Born in Switzerland in 1901, Béguin attended the University of Geneva and was graduated in 1923. In 1924 he left Geneva for Paris, where he studied at the Sorbonne, became bookseller's assistant, and discovered German Romanticism through the works of Jean Paul. In 1929 he became a French instructor in the University of Halle an der Saale; but he was expelled from Germany in 1934, when he returned to Switzerland to teach French and Greek at the Collège de Genève. By 1937 his writing shows the beginning of an interest in the mystical aspects of literature, an interest that may be seen in his doctoral thesis "Essai sur le romantisme allemand et la poésie française moderne" (later published as *L'Ame romantique et le rêve*) and in *Gérard de Nerval*, with its supplementary essay "Poésie et mystique." That same year he came to Bâle to fill the position left vacant in 1936 by Raymond's departure for Geneva. In November of 1940 he became a Roman Catholic. During the war years he and Raymond edited the *Cahiers du Rhône* for distribution by the underground in occupied France.

This period of his career is marked by a growing preoccupation with religious literature. As a teacher he tended to discuss writers who emphasized religious themes, and one of his former students has remarked upon an evident "conscious need to bear witness as a Christian." [1] Béguin's own writings illustrate, from now on, his desire to analyze a literary language that expresses religious revelation, especially novels and poems that express Catholic revelation. His essays in the *Cahiers* are notable for their Christian humanism, and his books concentrate on religious authors. These works include *La Prière de Péguy* (1942), *Léon Bloy l'impatient* (1944), *L'Eve de Péguy* (1948), *Léon Bloy, mystique*

1. Marie-Jeanne Hublard, "Albert Béguin à Bâle," in *Albert Béguin, étapes d'une pensée* (*Cahiers du Rhône, Série blanche,* 30 [96] December 1957, La Baconnière, Neuchâtel), pp. 185–186. A volume of *hommages* henceforth referred to as *Etapes.*

de la douleur (1948), *Patience de Ramuz* (1950), *Pascal par lui-même* (1952), and *Bernanos par lui-même* (1954). *Balzac visionnaire,* published in 1946, is Béguin's only book in this period that is not concerned with a religious author, but he has chosen here an author whose traditional religious beliefs buttress his visionary style.

With the publication of *Balzac visionnaire,* Béguin moved from the academic security of the University of Bâle to life as a free-lance writer and critic in Paris. In 1950 he assumed direction of *Esprit,* and from then on until his death in Rome in 1957 he added to his already voluminous production numerous articles upon literature, problems of civilization, culture, and religion. In this last period of his career he broadened the range of his essays to comment generally upon contemporary civilization. Most important for us, he recognized a certain development in modern criticism toward a "criticism in depth": criticism relying on the perception of a human element in literature, and therefore a humanistic reading close to his own ideals. Béguin was led to religion through a concern for the human being, and through his own discovery of humanity in literature. Even later, when he recognizes humanity in a work only if it also conveys Catholic vision, he remains strongly attached to the idea of the writer's profoundly human intuition.

Such a blending of subjective, humanistic, and religious elements characterizes Béguin throughout his career, so that his position appears to be clear only when understood in the light of all three. But to confine his criticism to the niche of subjectivism, humanism, or religiosity is to curtail its significance for existential theory. Existential theory in general is concerned with subjective perceptions and reactions in literature, and Béguin's struggle to identify himself with a new manner of perceiving literature makes him one of the early examples of existential reading. Here is a man whose every literary pronouncement reflects his inner life, a man who really lives with literature. Narrow as his later judgments may be, they represent an extreme degree of identification with the works he discusses. Béguin has chosen texts with which he can sympathize, and he uses his knowledge of religion to illuminate his literary perceptions. By choosing such authors as Péguy and Bernanos, who are inspired by religious themes, he is able to achieve a sense of identification with them which he could not achieve with others. Béguin is coeval with these texts (and such is the ideal existential reading) because his interpretation springs both from them and from himself. He lives an act of reading which is both personal and analytical. These two aspects—a combination of personal and professional instincts—dominate Béguin's criticism. In this criticism, with its alternating emphases, the great themes remain the Romantic soul, its vision of a double reality, and its literary creation as a version of spiritual catharsis.

Béguin is best known for his description of the Romantic soul in literature: a specially attuned, perceptive intelligence which dominates German Romantic and modern French poetry. The same soul will take on a religious cast in his later works, but its delineation in *L'Ame romantique et le rêve* remains essentially unchanged. It is a sensitive, perceiving instrument which intuits the existence of a universe beyond formal knowledge and communicates this intuition as best it can. Drawing on its own intuitions, it creates a literary work that is primarily amenable to categories of mystic knowledge and not of formal construction. By defining the Romantic work as the re-creation of poetic "knowledge," Béguin departs from ordinary literary criticism. Knowledge in the accepted sense, he maintains, need not be found inside or through the work; rather, the work itself should be an active communication of vision.

The Romantic soul is defined by its characteristic posture of perceiving reality, by intuition and re-creation. To Béguin, all literature embodies gestures and attitudes toward experience, and the Romantic attitude is merely the most clairvoyant.[2] Authors in *L'Ame romantique et le rêve* constantly appear as visionaries who re-create their experience of life in a fantastic interplay of material reality and its metaphysical dimension. Hoffmann's dreamlike world exists only by such a continual metamorphosis: "you glide from real objects to the intoxication of dreams, in a sort of dizziness which takes possession of the senses, plays with their perceptions, and draws matter into a dance where it loses its substance" (p. 310). For Proust time puts reality into a comprehensible, human perspective. By the technique of an affective memory the author marshals his sensations and creates a coherent image of his own existence. Béguin's essay on Jean Paul describes a

2. Albert Béguin, *L'Ame romantique et le rêve* (Paris: Corti, 1956), p. 401.

creative mind employing material perceptions in a ceaseless series of metamorphoses: "There is a perpetual birth of forms, a creative spawning . . . dreams seize the universe at the very moment when creatures take form" (pp. 170–171). The Romantic mind re-creates objective reality in subjective forms; in a technique of literary creation which can only be called a creative dream-perception, it seizes familiar elements of the everyday world as they are being rearranged in a new and psychic structure. Such dreams, according to Béguin, are for Nerval an actual means of knowledge: "he saw in them a means of discovery: not merely a discovery of self, but a knowledge of ultimate reality" (p. 365). In probing the soul to hear the faint voices of a subconscious life, these Romantic or neo-Romantic authors seek a universal knowledge. It is the aim of this tradition to discover such universal knowledge and express it in individual terms.

Béguin consistently rejects any formal discipline which is not directly related to Romantic knowledge and to literature as an interrogation of human existence. To him the Romantic tradition extends into modern times only through Rimbaud and the surrealists, not through Mallarmé or Valéry. Mallarmé is Romantic in that he wants to transfigure reality, but his technical idealism is foreign to the tradition. Béguin rejects what he calls Mallarmé's "angelism" as too distant from perceived reality and from human nature. As for the Romantics, he says "each of their attempts remains intimately related to an interrogation which comes from all layers of being, and aspires to personal salvation" (p. 383). This emphasis upon personal salvation will form, toward the end of Béguin's career, the bridge to religiously evocative literature. At the moment it is the identifying mark which links Romantic interrogation to the spiritual revolt of Rimbaud and the surrealists.

Rimbaud's role as seer or voyant connects him directly to a tradition that intuits reality, even though his flamboyant and precise imagery remains far from the German Romantics' muted tones and fluidity of being. "Never was anyone so far from 'literature,' so close to the essence of poetry. Rimbaud's use of language is justified uniquely by this will to grasp something that is not grasped by any other of the means at our disposal" (p. 386). His example is emulated by the surrealists, whose grandeur for Béguin consists in "this continual orientation towards what is essential" (p. 392). The quest for human essences is the distinguishing characteristic by which Béguin rejects not only Mallarmé but all formalism.

At the end of *L'Ame romantique et le rêve*, Béguin describes three great myths that lie behind the Romantic perspective. The myth of the Soul, which the Romantics adopted as part of their reaction against rational and dehumanizing tendencies in literature, is a mystic belief in psychic unity: this "unexplained but fervent belief reaffirmed the existence of an inner center . . . a living essence" (p. 398). Because the soul seeks to perceive reality it turns away from the illusory verities of Cartesian philosophy. It then hopes to establish links with the second myth: that of the Unconscious. Through the subterranean impulses governing the unconscious mind, the Romantic soul hopes to attain contact with an underlying reality that escapes formalizing philosophies. Both these myths culminate naturally in the third myth of Poetry as a "series of magic gestures" in which the poet apprehends reality. "The poet is a seer, a visionary; he arrives at what is unknown, finds what is new. Poetry is absolute reality; its truth is superior to historical truth" (p. 400). Poetry is superior because it embodies a human dimension. As the essence of creative literature, it most clearly describes the human condition.

At this time, in 1937, Béguin's perspective is largely ontological—concerned with the being of literature—and not yet either religious or systematically existential. His basic themes are already apparent, nonetheless. "Poetry and Mysticism," an essay published in the same year as *L'Ame romantique et le rêve*, restates the ideas to which he has been led by pondering the Romantic tradition. Poetry is a verbalized mystic experience which gives the reader "the certainty of communicating suddenly with something real, real *in another sense*."[3] Although the poet's thoughts end in words while the mystic's end in silence, the poet's words have meaning "only by allusion to an intuited Night" which is their common experience.[4] Béguin's themes, then, are largely set forth by this time: the communication with another reality by sig-

3. Béguin, *Gérard de Nerval: suivi de Poésie et mystique* (Paris: Stock, 1937), p. 102.

4. Béguin's "Night" is an appropriate image for a theory of dreamlike perception. It is also a convenient metaphor for formless, unknowable existence, and is used as such by many "existential" writers.

nificant language, the unity and interpenetration of all being, and the poetic soul's search for identity and psychic unity in the night of the Unconscious. These themes, however much Béguin altered them after his religious conversion, and however much he disavowed them as early "pagan" studies, remain a fundamental concern until the end of his life.

Because Béguin's image of the Romantic soul is similar to Raymond's idea of a new "baroque" perception, the question of influence must be considered. Raymond's education and career began before Béguin's, and *De Baudelaire au surréalisme* was published four years before *L'Ame romantique et le rêve*. What is more, Béguin and Raymond were friends and had exchanged letters at an early point in their careers. From a chronological point of view, then, it would seem that Raymond influenced Béguin's path of development toward an anticlassical, expressive literature, and that Béguin developed this given insight and already-existing taste into a single theory of visionary intuition. At no point does either critic completely adopt the views of the other, for there is a strong strain of mysticism and personal involvement in Béguin which is lacking until quite late in Raymond, the versatile scholar and historian. It is very likely, nonetheless, that Béguin's ideas, when they are not rooted in religious concerns, stem from Raymond's.

A common interest in perception links Béguin's work with Raymond's. In addition, Béguin's introduction to *L'Ame romantique et le rêve* uses phrases which recall Raymond's earlier statement that "the frontiers are being effaced between subjective and objective feeling." This same observation, several times repeated or paraphrased by Béguin in *L'Ame romantique et le rêve* and in *Gérard de Nerval* (both published in 1937) shows the influence of *De Baudelaire au surréalisme* in helping the younger critic to formulate his idea of interpenetrability. "Again," says Béguin, "the frontiers between the self and the non-self were being displaced or effaced." [5] He also comments that "the answers to these questions proposed by dreams depend on the frontiers we trace between what is ourselves and what is not" (p. ix). In speaking of Jean Paul, Béguin notes that in his "landscape of the soul," "at every moment, the frontier between dreams and reality is effaced" (p. 167).

5. Béguin, *L'Ame romantique et le rêve*, p. x.

Finally, the essay "Poésie et mystique" (whose title echoes the title of Béguin's review of *De Baudelaire au surréalisme* in 1934) states that "at the height of poetic experience the frontiers between an exterior and an interior world are abolished; everything is an image offered to the free disposition of a mind composing and ordering all data according to its own manner." [6] The process of recomposing reality in the mind and imposing upon it a human dimension is a familiar process for Raymond; both critics insist upon a close coordination of the introspective mind with strong sensations of exterior reality. Béguin, however, will add a religious dimension to the process, while Raymond retains a humanistic perspective throughout. Nevertheless, Raymond's perspective continued to interest Béguin, who wrote him a letter saying that he liked the "profound subjectivity" and "references to 'the human element'" in *De Baudelaire au surréalisme*.[7] When the human element no longer satisfies Béguin, he will begin to set himself off from Raymond and to arrive at his own idea of the existential "truth" (rather than mere existential humanity) to be perceived in literature.

Béguin is most himself when he speaks of the mystical or religious side of literature. As early as 1925, in a letter to Raymond, he describes Péguy's style as "mystical." [8] This preference for a mystical style is thus already established before *L'Ame romantique et le rêve*, and it eventually gives a religious interpretation to the idea of Romantic perception. Such an interpretation makes sense for Béguin, mainly because he believes that the spiritual soul in literature represents a universal experience through which men communicate. He has always looked beyond forms for a larger reality, and used this sense of reality as a practicable literary yardstick. From the beginning, he prefers Claudel's "whole" view and "truer order" to Valéry's "little arrangements." [9] He praises the Maritains' *Situation de la poésie* (1938) for setting poetry against a "clear, very firm notion of the human being conceived as a whole." [10] He does not look farther than the whole human being. Later

6. Béguin, *Gérard de Nerval*, p. 110.

7. Béguin, letter dated October 23, 1933, to Raymond, in "Quelques lettres d'Albert Béguin," *Cahiers du Sud*, no. 360 (April–May 1961), p. 210.

8. Béguin, letter in *Étapes*, p. 144.

9. Béguin, letter in *Étapes*, p. 205.

10. Béguin, "Situation de la poésie," *Esprit*, April 1929, p. 133.

he conceives of this human being as "whole" only when part of a religious framework. Béguin's Romantic soul develops into a religious soul through the truth and authenticity of its perception. An author, in the same way, must display the true perception of reality in order to prove his truly perceptive genius. Béguin, when he rejects "magical" for "true" literature, believes that he is rejecting a whole school of literature and proposing a completely new standard of appreciation. In fact, the religious dimension of his criticism only prolongs its original emphasis upon human perceptions of reality. Although Béguin turns his back upon the irreligious perceptions of the Romantics and the "disincarnation" of Rimbaud and Mallarmé, he welcomes the same intuitive attitude in Péguy, Bloy, and Bernanos when it conveys Christian revelation. As a critic he has passed through a period of technical experimentation and discovery, and is now ready to use these methods in a special framework: the analysis of literature as revelation.

Béguin's literary criticism shows the stamp of personal involvement at every stage. It becomes what he calls a continuing "promenade among the diverse forms of human expression." [11] His most famous and influential book, L'Ame romantique et le rêve, is for him only one stage in a process of self-discovery. Writing to Noël Devaulx on February 15, 1949, he speaks of his disappointment in the "sterility" of his first subjects. "You are surprised that I could pass from German Romanticism to Péguy. But I began with Péguy well before having any idea of Romanticism, and I have returned to him after this 'nocturnal' adventure which has been only a sort of accident, and finally an unadmitted deception. It is from knowing the sterile dizziness of a poetry of disincarnation that I have come to the Christian faith." [12] This extreme personal involvement with literature never actually means that Béguin abandons his profession for thinly-disguised evangelism. Curiously enough, he maintains a delicate balance by seeking out works which correspond to his beliefs, and by analyzing them in terms which he is careful to keep literary. He is moved to redefine the notion of literature, along with Raymond, but in doing so he is primarily concerned with supporting an anti-formal aesthetics. He does not reject literature for

11. Béguin, in "Entretien avec Albert Bèguin," *Esprit,* December 1958 (issue titled *Albert Béguin* and henceforth referred to as *Albert Béguin*), p. 762.
12. Béguin, letter in *Albert Béguin*, p. 816.

religion. There is no simple movement away from art in Béguin's career, and each phase of his inner development moves toward its literary corollary and reconciliation.

Béguin's personal tastes, as they emerge over the years from letters and editorials, are remarkably consistent. In the decade preceding *L'Ame romantique et le rêve* he is already seeking out expressive rather than formal constructions. Fragments of Gide's *Renoncement au Voyage* are full of an "inner fervor," and precious "for those who look for something besides literary construction." [13] Péguy's style, he says, cannot be understood without comparison to mystic style [14]—a comparison which he waits twenty years to elaborate. He reads Russian novelists, Dostoevsky in particular, to extract "a glance directed otherwise from our own upon the same objects." [15]

This period of humanistic interest in varying perspectives is shaken and altered by the prospect of another World War. In March, 1936, Béguin comments that "European humanity is looking for new moral bases, because the bankruptcy of everything we lived by is too obvious." [16] As editor of the *Cahiers du Rhône* he begins to assert a more narrow and strictly religious humanism which will set the tone for his later writings. The series of the *Cahiers* is to be a "Christian testimony" in literature, and contributions must be consonant with these aims. His first editorial essay in the *Cahiers* (March, 1942), rejects the older, broader humanism as an indiscriminate relativism. "We have been injured enough by becoming accustomed to a carelessness with truth and a cult of sincerity which, for a long time, have made us consider any attitude as valuable and 'interesting', provided that it was the authentic expression of a man." [17] When Béguin renounces the cult of sincerity, however, he does not renounce the study of literature as an expression of humanity. As late as 1954 a radio interview finds him reaffirming literature as a human expression and means of human knowledge,[18] and

13. Béguin, letter in *Albert Béguin*, p. 775.
14. Béguin, letter in *Étapes*, p. 144.
15. Béguin, letter in *Étapes*, p. 151.
16. Béguin, letter in *Albert Béguin*, p. 782.
17. Béguin, *Nos Cahiers* (first *Cahier du Rhône*, Neuchâtel, La Baconnière, March 1942), p. 71.
18. Béguin, "Entretien avec Albert Béguin," *Albert Béguin*, pp. 755–765.

he analyzes the metaphysical human being embodied in literature to the end of his career.

Béguin's vision of the Romantic soul prefigures his vision of the religious soul, and both Romantic and religious analyses refer to the same kind of perception. Two other main themes, the author's perception of a double reality, and his composition as a kind of spiritual catharsis, move similarly from a secular to a religious interpretation. Both are closely related to the theory of the soul, inasmuch as the embodied author *is* the soul. The development of all three themes reflects Béguin's own spiritual development.

The double reality which an author perceives is the sense of something in and beyond apparent reality. Both Raymond and Béguin insist that the first level of reality be present, and neither is willing for the poet to lose the sense of this world in intellectualized "classical" abstractions. Both critics also believe that this first level of reality is organized by human perceptions into a higher, second level—the metaphysical dimension of mundane reality. Béguin is still close to Raymond when he speaks of a subjective, neo-Romantic sense of "something beyond," but his interpretation of the "something" will go far beyond Raymond's broad humanism. The new "realism" which both seek to define, and which may have its roots in the medieval tradition, appears in Béguin as a revelation of Christian existentialism. It is a "feeling for things of this earth in their natural connection with mystery and the mind," [19] and is represented by Claudel and Péguy, not by Montherlant or Giono (p. 40). This "realism" becomes defined as an area of reality in itself, appearing more or less partially in various authors.

Béguin's emphasis upon this new reality as an existence above and beyond the text sets him off from Raymond, for whom the only analyzable reality is that in the text. Béguin realizes that he is going beyond the text proper, but his method proposes placing it in a larger context and returning to it with a more comprehensive illumination. In a *Cahier* ostensibly devoted to various essays on Bergson, Béguin identifies a "region of silence" in Bergson which is developed by Péguy, and calls his essay "Note conjointe sur Bergson et Péguy." The same technique

19. Béguin, *Nos Cahiers*, p. 59.

of filling in metaphysical gaps appears five years later in a volume dedicated to Mallarmé. Here "Notes sur Mallarmé et Claudel" compose an imaginary dialogue in which sentences from Claudel cap each quotation from Mallarmé. In each essay the earlier writer is seen to be groping toward the fulfilment which appears in the later one. Béguin thus feels justified in that he has cast light upon the complete spiritual dimension of the earlier author. Such a procedure is possible only for a critic who believes that literature is a metaphysical expression, and it leads to the logical possibility of analyzing unwritten works. Both Poulet and Richard explore this possibility, but a more textually minded critic, such as Jean Rousset, will argue that it borders on philosophy rather than on literature.

Once Béguin has definitely set himself the aim of revealing a Christian realism in literature, his task becomes much more straightforward, and possibly more imaginative. After his conversion in 1940 he never again studies an author who does not consider religious themes. From Pascal to Péguy, Bernanos, and Bloy (including the very conservative Balzac), Béguin concentrates upon various literary methods of communicating this one, agreed-upon vision of supernatural reality. Since the common vision does not change, the critic is able to explore new avenues of approach; paradoxically enough he can now be more "modern," more technical, and more "existential" than when he was elucidating Romantic myths.

The beginning of Béguin's literary shift away from his old sympathies comes with his analysis of Péguy. Péguy is to represent a newly discovered tradition of French poetry, one which Béguin can oppose to an older, purely humanistic tradition. In writing of Péguy's monumental *Eve,* he places it " 'to one side' of a tradition . . . perhaps 'to one side' of all poetry, or of what we are describing when we mean to speak thus of a magic and an art. But it is *on* the side of an expression in which poetry is closely related to truth." [20] Béguin does not intend to say that this new form of writing is unartistic, but he does maintain that it requires a different kind of reading. In *La Prière de Péguy* (1942) and the "Note sur la Litanie (pour servir à l'intelligence du style de Péguy)" printed with it, the critic describes a poetry that is

20. Béguin, letter in *Étapes,* p. 224.

closer to the poet's inner being than to any technical art form. Péguy's poetry is composed as a prayer and must be read as a litany. His repetitious, voluminous form is a means of creating another world where events appear in a poetic light not influenced or tainted by the everyday world of non-poetic values. Ostensibly the "Note on Litany" is an aid to Péguy alone, but references to medieval lyrics, Aragon, Rimbaud, Luc Estang, and Pierre Emmanuel make it appear that Béguin's real interest is in defining a larger manner of expression.

The culmination of Béguin's work on Péguy comes in *L'Eve de Péguy* (1952), where the critic returns to the analysis of repetitive form. Péguy's technique of repetition creates a calculated, hypnotic monotony which first lulls the reader and then forces him to concentrate upon any variation. This style deals in a series of emotions rather than in static forms. It is composed (in the poet's own term) of a series of "climates," or states of being, all of which refer to a poetic core.

This antiverbal, evocative conception of style resembles one already upheld by Béguin and Raymond (and Charles Du Bos): that a work of art must be considered from the point of a central *foyer,* an inspiring core of being from which the work radiates as a psychic entity. "The point of birth from which everything flows is at the same time the convergent point to which everything returns . . . everything is ordered and oriented around a generating source." [21] Béguin has come back to the idea of a generating, creative source such as the Romantic soul, but he now attempts to provide some description of its emergence into language. This soul is emerging in an act of self-discovery: "Péguy *discovers* the horizons of his poem . . . in the very words that are assembled by the pen. This is an extraordinarily structured composition; for in order to *discover* in this way, everything must erupt from a profound source in the self, not by chance and in formless waves, but in a continual reference to a central point" (p. 189). There are two implications to this discussion: first, that works must be understood in reference to their guiding inspiration, and second, that they must be evolved through the systematic expression of a writer's spiritual coherence. Any other organization, either intellectual or aesthetic, is a deceptive veneer of technique.

21. Béguin, *L'Eve de Péguy* (Paris: Labergerie, 1948), p. 18.

Béguin's new interest in a writer's manner of expression leads him away from Romantic themes and closer to existential considerations. In speaking of Pascal, who is already established as a religious author, he can afford to emphasize his existential vision and its modernity. *Pascal par lui-même* (1952) claims that "Pascal can easily pass for one of the precursors of modern thought and merits being invoked as such by existentialism." [22] Both Pascal and existentialism are preoccupied by man's fate, and both emphasize the need for choice or action in the face of a human condition which is "rather lived than thought." It is only because Pascal is concerned with religious issues that Béguin is able to make the equation, but he is quick to find here a prototype of modern Christian existentialism. "Pascal has never been more necessary to us than today . . . he knew . . . that the question of God is a 'question of man,' an existential question . . . that the answer from then on is not in a solution but in an act, a leap, a welcoming" (p. 111). Pascal makes this "leap" as a writer and offers it to the reader in his works.

Béguin's Pascal is not the familiar Romantic figure of an harassed, helplessly agonized being, but a style-conscious writer and philosopher. His real "anguish" is existential: "that of thought which is no longer certain of dominating its object . . . of establishing a satisfactory relationship between it and the living creature" (p. 45). From a recognition of the "very paradox of things," of the fact that "existants are relative, are the very places of relationships and of tensions" (p. 12), he evolves an "immediate" style which is to retain the antitheses and rhythms of life. "Pascal the writer is above all identical with the interior Pascal . . . from then on, fidelity to the object is fused with fidelity to the subject who writes, tracing the rhythm of his speech on the vivid gesture of his experience and grasp of reality" (p. 11). His immediate style suggests that he (like Péguy) discovers his truths at the moment he writes them down, and this close relationship between personal experience and its literary expression creates an extremely efficient, vital communication. In Béguin's analysis Pascal is an extremely competent writer whose existential vision exists on the stylistic as well as the metaphysical plane.

22. Béguin, *Pascal par lui-même* (Paris: Le Seuil, 1959), p. 108.

Supernatural vision and immediate communication are two ingredients which seem to make up the whole of Béguin's criticism. When he speaks of Bernanos, the vision is representative of a whole body of modern Catholic literature for which Béguin makes himself the interpreter and apologist. Bernanos as novelist tries to evoke a peculiar visionary knowledge, a sense of a "double world," or of each character's "supernatural situation." Incarnating this sense of double reality is the image of the child, whose unsullied personality reflects the real core of the later adult. Bernanos gives a childlike simplicity to all his main characters, and with it an intuition of supernatural circumstances. These children of God (such as the curé of Ambricourt) have a sudden, global vision into the existential condition of others—they see in another world. To Béguin, this vision contains religious truth. It is also important for his notion of poetic myth. The "myth," constructed out of the author's "data of experience," [23] gives form to any work of art and must be painstakingly extracted from the author's own consciousness. Béguin accentuates Bernanos' "workmanlike approach" to composition and his laborious exploration of the special meanings he feels in certain words and phrases. "The unique rhythm of his prose, which seems to reproduce the very rhythm of interior life like no other, is obtained at the end of a bitter pursuit . . . by the patient search for a movement which is first of all intuited, little by little called from the depths, and retained by words" (p. 64). This intuitive approach does not entail any lazy self-indulgence but proposes a new discipline involving the whole personality instead of merely the aesthetic intellect.

After his conversion, Béguin devotes only one book to a secular author: his *Balzac visionnaire* (1946). This book could seem a departure from Béguin's later perspectives, as its subject is more humanistic and less evangelical than the Catholic poets and novelists who interest him after 1940.[24] The study of Balzac, however, is no reversion into humanistic literature, for Balzac has an extremely conservative religious viewpoint that is touched only by an odd, Swedenborgian mysticism. Béguin's study may have been inspired by Ernst Robert Curtius, whose *Balzac*

23. Béguin, *Bernanos par lui-même* (Paris: Le Seuil, 1954), p. 44.
24. Marcel Raymond suggests that *Balzac visionnaire* was written soon after *L'Ame romantique* (from 1937 to 1939) and revised for its publication in 1946 (Raymond, *Étapes*, p. 17).

(1923) opposed the novelist's imaginative vision to a naturalistic, scientifically objective view of reality. But Béguin never mentions Curtius' book, which is much more scholarly and comprehensive than Béguin's analysis of Balzac's divinatory vision. Béguin continues to use his own key coordinates of vision and intuitive style, and outlines the figure of a visionary genius whose work is a world in itself.

From the very beginning, Béguin makes it clear that he considers Balzac's style more vital, more "real," and more adequately expressed than the insanely perfectionist art that lies under the shadow of "Flaubert's curse." [25] The critic's old hatred of formal structures comes to the surface again, as he compares the inner vitality of submerged, metaphysical organization to the superficial, brittle veneer of well-articulated prose. He looks upon Flaubert's language as a "maniacal perfection, with its interminable repetitions . . . and expected endings" (p. 21). In contrast, Balzac's "marvellously free" language has a style of internal relationships, of varying rhythms between episodes. It is Rabelaisian in its sensuous love of words, and these words convey not plots but the emotional undercurrents of situations. Balzac "chooses his expression according to the changing exigencies of the story" (p. 22). His language is suggested by the situations it attempts to describe, and must be judged "according to countless hidden analogies whose web, underlying drama and plot, forms the true theme of each of his novels" (p. 23). This "true theme" may be described as an inner structure of related emotions that take part in changing patterns. It may well be the unwritten part of literature, and yet Béguin feels that here is the creative shadow that looms closely and precisely behind each word of the written text. The writing succeeds when this background of experience coincides exactly with the words that describe it, and when there is an actual correspondence between words and the life they symbolize. Balzac has such an evocative power. He writes by listening to the inner voice of words, and "possessed, really possessed by his passion for language, abandons himself to the suggestions of words" (p. 52). In this ecstatic state all creative powers reach a fused point "where an exceptional participation in life is revealed by a no less singular participation

25. Béguin, *Balzac visionnaire* (Geneva: Ed. Skira, 1946), p. 22.

in verbal substance" (pp. 52–53). Béguin, like any formal critic, looks constantly to verbal substance, but his perspective requires abandoning the formal structures of words for their subterranean structures of meanings.

A familiar concept—that of a "knowledge" of double reality—underlies Béguin's discussion of "participation in life." If Balzac's characters are more convincing than those of Stendhal or Flaubert, and are "denser, closer to the true weight of carnal creatures" (p. 25), their creator has endowed them with a soul and a destiny beyond most realistic descriptions. Béguin constantly refers to such a hidden profundity. In "the most profound pages," he says, material objects that have been "described to such a point that we think we know them, suddenly give way to another world" (p. 55). It is in this sense that Balzac is the visionary of Béguin's title, for he has visionary insight into the simply material realities around him. His method is not to "paint current reality" but to push its details to hyperbole, "to force an everyday spectacle to metamorphose itself into vision" (p. 171). These special powers endow ordinary events with unaccustomed significance and eventually organize all life around a personal myth. Balzac's characters all reflect this myth, and "are only themselves because there exists below them . . . Balzac's mind" (pp. 205–206). His mind dominates all the disparate forms of reality in the *Comédie humaine*, and gives them a spiritual coherence which reflects a single source.

Béguin's notion of a unifying creative myth is frequently found in his criticism of texts that are highly religious in content. When speaking of Balzac, however, he avoids merely repeating this myth in the same terms. Balzac's universe is more human than theological, and its creator is only quasi-divine. The *Comédie humaine* combines two mythic forces: a gesture of creation "forcing the boundaries of knowledge," and the recognition of man's ultimate destruction by time. Balzac as author presides over a multiple creation in "the very gesture of God creating this universe." He projects his personal myth into the *Comédie humaine* by a proliferation of obsessed and desiring characters; his myth is not in a stated scheme of the universe but "in the humanity he begets, which is a humanity all poised towards a creative act" (p. 72). Béguin calls this visionary gesture a Promethean grasp of reality, a second

Creation which is "to approach the sacred mysteries of existence." [26] This mystery of creation entails an act of destruction, a destruction by time against which human will can give only futile resistance.

Béguin has said earlier that Balzac's style is made up of varying rhythms and changing relationships. Such variations may be called a manipulation of time sequences in the style of composition, and according to Béguin this stylistic use of time transforms itself into the dominant metaphysical concern of the later novels. Into Balzac's complete myth comes the realization of a wasting, destructive time which works to nullify the creative act. Both the novelist and his characters create by an effort of will, and time is an overshadowing element in the background which gives poignancy to the interplay of various wills. Balzac is fond of depicting a driving will in his central characters, and to Béguin "each of the beings inhabiting his universe is, like himself, a seeker after absolutes and thirsty for eternity." [27] In existential terms these figures create their own destinies. The major characters, be they Père Goriot and his fondness for his daughters, Pons with a mania for art objects and good food, or Gobseck with his passion for gold, are driven by a force that impels them to action. They are impressive because "they use their energy to create their own existence . . . they *act* more than they *are*." They feel, choose, and desire until their characters are formed of pure will. All their ideas and obsessions, however, must be measured against time, whose victorious challenge gives a sense of urgency to all human creation.

Balzac, then, creates his characters around a personal myth, and for this reason he represents the sort of author Béguin has admired throughout. All Béguin's subjects, from Pascal to Péguy, appear as subjective expressions and personal myths. Such a personalized view of the author is necessary in this theory, for which literature is defined as the successful expression of a man's existential experience. Attached to this definition are a number of corollary statements: that the organization of any work reflects the human coherence behind it; that an author must explore his own experience to grasp what is truly his material,

26. This concept of a Promethean grasp substituting itself for God is not necessarily approved. Elsewhere, Béguin comments that modern poetry's attempt to rid itself of the body is a "Promethean act," an arrogant opposite to Péguy's attitude as the "poet of incarnation" (Béguin, *L'Eve de Péguy*, p. 10).

27. Béguin, *Balzac visionnaire*, p. 58.

and constantly test the words he plans to use against the touchstone of his own experience; and that the critic must read with an empathetic vision of all these levels of creation. A simple theoretical statement of this position is not complete, however, unless it takes into account the critic's personal involvement.

This involvement goes deeper than the obvious influence of Béguin's religious development on the vision he analyzes in literature. Béguin has always looked to literature as a means of communion with reality, with oneself, and among men. Poulet suggests that Béguin's turning toward literature stemmed from an inability to feel strongly through primary sensations. He needed the humanized interpretations of language.[28] It is certain that Béguin, too, understands himself best through exposure to literature.

When Béguin describes himself as a critic, he thinks of himself as a creative author—only the medium is different. *L'Ame romantique et le rêve* is a "personal interrogation" of works studied: a means of self-development via other human expressions, but not a final statement about certain collected works. "Actually I conceived it and carried it out as a great obstinate question for which I myself have no adequate answer. Through this book, and while writing it, I arrived at certain convictions which were suddenly made clear one day by the composition of the last pages." [29] Béguin's emphasis on personal affirmation through writing leads him to envision, in a letter, a criticism based upon the stream-of-consciousness. Here the literary critic would use the surrealist technique of "automatic writing," and a literary work would be substituted for the surrealist's feeling of reality. "It seems to me that this experience could be taken up on a larger scale and that by such means (by listening before writing, and forbidding oneself any intention of putting things in order) one could arrive at some rather curious affirmations." [30] Béguin never seriously proposes any technique so limited and undisciplined as automatic writing, but he does emphasize the need to reach some sense of personal identification between the being in a work and the reader seeking to comprehend. In writing

28. Georges Poulet, "La Pensée critique d'Albert Béguin," *Cahiers du Sud,* no. 360 (April–May 1961), p. 178.

29. Béguin, letter dated January 27, 1938, in *Étapes,* pp. 203–204.

30. Béguin, letter in *Étapes,* pp. 202–203.

to Georges Poulet he speaks of a "sort of passion that grips me in the struggle with an author I love, and this insatiability that launches me— with the help of the work—beyond any work." [31] This "insatiability" for something beyond any work marks a point at which Béguin's work reaches past the unique human expression in a text and toward the generic human expression of literature. Through experiencing a text he is now able to make it a stepping-stone to a transcendent reality.

When Béguin reaches this culmination of his literary experience his personal work diverges from the realm of pure literary criticism. He is aware of the divergence and continues to encourage a non-religious empathetic criticism at the same time that he pursues his own religious interests in literature. As editor of *Esprit*, Béguin points out and approves the development of an empathetic criticism that is close to his own. After 1950 (the year he became editor of *Esprit*) he adds to his writings a number of general observations on criticism. Moreover, he shows a greater concern for contemporary criticism and literature.

When Béguin speaks of the role of the critic he maintains a professional distance between existential criticism and religious interpretation. He has always preferred human substructures to their exterior, textual forms, and now he works to distinguish this perspective from a psychological or philosophical criticism which may seem closely allied. The difference between the latter critiques and the existential criticism that is his own, appears in the original posture of the reader. The existential reader tries to adopt a position inside the text, while other critiques retain an outside point of reference. The existential reader is able to gain the confidence of his author; in Béguin's terms he is a "critic in confidence" ("*critique de confiance*").

This ideal reader is "generous" in that he yields to the work. He practices a kind of submissive reading which allows him to subordinate his personality to that of the author. "The critic in confidence recognizes that the true writer can write only to grip more closely, despite the illusions of art, what seems to him to be his truth or the part of truth which is worth being communicated to another. The connection of the writer to the reader, reflected here by the relationship of critic

31. Georges Poulet, "Albert Béguin, l'insatiable," in *Étapes*, p. 265.

and writer, is of generosity, of gift, and consequently of approach to, or identification with, the other." [32] This sympathetic identification occurs in a "pre-criticism" which precedes stylistic analysis, and which is sought past forms. It is destroyed by an outer orientation, such as that of psychology or sociology. Béguin distinguishes here between the "criticism in confidence" and the analysis of Baudelaire given in René Laforgue's book, *L'Echec de Baudelaire* (1931). Laforgue's analysis of Baudelaire's "failure," an analysis taken up by Sartre and the more sociologically minded existentialists, is a work of "Boeotian malevolence" which inaugurates a whole literature "grubbing in psychoanalysis" (p. 1014). In spite of its claims, such a perspective is not existential, as it carries along with it a whole system of outer values. To read in this manner is to become a know-better critic who automatically places himself outside the work by assuming that the author has hidden behind a screen of protective colorations and must be exposed. For Béguin any such exterior view establishes a hostile relationship and prevents the critic from reaching the existential goal of "seeing into" an author.

Béguin is continually hostile to psychological or philosophical solutions for the human experience in literature. It is not enough, he says, to take literature as an historical document or as a psychological symptom.[33] All men are insane only in relation to a given society, and the designation of insanity can be questioned when applied to men like Hölderlin, Nerval, Nietzsche, and Artaud.[34] He states repeatedly that a human condition that can be analyzed psychologically becomes subject to different laws and surpasses the original psychological area of analysis when expressed in a work of art. Philosophical criticism is unsatisfactory as well: "it always remains outside the truth of poetic language, because this language is precisely poetic insofar as it grasps what escapes the philosopher's reflection, even the philosopher who tries hardest to limit himself to the 'existent.'" [35] It would seem that Béguin quarrels with psychological and philosophical critiques because they reflect different systems of truth from his own. However, he also

32. Béguin, "Pré-critique," *Esprit*, June 1954, p. 1017.
33. Béguin, "Note sur la critique littéraire," *Esprit*, March 1955, p. 447.
34. Béguin, "Qui est fou?" *Esprit*, December 1952, pp. 777–788.
35. Béguin, "Henri Michaux, poète de la cruauté" in the literary supplement to the *Gazette de Lausanne*, October 30–31, 1949, p. 8.

defends the existential view of literature from unrelated disciplines and seeks to establish a definition and an approach which is solely existential and solely literary.

In 1955 Béguin wrote at length about the rise of a new criticism, a criticism much like his own but lacking in religious interpretations. This time the view he opposes is the historical, documentary style represented by Gustave Lanson and popular in the French schools. Béguin objects that "no work of art was ever created to be a document, but rather to set forth a supplementary world. Modern criticism, with a Bachelard, a Poulet, a Jean-Pierre Richard, a Blanchot, a Roland Barthes, is newly conscious of this particular existence of a work . . . which can be valuably interpreted only if the interpreter is situated at the interior of the author's created universe." [36] A new criticism is needed to sweep away ingrained historical habits and to introduce into literature the analysis of human experience "just as Malraux has shaken up the immobile showcases of art history" (p. 170). Neither formal, nor psychological, nor philosophical, nor finally historical perspectives are adequate for Béguin's new criticism.

Béguin favors the new criticism because it dismisses from the start all approaches founded on extra-literary values and asserts the author's unique creative act as its fundamental reality. This new vision is necessary, he feels, for any fruitful reinterpretation of the work of art. The definition of literature must put down deeper roots, for "there is literature as soon as a successful metamorphosis of language evokes a particular form of expression, one that is absolutely personal." [37] A knowledgeable critic must try to find the original creative gesture which distinguishes one work from all others and must identify in the author "a movement issued from the most irreducible part of the person— what constitutes him first of all in his profound solitude" (p. 449).[38]

36. Béguin, "Limites de l'histoire littéraire," *Esprit*, January 1955, p. 169.
37. Béguin, "Note sur la critique littéraire," p. 448.
38. It is this emphasis upon the personal structure of a work of art that distinguishes Béguin and his fellow critics from such contemporary "structural" analysts as Lucien Goldmann. Up to a point, their vision of the work of art is identical. Goldmann distinguishes between an "aesthetic" analysis, which is for him the purely technical study of the inherent structures in a work, and an "explication," which links the work to a larger significant perspective. The perspective he chooses is a vision of man, as it is for Béguin, but a vision of man the social animal rather than man the individual. The frame of reference is thus radically changed. In *Pour une*

Thus far Béguin has outlined a theory of criticism indistinguishable from his own. Although his own practice moves away from this purely humanistic approach, he does not attempt to introduce here any supra-literary religious interpretation. The "profundity" he finds in this criticism is an existential, human profundity.

In accentuating the human dimensions of literature, this newly "profound" criticism looks only to the work and to the concrete phenomena which are the source of its inspiration. "It is the work which is the datum, the reality valuable for itself, and which must be understood by itself, not as a symptom of something more important to grasp." [39] Exponents of the new approach, such as Bachelard and Richard, follow a path which leads from the first physical sensations to an actual knowledge of the existential creature revealing himself in a work. "That from verbal signs in which an unspoken fundament is condensed, you can come back up—not simply to a psychology of the author but to a concrete knowledge of this other being which ordinarily escapes us: such is the certainty which authorizes the new criticism" (p. 450). The hope of these new critics is to discover the total human experience incarnated in literature, and their method is to apply existential perspectives to retain "a more attentive feeling for experience, a feeling consequently better able to appreciate the testimony of poetry." [40] Béguin is in complete agreement with the methods of this new criticism, but he has long since committed himself to working them out in a religious perspective.

Toward the end of Béguin's career his interests veer away from literature toward literary revelation. The temptation to go beyond literature

---

Sociologie du roman (Paris: Gallimard, 1964), Goldmann agrees with a "genetic structuralism" that calls *"all* human behavior" (including literature) "an attempt to give a *meaningful answer* to a particular situation," an attempt that generates successive states of equilibrium responding to successive situations (Goldmann, p. 338). However, Goldmann considers "cultural creation" a "doubtless privileged sector, but nonetheless the same as all other sectors of human behavior" (Goldmann, p. 337). This claim of sociology, like the claims of psychology or historicism, is one that Béguin and his colleagues cannot admit. Goldmann himself sees that the main point of difference lies here, when he comments that "empirical, rationalist, and recently phenomenological" thinkers see this "meaningful answer" as individual, whereas he, along with Marxists, psychologists, and sociologists, sees it as keyed to a "transindividual" group (Goldmann, p. 339).

39. Béguin, "Note sur la critique littéraire," p. 449.
40. Béguin, "Etudes sur la temps humain," *Esprit*, May 1951, p. 803.

must always be strong for a subjective, existential approach, as one which already goes *through* the text to a pre-verbal experience. Béguin's digression is significant in that it shows some of the literary pitfalls of this perspective. One of the central theses of the existential approach is the subjective, completely sympathetic relationship between reader and work. In theory an indispensable method for perceiving and communicating the real author instead of a straw man reflecting preconceived critical attitudes, it hazards in practice an unconscious carry-over of the critic's personality. If such criticism does not become a type of self-analysis to avoid the pitfalls of subjectivism (this method has been tried by Bachelard), it may well fall into an unconscious system of evaluation. Toward the end, Béguin's religious convictions led him to discard certain works of literature that at one time he had loved. As Poulet describes it: "each time I saw him I was sad to remark that he had extinguished still another flame, that he had cast off an old love. We used to speak with equal admiration of Vigny, Rilke, or Mallarmé, and then, a year later, I met Béguin again and discovered that for him Vigny, Rilke, and Mallarmé were now only ashes. Even, at the end, I believe that his great passion for Nerval had almost dried up. Pascal was menaced. He was tottering on the razor's edge which, for Béguin, separated his loves and his hatreds." [41] Béguin ends, then, by limiting his existential communion with an author.

Béguin's ability to sympathize and communicate with given works should not blind one to the fact that he kept his own personal quest foremost in mind. In *L'Ame romantique et le rêve*, and throughout his career, he insists that he is testing his own experience by the echo it finds in "diverse forms of human expression." He almost finds a satisfactory mold for this quest in existential criticism, combining as it does literary and metaphysical investigation. The great models of Béguin's criticism (*L'Ame romantique, Balzac visionnaire*, and the works on Pascal, Péguy, and Bernanos) are still examples of that capacity for sympathetic identification which is the aim of every existential reader. At a given point, however, Béguin veers away from purely literary criticism to a set of values that he finds more important. Henceforth he will be regarded as a seminal but not a complete theoretician. He

41. Georges Poulet, "Albert Béguin, l'insatiable," p. 264.

will influence subsequent criticism mainly through his example: his concept of the author's visionary experience and "immediate" style, his championing of a sympathetic reading opposed to formal systems and extra-literary values, and his own involvement as a reader totally committed to the literary vision.

GEORGES POULET

Georges Poulet is the first critic to develop Raymond's and Béguin's concept of experience in literature as a systematic tool of analysis. Born in Belgium, he has taught at the University of Edinburgh (1927–1951), at The Johns Hopkins University (1952–1957), where he was associated with Joseph Hillis Miller and Jean Starobinski, and at the University of Zurich, where he is now Professor of French literature. Poulet's major works include three *Etudes sur le temps humain* (1949, 1952, and 1964), *Les Métamorphoses du cercle* (1961), *L'Espace proustien* (1963), and *Trois Essais de mythologie romantique* (1966). He is now preparing a fourth volume of the *Etudes sur le temps humain,* as well as an *Essai sur la pensée critique de notre temps,* in which he will apply his analysis of literature to an analysis of criticism. Poulet takes up

74

the subjective and sympathetic approach of Raymond and Béguin, but he is more systematic. Moreover, he is the first critic to propose analytical coordinates for the human experience in literature, and the first to focus this experience in time and in space. With the results of his analysis he is able to re-create the stages in which each author grasps a sense of his own existence. Finally, Poulet sets various existential careers into a pattern that allows him to rewrite literary history and that makes of it truly a "history of the mind expressing itself in forms."

It was Poulet's reading of *De Baudelaire au surréalisme* and *L'Ame romantique et le rêve* that gave him new insights into works of art and supported his dislike for traditional academic analysis. His view of the literary experience, however, goes beyond Raymond's and Béguin's emphasis on personality and character. Poulet's development of the existential perspective cuts their last ties with the formal and historical approach and lifts their argument onto a consistently existential plane. He shifts their focus from the individual author to the author's generic human experience—from the personal stylistic stamp of the creator to his unique experience, mapped out in existential coordinates.

Although Poulet recognizes Raymond and Béguin as the main source of his inspiration, his views can be traced to other men as well: to Arthur Lovejoy, Charles Du Bos, and Gaston Bachelard. From Raymond and Béguin he learned his concern for the pre-verbal substructures of literature. The actual form of Poulet's works, however, is closer to Arthur Lovejoy's scheme of intellectual history in *The Great Chain of Being*. The first two *Etudes sur le temps humain,* with their emphasis on shifting patterns of perception throughout generations of literary thought, are as much related to Lovejoy's lectures (1936) as to *De Baudelaire au surréalisme* (1933) and *L'Ame romantique et le rêve* (1937). A third element in Poulet's approach is its hypothesis that the work's structure is keyed to a central core or *foyer* that generates each work's interlocking themes and governs its spiritual identity. To focus on a creative human core is necessary and natural for any existential ideology, and yet the credit for developing the term *foyer* as a tool of literary analysis must be given largely to Charles Du Bos. To Du Bos as well goes the credit for formulating the idea of a "starting point" in creating the self, and for probing a writer's feeling of identity. Finally, Poulet's refusal to submerge himself in purely intellectual, purely "classical" formulations draws him close to the phenomenological perspective of Gaston Bachelard. Bachelard's literary phenomenology encourages Poulet to connect an author's metaphysical experience with the physical sensations which are its raw material. Jean-Pierre Richard, a follower of both Bachelard and Poulet, is the most notable adapter of Bachelard's phenomenological perspective to literary criticism. His analysis of existential patterns and the correlation of physical images and intangible emotions strongly influences Poulet's work around the time of *Les Métamorphoses du cercle* (1961). All these men embody separate perspectives which relate to the existential view of literature. Their work corroborates and partly suggests Poulet's own theory, but is not sufficient to explain it completely.

Poulet's own criticism is no mere jigsaw puzzle of influences. His sensitive analyses of the text, his intricate assessments of each author's metaphysical stance, and his systematic discovery and combination of existential coordinates in literature comprise a unique entry into the work of art which has become even more ambitious in recent years.

Poulet's early works (*Etudes sur le temps humain I*, 1949, and *Etudes sur le temps humain II: La Distance intérieure*, 1952) propose using categories of time and space to analyze the manner in which human perceptions organize a work's mental universe. His technique is largely that of extrapolation and synthesis, as he collects words and phrases revealing existential predispositions. *Les Métamorphoses du cercle* (1961) develops patterns of perception and existence based upon these coordinates. Here the concept of the circle and its emanating center represents man as a perceiving, active figure who reacts to his environment. The pattern of human experience, says Poulet, is a central emanating thought which proceeds in increasing concentric circles to vivify and unite the immense "interior distance" existing for man between himself and the ultimate range (the "circle") of his perceptions.

The emphasis upon patterns of experience fades with *L'Espace proustien* (1963), where Poulet concentrates upon the meaning for Proust of various spatial images and experiences. Here the critic is more likely to juxtapose similar passages than to extrapolate significant words or phrases. His approach is broader, with a greater use of analogy and compared experiences. Indeed, *L'Espace proustien* begins by contrasting Bergson's sense of an active, continuous time with Proust's creation of a static, panoramic (spatial) time. Time and space blend into a total experience, a *cogito* best revealed in its "starting point," and whose evolution it is the task of the critic to trace.

The contemporary feeling of time is the focus for Poulet's third *Etude, Le Point de départ* (1964). Although this book has some elements in common with the earlier two *Etudes* (an introductory essay on time, emphasis on revelatory words and images, and a general preoccupation with man at the crossroads of space and time), it stands apart from Poulet's previous works in several ways. It is the first collection of his essays to deal wholly with modern authors, and it considers them not at random but as so many responses to one overriding contemporary dilemma. This dilemma is an existential one: that of creating any believable sense of continuity after the elementary sense of existing moment by moment. For Poulet, the *cogito*'s of modern literature are so many attempts to provide a successful "departure" from a chaotic and momentary existence to continuous and coherent life. *Le Point de départ* is also an exception to Poulet's previous work in that it is a conscious attempt to establish the outline of an existential history of literature. Dozens of allusions to comparable authors appear, so that there is a pattern of historical relevancy both for epochs of thought and for individual writers. If Poulet seems to have returned to the nineteenth-century idea of a *Zeitgeist*, it is with this difference: along with the spiritual identity of each epoch, he recognizes the spiritual identity of types of experience. His existential history must be vertical as well as horizontal, if it is to create the desired "whole" effect.

From the rather limited calculation of coordinates in early years to the rather rigid patterns of perception in 1961, Poulet has developed a richer synthesis which pursues a *cogito* rather than coordinates, and a total experience rather than its component parts. His criticism has become freer of classifications and patterns, and there is more extended dialogue between the critic and his text. With the book-length essay on Proust he has demonstrated how an empathetic critic can re-create the varying steps of an author's spiritual career. The *Etudes sur le temps humain III* repeats this format in shorter separate essays analyzing different poetic *cogito*'s. Here Poulet seems to devote himself to the task of providing model chapters for the existential history of literature which represents the sum of his critical vision. Aiding him to shape this history is a renewed faith in the existence of an ideal human experience, a poetic conception of man integrated into a divine—or at least a coherent—universe. All Poulet's analyses are measured against this implied ideal, which serves to unify his literary history from a validly existential point of view. By 1964 he has provided a coherent system of existential interpretation which has its methods, standards, history, and philosophy. The existential approach is no longer mingled with formal historical or biographical considerations. Henceforth it must be accepted or rejected in terms of its own values.

Poulet's general approach to literature is outlined in two essays: the preface to Richard's *Littérature et sensation* (1954) and a "Réponse" to an inquiry of *Les Lettres nouvelles*, written in June 1959. In both essays the critic examines not only his own concept of literature as a human thought and an imaginary world, but also the implications of this attitude for a general reader.

The preface to *Littérature et sensation* defines literature as an "imaginary world" and a "thought." [1] The fact that literature is imaginary does not mean that it is a gratuitous formal exercise. Neither is it a true reflection of the exterior world, for it is a *subjective* perception of reality. It is a combination of the outer and inner worlds, shaped individually in each literary text. The reader of this text must adapt himself to its foreign experience—he must be "inhabited by thought."

The literary "thought" is no collection of thoughts, and may not be analyzed from the outside as "the author's ideas." It is a motivating impulse, an original birth which must be resurrected by the reader as he rethinks and re-creates the author's own expression. In this context Poulet coins the term "critique de la conscience," or a reading that explores the work's expression of a conscious, perceiving being. "For the critic, nothing exists any more except this consciousness, which no longer even belongs to another being, which is solitary and universal. The first and perhaps the only criticism is the criticism of consciousness." Such consciousness is solitary because it belongs always to a single being; it is universal because it is an experience shared by all mankind. Because of its universality a reader may hope to take a sym-

1. Georges Poulet, preface in Jean-Pierre Richard, *Littérature et sensation* (Paris: Le Seuil, 1954), p. 9.

pathetic leap into another mental world and to resurrect a solitary experience as it takes shape in universal human coordinates.

The criticism of consciousness has two alternative extremes: an introspective and an extroverted vision. Poulet describes the introspective vision as that of Maurice Blanchot, whose work he calls "literature of literature, consciousness of consciousness." Blanchot's exploration of personal consciousness, stripped of all possible outer references, is not an approach which Poulet can accept. There is another pole, that of an extroverted vision in which the subjective consciousness reaches out to take possession of the world. This is the criticism embodied by Richard in *Littérature et sensation*, and to Poulet it is the more meaningful approach. "Criticism cannot be contented with thinking a thought. It must work its way farther back, from image to image to feelings. It must reach the act by which the mind . . . united itself to an object to invent itself as subject" (p. 10). The criticism of the second type recognizes both subject and object; it exists "not *in a vacuum* but *in close contact*," and seeks to explore human experience at the vital point of artistic creation. With Jean-Pierre Richard as its representative, says Poulet, "a new criticism is born, closer both to genetic sources and to felt realities." The second pole of the criticism of consciousness is more comprehensive and hence more satisfactory.

Richard may be the first to set forth a true phenomenological literary criticism, as Poulet says, but his work is neither solitary nor unprepared. Poulet points out that Richard's criticism follows upon earlier analysis, in particular *De Baudelaire au surréalisme* and *L'Ame romantique et le rêve*. It was Raymond's genius to discover "beyond words, their contact with things, the vanishing of the frontiers between objective and subjective," and likewise, Béguin "revealed nature as the very matter of the dream which the mind pursues." In literary criticism, these two men are the most important forerunners of Richard's views, but there are others associated in a less literary, more philosophical genealogy.

Poulet mentions Jean-Paul Sartre, Gabriel Marcel, Jean Wahl, Maurice Merleau-Ponty, and Gaston Bachelard as writers who fall in the domain of "pre-philosophy" (similar to Béguin's "pre-criticism"). These men are all philosophers who situate themselves "in a domain close to criticism, a domain of pre-philosophy, where there appears a profound similarity between philosophy and literature in the fundamental act through which they turn towards their objects." The genetic critics and these existential "pre-philosophers" have their perspectives in common if not their media: both conduct an existential inquiry into man and his means of knowing the universe. Nonetheless, the "pre-philosophers" are in fact philosophers, and the genetic critics limit themselves to another chosen field: literature.

Poulet makes a point of distinguishing existential criticism from an existential philosophy which uses literature as evidence for its own general and abstract ends. Existential criticism remains literary because it is based only upon literature and has no medium and no goal beyond literary experience. There is a certain playing with terms here, as there is in the entire existential definition of literature: if literature is defined as a human experience, then a great many associated areas become by definition "literary." Richard's is "a thought which is marvelously apt, not only to plunge into the substance of works but to work farther back to the perceptive experiences constituting their source and—often— their structure as well. Beyond the work there is being; beyond being there is the world. A world of others, with which one must communicate" (p. 11). Literature is defined as the highest and most vital point of human expression, the only way for man to express himself. Hence the existential literary critic is not tempted to call upon other standards (be they psychological, political, sociological, or metaphysical) or to venture outside the area of literary analysis, for he has already defined literature as the consummately human expression. Such a definition is enough for his inquiry, and he is content to remain inside it.

When literature is defined as human expression, it appeals to intuition rather than to examination. The empathetic reader may not judge, and must sympathize, if there is to be any valid connection between him and human literature. In answering a questionnaire sent out in June 1959 by *Les Lettres nouvelles* (based upon Henri Guillemin's extremely personal, polemic criticism), Poulet defends the personal, subjective approach to literary criticism.

If the aim of criticism, he says, is "to arrive at an intimate knowledge of critical reality," then the critic must make a subjective attempt to parallel or re-create this reality. He must find a way "to re-feel, to re-think, to re-imagine" the work's basic impulse—to respond in such a way as to forget his own personality. "Nothing is less objective than such a movement of the mind . . . for what must be reached is a subject, or a mental activity that can only be understood by putting oneself in its place and perspectives—by making it play again its role of subject in ourselves." [2] This notion of extreme empathy resembles that of Albert Béguin, although Poulet does not imitate Béguin's selection of texts close to his own opinions. Both men reject any critical distance or objectivity, for, as Poulet says, "what is not grasped as subject will be inevitably, and erroneously, grasped as object" (p. 11). To grasp literature as an object is to contravert the very premises of this literary theory, which defines literature as expression and experience.

Any reader who puts himself in the place and perspective of a work must necessarily neglect all ordinary formal objects of study: he must refuse to be concerned with formal style, diction, structure, interplay of words, character relationships, or contextual shadings given to words and phrases. Rather, he must discover in the text the overall, nonobjective reality of the author as subject. This reality, moreover, may not be confined to any one work or aspect of a work, for "it is in the nature of a work both to invent its structures and to go beyond them . . . revealing by that very fact a movement which is a liberation from structures" (p. 12). Anything the reader takes from the work and studies at a distance is automatically excluded from Poulet's analysis—just as the "pure poets" refused to consider "poetry" anything that could be put into prose. Literature is not, in effect, language; nor is it a structure composed of language: "a literary text is above all a living, conscious reality, a thought that thinks to itself and which, in thinking, becomes thinkable to us—a voice that speaks to itself and which, in so speaking, speaks to us from within" (p. 11). The image of literature as a voice allows Poulet to direct his argument beyond the voice to its speaker, and away from the blank, inhuman paper that underlies writing in formal theory ("le vide papier que sa blancheur défend").

Formal critics, proceeding from their entirely different premises, tend to criticize Poulet on the grounds that his general analyses do not correspond to the particular reality of a given text. But here it should be understood that Poulet is not trying to give a comprehensive view of the

2. Poulet, "Réponse," *Les Lettres nouvelles*, June 24, 1959, pp. 10–11.

text, as in ordinary textual criticism. His theory forces him to ignore formal structures and to wrench words and phrases out of context; for these words and phrases have a more vital context for him in their existential framework, where they communicate certain attitudes of perception and indicate the unique spiritual existence of a work or works. Poulet's analysis treads a narrow path between biographical criticism and inspection of the text. It attempts to combine the personal method of the first with the objective methods of the second, without assimilating itself to the aims of either.

Poulet naturally uses his answer to the questionnaire to express his views on literature and criticism: in it he pleads for a special history of existential analyses, a history that is clearly based upon Raymond's and Béguin's example. In *De Baudelaire au surréalisme,* Raymond follows the historical framework typical of French academic criticism, but breaks it occasionally to include spiritual affiliations from different times. In *L'Ame romantique et le rêve,* Béguin uses a similar historical comparison in order to frame his central study of dream-perception and artistic creation. Poulet, however, wants to carry the technique of these tentative spiritual affiliations to a logical end, and therefore analyzes individual authors in the light of an actual "history of the human consciousness." He accepts the manner in which Raymond and Béguin broke away from traditional historical analysis to include spiritual comparisons, and transforms such comparisons into the very form of a new, "historical" analysis.

Poulet defines literary history in much the same way that he defines literary criticism. "Taken in the highest and deepest sense," he writes, "literary history is a history of the human consciousness" (p. 12). Human consciousness can be studied in chronological phases, which may in turn be linked to separate works. Poulet believes that a total history must contain both elements, and hence his individual analyses are accompanied by a broader outline of the human mind in its various metamorphoses. Such an outline has value, as does literary history, in that it helps to show how a work has been influenced. The historian is able to understand how a work expresses the consciousness of its age, and to recognize after that its unique characteristics. In theory, says Poulet, it is difficult to group unique minds under a generalized consciousness for each epoch. "How can one become conscious of all these consciousnesses, whose very originality seems to forbid their being considered together?" The new history solves this problem first by distinguishing a *Zeitgeist* felt by individual authors, and then by distinguishing from it their separate personalities.

Such an existential historical plan appears throughout all three *Etudes sur le temps humain,* which begin with an essay on time and proceed with separate literary analyses. It is most important in *Le Point de départ*, where Poulet draws his historical comparisons most freely, and where he also takes up again the question of existential literary criticism.

At the end of the introduction to *Le Point de départ* the author explains in some detail a term defining his approach to literature: "genetic criticism." This term is not new, any more than is the term "Geneva School," which he has already used to describe himself and his associates. Poulet, however, has his own definition of both terms. "Genetic criticism," for him, is the same as the earlier "criticism of consciousness," with a more specific reference to literature's point of emergence from subconscious to conscious existence. It is not to be confused with the study of scraps, notes, and rough drafts, but is a study of the creative movement "in which the work of art passes from a shapeless and momentary state to a formal and lasting state." [3] As a term it permits Poulet to include all his earlier definitions of literature and criticism and to rephrase his discussion of time and space on a more "aesthetic" plane. The "time of the work of art" goes not from past to present to future, but from the moment to coherence, from the ephemeral to the eternal. The space of the work of art (an "aesthetic space," as he permits himself the use of the word for the first time in *L'Espace proustien*) is the mental space of this same movement, so that both of Poulet's coordinates are finally bound up in one comprehensive vision of literary genesis.

Poulet's works embody a consistent approach which is broader than the identification of temporal and spatial phenomena. He himself protests against being known as "that 'time' man" and insists that his attitude is not to be confined to the narrowness of two fixed categories. These categories themselves have not remained fixed. Poulet's first three volumes focus upon a special facet of human perception described in the preface, with separate essays illustrating this facet in different au-

3. Poulet, *Le Point de départ* (Paris: Plon, 1964), p. 40.

thors. There is an initial hypothesis that each work reveals its special nature in the same coordinates as a human being: time and space. An author's perceptions of time and space constitute his personal means of comprehending his situation, and are in the text the key by which he may be analyzed.

Poulet's early emphasis upon describing these perceptions gradually yields to a tendency to see the work as a struggle for identity. Space and time are tools of vision, tentatively manipulated into a coherent perspective. Poulet's analysis now develops a sense of direction in which the resolution of an existential dilemma is just as important as an earlier description of its nature. His latest two books use the insights of earlier technique, but evolve from it an "aesthetic" rather than a scientific interpretation of time and space. The critic's aims throughout have not changed, but he has refined his practice to fit his theory in a fascinating series of tests and adaptations.

The beginnings of Poulet's interest in an author's existential situation appear in an early essay in the *Cahiers du Sud*: "Sylvie ou la pensée de Nerval" (October 1938). The essay seems to show the influence of Béguin's *L'Ame romantique et le rêve* and *Gérard de Nerval*: the emphasis on dream technique, on the non-biographical value of the work, on the moral significance of Nerval's images, on double realities and the sense of an ideal quest (although certainly applicable) recall similar themes in Béguin's earlier studies. "*Sylvie* is the story of a man who betrays himself in his pursuit of the ideal," [4] and the story unfolds in a double reality where each event has spiritual significance. It is a "metaphysical allegory, whose subject is human destiny," and takes place "on two identical planes" (pp. 667–668). Nerval writes to examine his own consciousness: "It could be said that Gérard wrote *Sylvie* to become more keenly conscious of the order which he was trying to bring to his own mind." Poulet's analysis is still far from his later interpretations of space and time, but elements of these categories are already present. The ambiance surrounding Aurélie is an "*empty space*," whereas for Sylvie it is a "*full space*," and Nerval's dream technique attains direct consciousness of reality by evading the restraints of precise time. In spite of these early signs of existential categories, "Sylvie" is not a philosophi-

4. Poulet, "Sylvie ou la pensée de Nerval," *Cahiers du Sud*, October 1938, p. 666.

cal essay in the manner of the *Etudes sur le temps humain,* and it was
not reprinted until 1966, when it appeared as one of a series of "three
essays in Romantic mythology."

After "Sylvie" Poulet turns to developing the philosophical criticism
for which he is now known. His first important work in this field is a
collection of essays published at Edinburgh in 1949 as the first volume
of the *Etudes sur le temps humain.* The preface to the *Etudes* presents
an historical study of changing concepts of time in human existence
and underlines the implications of a given atmosphere of thought for
writers living in a particular era.

This preface discusses the concept of time as it influences human
creation. Poulet sees time not as a measurable dimension, a mere chron-
ology, but as a feeling of transitory existence which works alternately
for and against the creation of human identity. In the Middle Ages
time is a "continued creation" whose impulse is constantly provided by
God. With this continual divine support man proceeds to the fulfilment
of his divine nature. He finds worldly elements only temporary obstacles
to this end, or rather, they are the actual medium of his development.
A similar belief in a stable, continuous creation of identity will not be
possible again until the twentieth century, when the motivating force
will no longer be God but an existential consciousness.

Intervening epochs show different attitudes toward existence in time.
The age of Descartes tries to raise itself above illusory material reality.
"Human thought no longer feels a part of things. It distinguishes itself
from them in order to think them." [5] Descartes himself seeks to find
beyond his impressions, "outside of the duration of things," a moment
of pure intuition to give him a foothold on reality. Living in the moment,
seventeenth-century man cannot perceive anything outside his immediate
relationship to a fleeting creative act (p. xvi). Eighteenth-century man
is also limited to the moment of existence, which he tries to intensify
in order to possess a fuller life. In the literary creation of this century
intensity is heightened by sudden twists and changes between states of
being: "either by a sudden reversal of situation, which makes the soul
pass with no transition from one to the other pole of affective life . . .
or in procuring new and cruel sensations for the soul" (p. xxvi). In the

5. Poulet, *Études sur le temps humain* (Paris: Plon, 1956), p. xiv.

next century the Romantic's variation upon the intensification of the moment is to give it all its potential depth, all the infinity of human existence possible in an instant. "Possessing his life in an instant—such is the claim or fundamental desire of the Romantic" (p. xxxii). It is not until the twentieth century that existential thought proposes a new unity of time and existence, after the disunity of preceding centuries. Bergson's work implies a new acceptation of the term *devenir,* in which "continued creation" becomes a purely human term. "Each instant appears to embody a choice, that is to say, an act, and at the root of this act, a creative decision" (p. xlv). The struggle for existence in time has come full circle and has reacquired a coherence in which man, not God, makes the creative decision.

In order to categorize each of these variations, Poulet adopts the Cartesian formula of the *cogito.* A *cogito,* or each person's perception and creation of his own existence, is a human conception linking man's experience with his impulse toward creation. As such it appropriately describes the synthesis of experience with which Poulet continues to be concerned.

The *Etudes sur le temps humain* express each author's sense of being —his *cogito*—as he envisages and works out his identity in time. From the point of view of the author as a creative being, time is an element to be worked with or against; it is something he perceives as part of his *cogito,* and perceives as it reacts upon his experience of the subject-object relationship. From the point of view of the critic, time is an element of existence that is revealed by the author's attitude toward it.

For many, the sense of time is only the sense of a continual passage— the constant metamorphosis by which everything escapes our grasp. This time has tragic overtones, for it brings with it a feeling of loss and instability. For Montaigne, the quest for reality directly concerns time: he cannot portray any stable identity, but merely a sense of "passing," "that is to say the movement by which a being abandons being, by which he is hidden from himself, by which he feels himself die" (p. 7). The same sense of the passing (or the pastness) of events in time haunts Baudelaire: "At the very instant when the instant *is,* it detaches itself, it falls away, and in its fall there begins a second existence—an existence in which instants do not stop, never stop, *having been*" (p. 337). Benjamin Constant can recognize his identity only in a continuing series of past moments, and Mme de La Fayette tries to create a "true duration" in a neutral zone free from passion. Time, for these writers, is a fatal element that weakens their frail sense of existence.

It is with Proust that one finds a conscious and methodical use of the experience of time. Proust's *cogito* uses an affective memory to establish a consistent identity. Only by memory can the author give meaning to a past experience while making it present in the mind, and thus link the various stages of his existence. Poulet describes this overlay of experience and memory as "the operation by which, *in mimicking in one's depths the exterior gesture of the perceptible object*, one *imagines*, one creates something which is still the perceptible object, but this time no longer outside: inside, no longer something strange and impenetrable, but penetrable, recognizable, identifiable, for this thing comes from us, it is us" (p. 386). He accepts Proust's claim to use time as a fourth dimension knitting together the scattered perceptions of space and attaining a "human eternity" of the memory.[6] Proust has thus used time to his own advantage, to establish a durable sense of identity.

Just as a man's perceptions shape his identity, so an author's perceptions organize his literature. Poulet does not confuse the historical author with his literary image, but he insists that a literary work is based upon a perceived reality which it transforms. The author remains a man, but the work becomes a new, integrated human existence.

In this transfigured literary life, the "author" creates his own personality. For example, the literary identity known to us as "Montaigne" is created by the actual process of composition. In writing the essays which reflect his experience, he adds meditation to perception. "To the multiplicity of reality he opposes the multiplicity of his activity." This is the work "by which one gives oneself an existence" (p. 10). Even in Flaubert, archexample of a formal composition, Poulet finds that there is an existential choice governing the structure of his works. Flaubert's novels are so many attempts to come to grips with the realities of the exterior world, and his love of the picturesque is directed "toward a grasp of what is not self, a representation of the world" (p. 309). The abbé Prévost's perception of ruptures in time leads to a technique of

6. In *L'Espace proustien* (1963) Poulet rejects the idea of a fourth dimension (pp. 134–135) and prefers to describe Proust's integration as a static, spatial phenomenon. Apparently there is room for discussion, even with existential empathy.

catastrophes multiplied in time: "It is a sort of break occurring in existence, and from then on the hero and the novel are left no other alternative but to begin anew" (p. 147). As Poulet spoke of the role of affective memory in creating an identity for Proust, he shows how memory may also be used as a method of stylistic composition: Vigny's image of the pearl as a luminous accumulation of translucent layers represents the structure of his work as well. "At this height, all human life blends with the work whose substance it is; and the work itself tends to be only the most lucid and emotional interpretation of conscious life, an interpretation of such *crystalline* transparency and of such *prismatic* coloring that, in the same reflection, all existence appears in its unique moments and in its totality" (p. 277). Poulet proposes that all these authors, consciously or unconsciously, used their own experiences as the theme and organization of their literature.

The experience that Poulet considers is the recognition of other existence; its *cogito* is not merely the statement that "I think, and therefore I am," but that "I perceive" something else. Poulet never neglects to consider the existence of objects giving rise to thought, and of what Raymond first called the "frontiers between subjective and objective feelings." In speaking of Flaubert's creative method, he comments on the outward turn of the *cogito*: "Flaubert's point of departure is not Flaubert himself; it is the relationship of the perceiving self to the object perceived" (p. 309). Objects for Montaigne have no personal significance —mirrored in the mind, they become an "opportunity for thought, a pure pretext to think and to see oneself think" (p. 3). The human mind assumes its identity only through objects. "The point of departure for this wisdom is a *grasp*: not in the sense of taking something for oneself, but of taking it *in* oneself, of making it one's own. This grasp does not belong in the category of having, but in the category of being" (p. 11). It is the integration of subject and object which creates a full *cogito*.

Certain authors explore their experience of subject and object until they develop a new frame of references and a new consciousness of reality. Poulet's essay on Rousseau describes an early, pure identification of subject and object, a rupture between the two, and a rediscovery of the *moi* which occurs at the same time as a rediscovery of pure sensation. Benjamin Constant finds new meaning in the subject-object relationship when the object becomes, this time, another human being. For Constant, whose devouring passion is to discover and to seize something authentically real, love shared with another person enables him to escape from the solipsistic limits of his own being. The miracle for Constant, says Poulet, is that he is able to accept the sentiments of another being as paralleling, and thus authenticating, his own "unique" experience. "From the moment in which a being quits his isolation to admit the reality of an existence different from his own, he finds himself obliged to recognize in this different being feelings and tendencies which, in himself, he considered only elements of the play of the mind" (p. 232). It is to this point of shared recognition that Poulet wishes to carry the literary *cogito*. Constant's shared recognition becomes an experience shared with the reader, and a chain of human perception and expression links men in the bond of literature.

The *Etudes sur le temps humain* discuss literature as a series of consciousnesses (the *cogito* in each author) and do not refer to the formal structure conceived by an objective critic. It is nonetheless tempting for a formal critic (who may be more eclectic than his existentialist colleague) to set these existential analyses against prevailing stylistic interpretations of an author's work. Poulet's approach is rewarding and explanatory in the essays on writers who recognize particular attitudes of perception: Rousseau, Vigny, Constant, Guérin and Flaubert. However, these writers fall inside a certain Romantic-modern tradition already described by Raymond and Béguin, and are perhaps amenable to this approach. A more judicious assessment would have to consider writers outside this tradition as well: for example, Poulet's analyses of the three great classical playwrights Corneille, Racine, and Molière.

In the *Etudes*, Poulet is always concerned with the dominant impulse in a man's work, and such a monolinear approach can be applied most easily to a monothematic playwright. Corneille's plays reflect such a single system of values, and it is therefore not surprising that the essay on Corneille is the most satisfactory as a "formal reading" and that the studies on Molière and Racine more closely resemble a *tour de force*.

Corneille's plays, although rich and varied, are well known for their emphasis on certain essential traits of will which set off the heroic characters. Poulet considers Corneille's central willing character in the perspective of an existential analysis. The will creates a character and fixes him in a perpetual present. Says Poulet: "a being is portrayed who escapes suddenly from the tyranny of successive time to situate himself solidly in the realm of the decisive moment" (p. 91). The will is a means of possessing one's identity: one chooses oneself. "Will establishes being" continues Poulet, "from then on I possess myself" (p. 92). The structure of Corneille's theater consists in a series of acts of will through which the main character repeatedly affirms the choice of his identity. Corneille's character cannot envisage a future, or anticipate one, because he cannot wish himself different from his present chosen identity. Poulet finds a self-contained eternity in this constant self-creation of the will, for "in the instant when his will affirms itself, it possesses itself, contents itself at the same time . . . a little eternity which reproduces exactly the essential traits of divine eternity" (pp. 98–99). The reader must then "read" Corneille in the central act which proclaims the reality of the hero. "Being appears suddenly . . . in a voluntary movement, creator of being, *causa sui,* beyond which there is no need to go" (p. 96). Corneille's hero embodies what is most important in the plays, and ends by standing for all of them.

Poulet analyzes this hero to establish his own conception of Corneille's *cogito,* and the same general analysis also may help a formal critic to interpret specific heroes in Corneille's works; but this coincidence of formal and existential analysis does not hold true for Poulet's interpretation of Racine and Molière.

Poulet bases his study of Racine on "a problem which is so urgent, so fundamental, that all Racine's work will consist almost completely in its exploration" (p. 104)—the fatal intervention of past time into present events. "Racine's tragedy is an action *in the past*" (p. 112), and Poulet's existential inquiry shows how this past action stifles any genuine present or future. This despairing *cogito,* however, comes to a climax and changes with "Phèdre"; a statement of religious faith takes the place of despair. Whether or not Poulet is convincing in his presentation of Racine's existential career, he is unconvincing when he tries to assimilate the passionate and pagan Phèdre to a Christian Racine. This interpretation rests upon Poulet's analysis of Phèdre's final couplet. Her last speech (that, by dying, she gives back to the light of day all its once-sullied purity) is taken as the recognition of a higher divinity into which she is absorbed. It is a "discovery and a belief . . . a purgation and an act of faith." Poulet paraphrases Phèdre as saying: "O my God . . . what does it matter if I no longer am, since you will not cease to be, and to be the one who washes away the sins of the world, but whom the sins of the world do not touch" (p. 119). This interpretation of Phèdre's words omits all possibilities of bitterness and double meanings; it weakens and suddenly dilutes a complex dramatic personality. As a reflection of its author's beliefs, it may well be valid in reference to an existential picture which would change during and after the composition of the tenth play. The simultaneous application of such an analysis to Phèdre's character, however, does not fully apply to her tormented personality as it has been already described.

Poulet's interpretation of Phèdre is evidently inspired by his interpretation of "Phèdre" as an existential document referring to Racine. Such an abstract approach can rarely be reduced to individual figures and plays. For a play to remain a play and not a sermon, it must furnish a strong sense of each character's dramatic and verbal identity. This feeling of separate identities inside a text is thus far untouched by Poulet's approach: his "Phèdre" exists almost independent of its heroine, Phèdre.

The essay on Molière is the shortest in the collection. It is also the weakest in its substance and conclusions. Extremely general, and indebted to Bergson for several of its *dicta* on the comic moment, it cites only the "Critique de l'Ecole des Femmes," and refers briefly to the "Médecin volant," "La Jalousie du Barbouillé," and "Les Femmes savantes." For the most part, it draws upon the counterfeit "Lettre sur la comédie de l'Imposteur," which Poulet assumes to be representative of, if not written by, Molière. The essay itself attempts to define the comic moment. As opposed to the tragic moment, which evokes sympathy, the comic moment evokes ridicule. Ridicule, moreover, is a "cold sentiment" that leads to a "moment of rupture." In the end, Poulet concludes that Molière's spectator does not associate himself with comic characters.

For Poulet, Molière appeals to the spectator's cold, judging ridicule, and to his instantaneous grasp of the comic moment: "there are two universes in Molière: one of customs, another of passion" (p. 85). The latter contains an aspect of tragedy, for there is a recurrence of unfulfilled desire, or a "rhythm of passion," which characterizes the plays. The tragic aspect is undercut by the fact that it appears in a disassociating and objective approach, "like the behavior of an object which repeatedly strikes our attention" (p. 86). This approach typifies the object, and effectively removes it as a character from the realm of our sympathies. Poulet describes it as an "essentially nominalist procedure, by which Molière again shows his relationship with Gassendi" (p. 87). Thus emerges the real central reference of the essay: Poulet is describing a mental universe à la Gassendi as the basic existential fact for Molière. "Such a mental universe invincibly recalls the conception of life associated with Molière's master, Gassendi" (p. 85). Neither an existential nor a formal explanation of Molière, however, can be given life by references to Bergson and Gassendi.

The particular difficulty of this essay (for both existential and formal criticism) is that the tone of philosophical inquiry has become too general. It misses the uniqueness of Molière, for it could refer to any playwright at any time, or (as the reference to Gassendi implies) to a philosopher as well as to an artist, to a writer of satirical novels as well as to an author of plays. The essay is not typical of Poulet's method, but it serves to show its possibility for error. Poulet himself, in a letter to Professor René Wellek, comments that this essay fails to reach Molière's "substratum and temporal principle . . . not because there is no Molièresque time, but because I was unable to grasp it." [7] The deductive method by which Poulet collates numerous and varied references from an author's complete work is lacking here, and he seems to have started from an idea which is to be proved by the "Critique" and by a hypothetical letter from Molière. The essay is useful in that it shows how dangerous overly abstract thought can be in Poulet's subjective approach, but it is not typical of the main body of his work.

The English edition of the *Etudes sur le temps humain,* translated by Elliott Coleman as *Studies in Human Time* (1956), includes a new appendix on "Time and American Writers." Brief "thumbnail sketches" of Emerson, Hawthorne, Poe, Thoreau, Melville, Whitman, Emily Dickinson, Henry James, and T. S. Eliot do not reveal any change in Poulet's methods of analysis. He first selects a significant writer, compares his various statements on the subject of time, and then attempts to describe his existential situation. In this appendix, Poulet has launched his first

7. Letter dated October 6, 1956, and quoted by permission of the author.

book translated into English with a series of limited experimental sketches based on the method of the *Etudes sur le temps humain*.

The second volume of the *Etudes sur le temps humain, La Distance intérieure* (1952), is less dominated by a single form of perception than was the first. Poulet has moved away from the exclusive consideration of the role of time and into a more comprehensive attitude which collates both time and space. This space (like time) is always subjective and never an objective measurement. As "interior distance" it is both the mental distance in which perceptions take place, and also the distance between an object as perceived and the object as it actually, unknowably, *is*.

As in the first of the *Etudes*, Poulet prefaces his book with a definition of its theory and aims. Here he will concentrate on the mental landscape in which thought and literature take place. The objects of thought are temporarily set aside while he emphasizes the mind that thinks them. "All thought, it is true, is a thought *of* something . . . But all thought is also simply a thought . . . Whatever its objects, thought can never fix them, never think them, unless inside itself." [8] This thought arranges its perceptions in a separate space, parallel to reality. "My thought is a space where my thoughts take place, and have their place . . . it is made . . . of all the *interior distance* which separates or connects me with what I can think" (p. i). Thought creates a mental world as the human reflection of an unknowable, outside world, and expresses this reflection in words which are literature.

Such is the subjective, existential definition of literature. It is opposed to literature defined as a formal object with "external" forms and techniques. "Objectively literature is made of formal works whose contours are outlined with more or less precision . . . Subjectively, literature is not at all formal. It is the reality of an always particular thought —always anterior and posterior to any object" (p. ii). The goal of a subjective critic is to "make appear this interior vacancy in which the world is redisposed" (p. ii). This critic outlines the private mental space which frames each author's experience, shapes his literary expression, and defines his special manner of being: his typical act of consciousness. Balzac's basic experience, for example, is that of a "liv-

8. Poulet, *La Distance intérieure* (Paris: Plon, 1958), p. i.

ing gap" between desire and fulfilment. He is "a being immediately oriented toward what he is not, toward what he wants to be" (p. 122). Hugo's first experience is the recognition of an overwhelming reality: he "suddenly arrives at consciousness when the formidable mass of things has broken over him and when he feels its moving and multiple contact everywhere" (p. 206). For any author, the total reaction does not come at once: it is through writing that he expresses and comes to grips with his experience.

A writer, says Poulet, shapes his own nature when he chooses the form of his literature. Mallarmé creates a special existence through thought alone. "At the summit of the Mallarméan *Cogito*, the being who thinks himself establishes his existence" (p. 332). In Laclos, shaping the future implies "a re-creation of time by voluntary thought" (pp. 70–71). Balzac's original sense of lack and desire is transformed by the exercise of his will: "I am, first of all, only my will" (p. 123). Consequently, Balzac becomes the creator *par excellence*: "no universe, no plurality of real combinations, can exhaust the desire of a demiurge who no longer wants only to mold and knead reality, but to play with all the forms of possibility" (p. 188). Implied in the exercise of the will, then, is the creative force: force to choose and create one's own existence, but force also (since literature is a human expression) to write.

In *La Distance intérieure*, as compared with *Etudes sur le temps humain*, there is more emphasis on creative activity through existential choice. This choice is both personal and verbal at the same time, and it frames itself in spatial images. Marivaux' art rests upon the parallel creation of supple, variable language to represent the numerous metamorphoses of reality. In Vauvenargues, the central being is able to surmount his ontological imperfections in a "moment of consciousness when . . . [he] touches simultaneously at all the points of the universe" (p. 55). A similar act of the will governs Balzac's creation, but this author's creative energy is so immense that it surpasses the objects it describes. His "imaginative power is such that it surpasses somehow its object—all its objects—and the mind, in a sort of frightful intoxication, finds itself invaded and engulfed in its turn by the universe it had devoured" (p. 139). In speaking of Hugo, Poulet again expresses a literary experience in terms of spatial images. Hugo's world is formed of an immense accumulation of words which attempts to represent reality from vaporous forms: "Hugo's whole poetic effort consists in trying to condense in a vacuum—the vacuum of thought—a vaporous core of images, to make all of reality from them" (p. 222). Throughout, the creation of a mental world rests upon the author's ability to re-integrate perceptions from the real world. "Interior distance," however, need not always be a reflection of real distance.

In an essay on Mallarmé, Poulet gives his most extended analysis of willed creation in the mind. Mallarmé's world is totally abstract and does not depend on reactions to reality; the poet composes an ideal space from nothing. There is only an "initial situation," the paralysis of a negative feeling which becomes the starting point for a purely "notional" composition. Language, not sensation, is the medium of this creation. "To suggest this new existence, and to accomplish the fictive installation of a new world, it suffices to arrange patiently terms which one has mastered, in a certain order, in a certain hymn . . . this poetic universe . . . is outlined not in them, but between them, through them, above them" (p. 342). Mallarmé's poem is entirely a product of the mind, and its words do not reflect interacting sensations. Rather, the words react upon one another in a voluntary arrangement. "They suggest, they recall. They prepare the words which are to come, they reflect those which have disappeared" (p. 347). Although the poem exists in the mind only, it is no less real than its more worldly fellows. All poetry exists ultimately in the "interior distance" of mental creation, says Poulet, and "a poem must ultimately be recognized for the 'mental space' of the one who thinks it, and for the site of the mind" (p. 353).

This interior space, which is the site of the mind, may be described in several ways. Sometimes it is the totally interior arrangement of one's human situation; sometimes it is an invisible, unmeasurable distance between the subjective author and the life around him. For Hugo and Joubert, space symbolizes a metaphysical possibility, a field to be populated. Joubert's "intuition of extended space" is the intuition of an immense reality as the proving ground for his existence. "Joubert believed that he saw opening in him and before him an immense, transparent, and invisible reality in which we all exist and move" (p. 93). He orients himself toward "a grasp of space" (p. 89) in that this space is an integrating distance which allows human personality to assert itself.

Hugo's experience is more complex, and moves toward a gradual conquest and transcendence of space. His poetry emerges "in a vague place" and appears initially "as something which vaguely takes shape in the total emptiness of thought" (p. 194). An "amplifying movement" follows as his poetry expands to take possession of space (p. 196). Hugo feels himself one with a mass of various concrete perceptions aimed to fill his original vague emptiness. "He *is*, but is *in* things" (p. 207). Striving to reach a fullness of being, he places himself "perennially inside the object, or at least *with* it" (p. 210), only to find a perpetual nothingness behind the accumulation of forms. Here are the familiar images of the gulf, and the terrified searches and doubts of the *Fin de Satan* and *Dieu*. A real absence of being appears in this originally vague emptiness, and Hugo must reverse his methods. In *Dieu,* images are no longer concrete presences, but negative symbols and empty forms. "Hugo attains the highest poetry, not when he tries to fill his mental space with a forest of pseudo-real forms, but when he succeeds in expressing—by means of forms which successively appear hollow and empty—the very reality of emptiness. Before Mallarmé, Hugo had discovered negative poetry" (p. 225). The same interior space may take many forms: it may be an element in which the mind moves freely to develop, or it may become a limitless gulf that swallows up any developing sense of reality.

Although *La Distance intérieure* concentrates on the sense of space, it continues to analyze both space and time inasmuch as they interact to shape a *cogito*. Poulet's essay on Vauvenargues describes both time and space as existential gaps which must be filled by human will: "Since being is action and being is never finished, there is nothing else but to continue, to prolong action, to fill one's task, to fill with being and with action the double hollow of time and of space (p. 42)." Time and space are complementary aspects of the mind's perception, for it is impossible to conceive the one without the other. "True human time" is a "web of relationships," and distance is "the milieu which binds us to our past or to our thought" (p. 118). This milieu in which space and time are combined is the "mental site" of poetry, the "interior distance" which gives the book its name.

La Distance intérieure develops Poulet's early use of time and space perceptions, but still in their rather limited function as dual coordinates.

In *Les Métamorphoses du cercle* (1961), a third volume which is not part of the *Etudes* but is based on their technique, he synthesizes patterns of experience from this dual analysis. The dominant metaphor in *Les Métamorphoses* is that of a series of emanating concentric circles which unite the author as central perceiving agent to the periphery of his perceptions.

The series of essays leading into *Les Métamorphoses* shows Poulet looking for an image to concentrate and symbolize his method. In "La Pensée circulaire de Flaubert," "Baudelaire et la circonférence change-ante," and "Les Métamorphoses du cercle et la toile d'araignée," all published earlier and reappearing now, he organizes exterior sensations as patterns tending toward diagrammatic resolution. Such an approach is reminiscent of Jean-Pierre Richard, and Poulet's "Baudelaire" is strikingly close to Richard's essay in *Poésie et profondeur*. The guiding motif at this time is a spiderweb (first outlined in "Les Métamorphoses du cercle et la toile d'araignée," 1958). A spiderweb organizes space between center and circumference in a network of perceived relations; it is the "universe's consciousness of its web." A web, however, is a statically perceived organization, and Poulet cannot be content with a system that occurs on what he calls the "lowest level" of spiritual experience. This "level of feeling" is not enough to create a *cogito*, and a way must be found to incorporate choice and direction. Poulet's original image of the web gives way to a movement of emanating circles inside a given framework. In the book, his discussion of the web is relegated to a chapter on the eighteenth century, and his later essays grow away from their temporary proximity to Richard's purely phenomenological approach.

Poulet's adoption of the circle as a symbol for literary and existential coherence is based on a specially interpreted organic theory. *Les Métamorphoses du cercle* redefines the "organic" nature of a work of art to remove it from any mistaken association with formal criticism. This existential organism is a network of perceptions, not language. The circle, as a "privileged form" [9] in human consciousness, becomes the metaphor of its literary organization. It is a natural metaphor for existential thought, since it represents the uniform horizon of perception

9. Poulet, *Les Métamorphoses du cercle* (Paris, 1961), p. i.

around each person: "the field of human consciousness" (p. xxiv). Because the circle symbolizes the expansion and limitation of human personality, it can also represent the literary structure which is its parallel form. For Poulet, who believes in art as a concentrated single expression, it is the only possible organic form. "If the work of art has a center, around which the other parts are distributed to form a whole, it becomes possible to analyze the relationships of the center with the different parts of the whole, and to re-create its synthesis" (p. 84). Not all art succeeds in living a perfect circle, of course. Some existences are patterned in straight lines, and are not rich enough; some follow curved, "sinuous" lines, and become futile (aimless) gestures (p. 78). Occasionally, a thyrse-like resolution appears (Baudelaire, Goethe). In *Les Métamorphoses du cercle*, Poulet analyzes curvilinear patterns of existence as the symbolic expression of each author's growth and self-realization.

The appeal of the emanating circle as a satisfactory spiritual motif rests on the belief that human thought needs a dynamic balance between center and circumference, between subjectivity and objectivity; for more than a static form, there must be a reciprocal activity. Poulet uses the circle as a symbol to distinguish between two existential approaches: a circumference-oriented viewpoint, which he associates with Plotinus, Nicolas of Cusa, Boehme, Amiel, and Blanchot (p. 465) and a viewpoint closer to his own, which emphasizes the subjective perceptions of the center. The former approach locates its "center" as a constantly changing point on the circumference of the circle, a "center" which denies any constant centrality. It maintains instead a sense of varying, "objective" movement inside the circle. The latter approach, clinging to an orthodox center, hypothesizes a constant relationship of center to circle and works within such a given framework. To Poulet, all thought is "misdirected," be it through centrifugal or centripetal excess, when it ignores a true balance between the self and the surrounding universe.

It is consistent with the mystic humanism of Poulet's approach that he should qualify the Romantic discovery of "self-centeredness" (p. 136) as an essentially religious discovery, and a return to sacred sources. To return to one's innermost feelings is to be renewed at a mysterious source, which itself inspires a "new return toward nature and, consequently, a new expansion of being out of the center where it was re-invigorated" (p. 138). Such an experience is an "ontological expansion" in which "to expand is to create one's being" (p. 141). These moral concerns reappear in *Le Point de départ*, and are never far absent from an approach focused on man and his human universe.

The "history of the human consciousness," or of man discovering himself and his universe, follows much the same course in *Les Métamorphoses du cercle* as it did in *Etudes sur le temps humain*. In each, Poulet follows a development from Renaissance to Romantic to modern concerns, although his point of reference widens from the concept of time to a universal *cogito*. Each study describes the coherence of an early, centralized outlook, and the disintegration of this coherence over succeeding ages. In *Les Métamorphoses*, the Renaissance represents an age where belief in God as an active center gave coherence to the worlds of its poets. Renaissance poetry is "a poetry of revolutions operated around a center" (p. 13). In the baroque age, the centripetal orientation of these revolutions gives way to an aimless proliferation of tiny, subjective and transitory universes. Baroque artists seek to fill and to possess space: they retain the notions of macrocosm and microcosm from the Renaissance, but their intense creativity multiplies forms of existence without possessing it. The eighteenth century, a "relativist century" (p. 91), is the most disoriented of all. The lines of its meditations are curved, endless, and helplessly free. Objects lose their implied orbits around a center and depart on an aimless trajectory in which the principle of variety is substituted for that of unity (p. 74). There are too many centers and too many possible orientations. With Romanticism, the human being rediscovers his identity as center of the universe, and discovers the impulse of creativity in his own depths. The circle is once again controlled by its center, and the work of art reflects a new kind of organic coherence.

In the metaphor of the emanating circle, Poulet has found an existential criterion by which to measure the achievement perceived through his accustomed tools of analysis. A certain standard, and with it a sense of judgment, re-enters this empathetic approach. Unsuccessful resolutions of metaphysical conflicts are pointed out, and a resolution into non-existence (Amiel, Blanchot) is seen as a failure. The centrifugal impulse in Lamartine is called futile and aimless; the "evaporation" of his soul is the consequence of an earlier "evaporation" of reality in his poetry, and both lead to a general loss of any sense of existence (p. 199). The loss of a sense of being is, of course, a failure according to these existential tenets.

Poulet is characteristically subtle and sympathetic as he points out this existential shortcoming. He recognizes the failure of an "inexpressive" poetry, but he also comments on the successful coherence of an anti-Cartesian principle of beauty. Until Lamartine's poetry reached a final impotent vaporization, it approached the perfect expression of the poet's "evaporated" experience. A formless experience, which no longer recognizes the separate nature of material objects and of the perceiving subject, can only be expressed in a "formless" literature. "In one sense, there is here an extraordinary success. Never has poetry so completely escaped the Cartesian spirit, which makes clarity and distinctness not only a principle of truth, but a principle of beauty . . . With Lamartine there comes . . . an almost formless poetry, *a poetry*, consequently, *of the unformed*" (pp. 199–200). Poulet's analysis displays two aspects of his criticism which do not always harmonize: a sympathy for the author's essential attitude, and a desire to place this attitude in a scientific framework. In this essay he is able to sympathize with and to express what he feels to be Lamartine's essential quality—"the movement with which every image travels toward absence" (p. 185)—even while he disapproves of the poet's specific existential trajectory. The success of the analysis lies in its interpretation of a consistent movement for the poetry: instead of a more coldly deductive argument from selected phrases, it concentrates on the interpretation of a typical existential gesture.

A study with a more cut-and-dried, purely methodological approach is the essay on Balzac. Perhaps it is impossible, in one short essay, to comprehend such a richly varied writer as Balzac. Nonetheless, Poulet's attempt to demonstrate circular motifs in Balzac's work leaves the impression that his analytical patterns overlay and obscure the human variety of the novels, and that the circular motifs the critic extracts are not always essential to the universe interpreted. One can hardly object to Poulet's remark that the *Comédie Humaine* forms a coherent whole, or to the idea that Balzac's world consists largely in expansion and reaction to expansion (otherwise phrased, the battle of two wills).

However, the "circle" that Poulet professes to seek is the necessary symbolic expression of a mode of existence: as such, it can conceivably be used to express a world in which circles are never mentioned, but it need not be the proper existential explanation of any world which speaks of circles. Such an explanation is too often given in the essay on Balzac.

Poulet's discussion of circles in Balzac tends to become a technical exercise rather than a demonstration of existential necessity. He points to Balzac's conception of the social order as a series of worlds surrounded by their own atmospheres—which proves only that the novelist liked to justify his particular conservative-Catholic-royalist viewpoint by parallels with physical or occult science. His description of *L'Histoire des Treize* as a central activity governing a concealed but affected periphery is no more than a useful symbol for such group organization. There is a confusion between the circle as a useful descriptive image, and Poulet's hypothetical circle, which is the symbol of human metaphysical activity. When Poulet states that in each of Balzac's novels there is a "circle of avid wills surrounding a figure who is both victim and enviable object" (p. 209), and when he mentions that "so many interests converged" on one woman (p. 210, quoting Balzac), he is reporting a rather pedestrian use of the circle motif: functional in the plot rather than spiritually symbolic.

Poulet often applies the image of the circle in a sense that is useful rather than especially significant. For example, Balzac's celebrated monomaniacs are always "oriented toward the same object, seeking their unity at the same converging point" (p. 214)—but here the reader is simply given a definition of monomania. Poulet then paraphrases the *Comédie Humaine*'s familiar battles of wills in circular terms: "In opposition to the concentric movement squeezing in upon a blockaded center, there appears an inverse, eccentric movement by which the threatened being turns to attack and beats back the surrounding invader" (p. 215). It is difficult, however, to see any special circular significance in this projection of will, even if "a character of Balzac likes to sit at the center of a world on which his will streams out" (p. 222). When the critic ends by proposing that the extreme end of Balzac's development is the absorption into a central, causal point—which replaces "the marvelous circular development of concrete figures who fill the *Comédie Humaine*" (p. 227)—his conclusion does not appear to be based on a logical progression of significant examples.

Poulet again makes use of patterning impulses in his chapters on Flaubert and Baudelaire. In discussing Flaubert, he uses existential and creative patterns in an effective way; but with Baudelaire his approach seems artificial. Poulet notes that Flaubert's novel is a "novel of ambiance" (p. 393)—the ambiance of a central perceiving intelligence. Such an intelligence expands and contracts as it perceives: "it is an existence which alternately contracts and expands, which is sometimes reduced to being only a moment . . . and which sometimes . . . extends to become a circular consciousness" (p. 389). Flaubert's experience leads him to become the first novelist to abandon a unilear conception of novel construction, for he "constructs his novels in a series of *foyers*" (p. 390). Such a method of composition, says Poulet, at last makes it possible for the novel to reflect human consciousness actually perceiving reality: "in making itself both center and circle" (p. 391), it endows its characters with extraordinary density and humanity. It may be that Poulet overemphasizes the novelty of this construction by *foyer*: Béguin, in *Balzac visionnaire*, has already spoken of the dominant role of a central, influential personality. However, Poulet is discussing Flaubert's simultaneous integration of the *foyer* with objective, peripheral reality: "the novel then becomes the constant relationship by which the disordered variety of the universe is ceaselessly ordered around a central object" (p. 391). This aim, thus attributed to Flaubert, would indeed place him in the forefront of the "existential" novelists.

Poulet's analysis of existential patterns in Baudelaire reaches much more abstract conclusions. Poulet has written two essays on the French poet and moves from an earlier discussion of will conquering time to an analysis of the actual patterns organizing Baudelaire's existence. Baudelaire's experience, says Poulet, reaches out in a kind of "vibration" to a circumference from which he is then pressed back into his own identity. Everything begins with a "shiver" (p. 397), when a wave of thought taking possession of space meets a corresponding wave of sensations emanating from things. Baudelaire achieves a temporary sense of identity in this vibration or resonance (*retentissement*), but his reaching outward is soon halted by the realization of its futility.

A "poetry of presences" is supplanted by an immense absence (p. 414) revealed in prison-like, repressive motifs, but neither expansion or contraction is possible on an absolute plane. Poulet, like Jean-Pierre Richard in *Poésie et profondeur*, finds that the two impulses resolve in a spiral movement which directs the circular experience. Drawing upon repeated descriptions of spirals in Baudelaire's poetry, he postulates a final thyrse-like movement as the spiritual pattern resolving two conflicting impulses. "The poetic act is thus a spiral which rolls and unrolls itself around a directed thought. It is a thyrse" (p. 426). With this abstract, even "formal" conclusion, Poulet ends his interpretation of Baudelaire.

This essay soars to heights in which the analysis is increasingly removed from Poulet's usual deductive process; it tends to become an experiment in symbolic patterns whose actual, existential correlations are not always maintained. Textual moorings are seen as bits of evidence and not as vehicles of creation. Baudelaire's obsessions with expansion, with lid-like oppression, and with spiral patterns, fit together extremely well in a discussion of pattern, but they are not necessarily the direct and total revelation of his existential premises. Poulet gives a convincing description of the poet's manipulation of space and of time. His essay, however, needs more direct proof of the relationship between manipulating patterns and an overall existential outlook which is, in effect, with difficulty reduceable to patterns. To minimize the discussion of these connections is to risk making the original text —the creation itself—disappear. Without a constant chain of relationships, the pattern of an existential personality may become completely independent of the text on which it is based. Poulet has succumbed to this temptation elsewhere, when he writes, "Such is the poetry of Edgar Poe; at least, the poetry which he did not write, but which remains indicated or suggested by his words" (p. 272). At this point the analysis has left the realm of public verification and has entered that of speculation.

Poulet's interpretation of the circle varies according to the manner in which he is able to apply it to different authors. Like his discussion of time in the *Etudes sur le temps humain*, it meets with varying success. When discussing Claudel, he is aided by the fact that Claudel consciously created in terms of circular motifs. Claudel's space is a volume, a three-dimensional profundity in which all activity emanates outward from a central point; concurrently, time is a moving dial in which the figures revolve but remain fixed in relationship to their center. "Space and time are 'reporteurs circonférents' . . . Everything forms a peripheral reality upon which he feels deeply dependent" (pp. 489–490). Claudel does not lose himself in futile, aimless expansion because his perception of reality finds its center not merely in himself but also, potentially, in each separate object. Poulet names this phenomenon a "removal from subjective to objective knowledge" (p. 490), reaching towards an eventual all-inclusive and reciprocal perception. "In Claudel's universe, every object and every being may become the center of the circle" (p. 491). There is a play of reciprocal pressures leading to an "undulatory double movement" or, in the poet's terms, to a *co-naître*. Such an integrated experience of center and circumference exemplifies the ideal phenomenological experience in Poulet's system.

A reversal of the same circle cosmology describes Amiel's existential "failure." In an essay on Amiel dedicated to Maurice Blanchot, Poulet analyzes and implicitly rejects an approach of non-centrality which is the exact opposite of Claudel's. This approach, which he compares to Blanchot, attempts to live on the periphery while contemplating a vast and empty central area. The self is abandoned for an impersonal feeling of being, and personal existence becomes a part of external objects. From the vantage point of these objects, the self may then focus on the universe with different perspectives. Most important is the very movement of consciousness, which is itself the only possible "knowledge." Ultimately, the individual arrives at an "empty eternity" and a sense of "non-existence" (p. 362) by rejecting all the concrete moorings of the thought it wishes to explore. "Actually, consciousness without an object is a thought which forbids itself to think anything—at least anything explicitly thinkable—and which, with this aim, seeks and flees itself in an endless movement described often and unforgettably by Maurice Blanchot" (p. 331). Here the circle is only a geometric shorthand for a philosophical position.

Claudel and Amiel lend themselves to this geometry when they speak of the horizons of perception, but the relationship is not so evident in Mallarmé. The chapter on Mallarmé is exceptional in Poulet's work because it stands as his only example of an *explication de texte,* the familiar traditional analysis of a single given passage. There is no accumulation of selected "circular" terms from which to deduce an inner perspective. The circle itself is introduced only at the end to symbolize Mallarmé's self-contained universe; in this position, it is merely a useful frame of reference.

The text for Poulet's explication is Mallarmé's "Prose pour des Esseintes," for which he outlines a pattern of coordinate affirmation and negation. This pattern governs a universe which is subjective and hermetic, and where the only form of perception is an expanded or contracted vision of the self. "It is the spectacle offered by the self to the self in projecting itself circularly . . . but always inside itself, so as to bring back ultimately its own magnified image" (pp. 443–444). The difficulty with this analysis is that it makes a whole interpretation rest on one vision of Mallarmé's poetry and carries out the technique of explication only insofar as it serves this vision. The selective approach that has served Poulet's purpose in other essays is not transferable to an *explication de texte.* Here the omission or slanted interpretation of various figures leads to puzzlement rather than to persuasion. Other interpretations rise immediately to mind: ones based on a different identification of the same material. One could contest Poulet's identification of the two figures and of the garden, or the proposed dialogue of contradictions and its end in an admission of emptiness, or the falling away from an original unity; and yet the reader is left without any common basis for discussion. Even Poulet's concluding description of a fully self-reflecting universe is not substantiated against counterclaims. The argument as it stands is convincing on its own level, but not comprehensive enough to deal with poetic images which are remarkably concrete for all their abstract significance. Poulet's experiment with a partial *explication de texte* does not prove so satisfying a technique for his approach as the wider-ranging selectivity of his other essays.

This explication is not typical of Poulet's work, however. Nor is his use of forms and patterns at all typical. Both techniques are too limited in scope for a theory which seeks to reveal a man's total sense of existence developing throughout his works. The analysis of circles and other patterns shows Poulet manipulating his own coordinates in an experimental way: a temporary response to his desire for scientific accuracy, but inadequate for his larger existential goals. The circle plays an uneasy role in this criticism: a role that is occasionally apt, but often only generically human (not particular to any author), or coincidentally useful. Poulet is mainly interested in an author's attitude, and soon discovers that this attitude cannot be fully expressed by visual patterns. After *Les Métamorphoses du cercle,* the coordinates remain but the patterned resolutions disappear.

Coordinates of space and time remain as a kind of analytical grid placed over a text, and from which Poulet plots increasingly subtle conclusions. In *L'Espace proustien* (1963) there is a greater sense of the actual feelings of time and space, and fewer graph-like projections of these feelings. The difference, however, is one of technique rather than of aims. Poulet still sums up Proust's experience in a perspective combining space and time, but the analyses bring out more of the personal significance of the author's perceptions. No longer is the perspective metaphysically abstract and generically human. If Poulet shows that Proust thinks in terms of place instead of space (*lieux* instead of *espace*), he enriches this concept by associating it with Proust's love of noble names, his manner of seeing characters in localized frames, and his habit of superimposing and juxtaposing various scenes. The existential conclusions he then reaches, and which must necessarily be phrased in abstract language ("Proust's time is spatialized, juxtaposed time") [10] remain rich and personalized by a cluster of literary associations.

Poulet's *L'Espace proustien* is the second of his two essays on Proust. Signs of the second essay are already present in the first: the opposition with Bergson, the sense of places and of empty distances, and the integrated vision symbolized by the steeples at Martinville. However, the differences are even more important. *L'Espace proustien* is an essay in nine parts, tracing Proust's gradual creation of a coherent sense of existence. The first seven parts echo Poulet's earlier essay, and yet they lead to a new beginning. After this point, Poulet frees himself from the orthodox focus on time in Proust and from Proust's own claims to establish time as a fourth dimension. He conceives of Proust's

10. Poulet, *L'Espace proustien* (Paris: Gallimard, 1964), p. 136.

time as a static, panoramic, *spatial* vision, and develops a new analysis along these lines.

This analysis shows that Proust arrives at a panoramic vision as the only satisfactory way to frame his existence in coherent terms. Tracing the steps of this discovery, Poulet finds that the author has initially to cope with a feeling of emptiness and loss. This initial feeling, moreover, is one that Poulet discusses in *Le Point de départ* as typical of the twentieth century. Modern man, he maintains, exists in the moment and knows no real continuous or coherent life. To be sure of his identity, Proust must establish an enduring personality; and to do that he must be able to recognize the same personality as continuing in space and time. It is not new for Poulet to be analyzing the framework of an author's experience, but he is more than ever successful here in keeping the human figure at the center of his analysis. The nine sections of this essay reflect more closely than did the academic divisions of earlier essays the gradual evolution of a single perceiving subject.

This subject evolves from an initial sense of helplessness to a state in which he possesses certain aspects and fragments of his existence and struggles to piece them together. For awhile he is torn between two universes: one "real" universe which has no relation to his own private being, and another separate universe which is his own but exists only in fragments. There is a tremendous internal discontinuity between these fragments, and a tragic sense of the distance separating them. Through this tragic distance Proust discovers the "depth of existence": "in place of life, only an empty hole where it had been" (p. 68). Each space and each moment exists by itself in a "sort of emptiness sprinkled with sites" (p. 73) and "a few moments in time" (p. 87). Thus the hope held out by Proust's sudden memories at the beginning of *A la Recherche du temps perdu,* when he dips the *madeleine* into his tea, indicates only a clue and a beginning. These places and moments are fragmentary indications of a still unseen unity. They are so many pieces of a spatial existence to be fitted together, so that Proust's real task is to accumulate a sufficient number of consistent pieces to establish a comprehensive pattern.

The end of this task is not temporal, but spatial. There are too many gaps in the memory, and what is remembered does not always fit conveniently into Proust's ideal universe. Memory is a tool that is based in time, but what it calls up need not end as a function of time. Poulet observes that all memories in Proust are connected to a place, are "localized," and that all characters appear framed in a setting which they never completely leave. Proust's memory of one character becomes the memory of all the various situations and places in which the author has seen him, so that he exists in a "system of places" (p. 41) coordinating his universe.

At this juncture Poulet breaks away from the main theme of his early essay. The first essay accepted Proust's claim to have described time as a fourth dimension uniting existence, but the terms in which Poulet accepted this claim show that he considered the dimensions of time and space to be approximately the same. The second essay gives space a new and separate importance. Poulet now goes beyond the earlier essay's vision of the superimposed steeples at Martinville as a sufficient symbolic coordination of Proust's universe. This earlier conclusion shows Proust accumulating numerous overlaid memories in what Poulet calls "a series of steps calculated to approximate reality" (p. 105). By discovering a great variety of remembered aspects for each object, Proust is to establish their relationships and hidden unity. However, this method works against itself, as Poulet shows in his second analysis. It does unite the distant steeples of Martinville and Vieuxvicq, but it explodes into excess when it gives multiple visions of Albertine. "Albertine multiplied ten or more times has already disappeared" says Poulet (p. 110). Quantitative memory is not enough; what is needed is a qualitative selection of ideally suited visions. Beyond variety—even beyond superposed images which obscure one another—there is an ideal juxtaposition, "a collection of images which, put together, furnish a place and form an *illustrated space*" (p. 134). This space is the ultimate, static, but comprehensive vision Proust attains. In this second essay, Poulet undertakes a new conclusion to an old analysis, and a more ambitious attempt to assess the quality of experience.

Along with a new vision of Proust's existential career, Poulet gives a more personal and less methodological examination of the text. His manner of approximating an author's experience is closer to the ideal he has always maintained: a refeeling of original sensations, and an appreciation of their personal significance. There is a slight alteration

in the choice and treatment of source material. In earlier essays Poulet
was more likely to collect a large number of short phrases revealing
attitudes towards space and time. Such a quantitative approach gives
a rather skeletal, intellectualized version of the text's experience. Gradually, he draws upon larger chunks of material to discuss at greater
length. In *L'Espace proustien* he enriches the same basic investigation
with a discussion and comparison of larger passages embodying more
complex attitudes of experience. To a scene showing Proust as a be-
wildered child, suddenly recognizing the gate to his back yard, he adds
a similar scene showing Proust's sudden recognition of Vinteuil's sonata.
The two scenes are evidently meant to be compared, as Poulet points
out, and yet it is this sort of extended sympathetic comparison which
is often lacking in earlier essays. Rather than simply stating that a
being comes from emptiness to a sudden understanding of his environment (and quoting two short phrases), Poulet traces the evolution of
two complete experiences: one in real space, the other in interior space.
A central figure experiences first the vague, helpless feeling of being
lost, and then a sudden reassurance, familiarity, and "localization" of
his environment. By coexisting with the process of discovery in each
situation, Poulet has brought out more of the feelings involved, and
ultimately given more personal density to the same extrapolated experience.

Other passages confirm this approach. Poulet, for example, compares
Proust's attachment for unique places to his feeling for individual identities. Places for Proust are not simply sites in space, "any more than
Charlus and Norpois, Françoise and M. de Bréauté, the Duc de Guerm-
antes, and Marcel's grandmother can be seen as simple interchangeable
specimens of humanity" (p. 50). They are unique identities, comparable at times but never to be generalized. Proust's attachment to places
explains in turn his love of noble names as the personal embodiment
of a place. This feeling for separate identities also petrifies each memory in its visual frame. Objects always appear the same in Proust's
space, for they never develop a continuing existence from one frame
to another. Poulet compares them to a sculpture by Giacometti which,
"from whatever angle you look at it, presents the same drawn-out sil-
houette. Thus what Proust looks at can never grow or disappear . . .

an eternal stranger and eternally absent" (p. 69). Poulet is speaking now in terms of attitudes of existence, and of human reactions to the plotted coordinates of time and space.

These human reactions are not in themselves literary, although they are best expressed in literature. They can be compared to the reactions of artists and philosophers: to Giacometti, to Leibniz (p. 57), and to Bergson. Poulet's first essay on Proust already contrasted his vision with Bergson's. Struck by the philosopher's criticism that the intellect "projects time into space" and destroys the real continuity of existence, he set out to show that Proust exercises this same spatialization of time as a unique creative method. "To the bad juxtaposition condemned by Bergson—intellectual space—there is contrasted a good juxtaposition—an aesthetic space—where moments and places take on the shape of the work of art, a memorable and admirable combination" (p. 10). This distinction appears in the foreword to *L'Espace proustien* and is carried out in its appendix: "Bergson: le thème de la vision panoramique des mourants et la juxtaposition" ("Bergson: the theme of the dying man's panoramic vision and juxtaposition"). After describing Proust's panoramic vision, he outlines a complementary panorama in Bergson. Bergson's panorama is a moving synthesis that does not recognize fixed distinctions between images. "Total, living, moving, composed of a multiplicity of heterogeneous, interpenetrating instants, existence appears in its indivisible surge" (p. 177). Bergson, the believer in continuity, believes in a total, present, continuous flux of life; Proust, the "intermittent thinker," desires the static coexistence of elements that are chosen and juxtaposed. Both the moving and the static panoramas are views of an inner world: a world that becomes philosophy when written by Bergson, and literature when written by Proust. If the comparison of such different genres as philosophy and literature is valid here, the reason is that Poulet is referring to a system of organization which precedes genre. His appendix on Bergson shows once again that Poulet does not turn to literature for aesthetic concerns, that he is primarily concerned with existential attitudes, and thus that he analyzes literature believing that it is the most immediate expression of existence.

L'Espace proustien is a long essay on one author and thus differs from Poulet's next book, which contains nine essays on separate authors. *Le Point de départ* (1964) is the third of his "studies in human time." It is much shorter and less technical than the other two, and shows a broader and more personal attitude of mind. Like *Les Etudes sur le temps humain I* and *Les Métamorphoses du cercle,* it begins with a lengthy introduction that outlines the philosophical and historical hypotheses to come. In this volume, however, the introduction avoids abstract thought and concentrates on a comparative analysis of Gide, Valéry, Claudel and Proust. Human experience as a whole, as it affects individual authors, now takes a larger place in Poulet's analysis.

For Poulet the problem is now to find a mold in which to cast the results of his analysis by coordinates. He seems unsatisfied with visual patterns, although his analyses retain occasional echoes of circular symbolism. If he is to find a personal relationship with the text, he needs a more sensuous contact than abstract patterns provide. On the other hand, if he is to erect any larger system of analyses to give substance to his existential theory, and to frame a history of the human consciousness, he needs a consistent technique of deduction and comparison. In *Le Point de départ,* this technical mold is the moment in which both coordinates lead to creation—a crucial starting point which is both human and literary, and hence represents both aspects of existential theory.

In the introduction, this "starting point" appears as an abstract and an historical argument: it is both the absolute moment of artistic genesis and a newly rediscovered basic instant in human existence. As a feeling of the moment it creates a modern dilemma which each artist tries to solve in his own way. If he succeeds in freeing himself from all accepted notions of permanence and continuity, he lives profoundly from moment to moment; at the same time, however, he is unable to conceive any larger continuous life. Gide, Valéry, Claudel, and Proust "all chose, as the starting point of their spiritual careers, the grasp of a moment different from all other moments." [11] Gide never surpasses this moment of ardor, says Poulet, "but the question is to know if this adventure was condemned to turn out badly, and if the experience of the moment could never end in creation or in the possession of an authentic duration" (p. 27). He proposes this attempted creation of continuity as the spiritual adventure of the twentieth century, whose literature,

11. Poulet, *Le Point de départ* (Paris: Plon, 1964), p. 23.

he maintains, "seems situated in an original point of time, starting from which it must invent or rediscover this time" (p. 37) as a whole. Poulet has found a subject of analysis that is both comparative and comprehensive: it lets him discuss twentieth-century authors from a single standpoint, and permits historical comparisons as well.

The essays in *Le Point de départ* begin by discussing an author's recognition of this basic point in time, and continue with his attempt to create past it a new feeling of permanence and duration. This genesis or "starting point" functions on two levels: in the mind and in art. In the mind it attempts to create a lasting experience; in art it moves from a similarly shapeless, momentary feeling to its expression in tangible, durable form. The point at which artistic creation begins is also the starting point of self-recognition in time.

This double aspect of literary genesis makes it the proper focus of an existential criticism which now calls itself "genetic" rather than a "criticism of consciousness." (Although Poulet defends and defines "genetic criticism," it is clear that he is merely adopting a new name for the criticism that he has practiced all along.) True genetic criticism, says Poulet, is not the study of sources, rough drafts, and their antecedents. Rather, it allows the reader to coexist with the author's developing grasp and formulation of his own existence, and with the work's simultaneous emergence from unconnected bits of raw material to an ideological, structural, and formally cohesive whole. The moment in which both the artistic work and the existential consciousness emerge is the "time" of this third "study in human time." Such a creative *moment* seems close to the aesthetic *space* he described for Proust. This time does not go from past to present to future, but "from the isolated moment to temporal continuity." "The time of the work of art is the very movement in which the work passes from a shapeless, momentary state to a formal and durable state. It is thus a *genetic* movement, deeply subjective and lived from within" (p. 40). It is a moment of consciousness, so that any criticism of it is a "criticism of consciousness," but it is also the focal moment of this consciousness, and of the artistic creation linked to it.

Poulet's notion of this moment as a "starting point" is not quite the same as the concept of the soul's rebirth in Raymond and Béguin. It is a larger, more intellectualized concept which includes and surpasses their concentration upon the Renaissance-Romantic-Surrealist tradition. If the twentieth century inherits the emotional sensitivity of the anti-formal tradition, it also inherits the intellectual attitudes of the classical centuries. It is attached to the seventeenth century by its perception of each moment's creative activity, and to the eighteenth by its emphasis on immediate perceptions, on starting anew, and on the genesis of psychic beings. "From the epoch of 'continued creation' to that of 'continuous feeling' to that of our modern 'continuous grasp of consciousness' a sort of logical connection is established: the repeated recognition of the present moment's basic importance" (p. 23). Poulet's more inclusive philosophical approach leads him away from the original anticlassical reading experience which prompted the study of consciousness in literature. He emphasizes the same sense of emotional discovery and creation, but integrates it with concomitant philosophical attitudes. This integrated experience is Poulet's own development, and becomes an ideal standard against which he measures all periods and literatures.

Le Point de départ uses this focal experience as a standard for historical comparison. Up to this point, Poulet has always set his analyses against an implied ideal experience, but he has never compared them to such an extent or gone so far toward establishing an historical pattern of consciousness. He has also preferred to take the relatively safe position of analyzing the complete works of men long dead, and thus assured of having completed their existential careers. Now, however, Poulet is able to use the idea of a "starting point" of self-recognition and creation in order to treat contemporary and incomplete authors. *Le Point de départ* is completely devoted to modern authors, most of whom are still alive even if they have already produced the bulk of their work. In analyzing the point at which they start into artistic creation, Poulet condenses a whole existential experience and makes it comparable to that of other, past writers.

The historical aims of *Le Point de départ* appear not so much in its unusual preoccupation with one century as in its proliferation of literary comparisons. These comparisons are often apt, but also often fleeting and undeveloped. At times they seem inserted to suggest a pattern of existential relevancy that can be developed at a later date. "From Rousseau to Gide, it is not hard to point out a whole series of this kind of experience: in Senancour, Biran, Guérin, Flaubert, Baudelaire" (p.

11). Comparisons and contrasts abound. "Whitman's enumeration is already that of Péguy" (p. 45). "As in so many passages from Baudelaire, Flaubert, or Mallarmé," there is in Bernanos a "desperate reiteration of existence" (p. 50). Bernanos' liquid passivity does not end in a clear stream, "as in Mme Guyon or Fénelon," but in a swampy plain "like the pools of the house of Usher" (p. 55). There is no equivalent to his feeling of initial paralysis "unless perhaps in the first poems of Mallarmé" (p. 60), and his novels "are diametrically opposed to all other novels (except perhaps the novels of Dostoievsky alone)" (p. 72). In René Char, the mind risks itself in a way which is "the exact opposite of Mallarmé's attempt" (p. 92), and Char's poetry resembles "another hard, laconic, and voluntary poetry . . . Corneille's poetry" (p. 95). Supervielle is like Diogenes, Robinson Crusoe, Proust (p. 111), La Palice, Hugo, and Péguy (p. 112). Eluard is like Proust, Valéry, Supervielle, Hugo (pp. 128–129), Dante (p. 135), Rimbaud, Gide (p. 143), and Breton (p. 144), but unlike Alain-Fournier (p. 130). In Perse the perfect instant is a goal, not a beginning as in Proust (p. 166). Perse's sense of time is an accumulative progression to be contrasted with Valéry's anticipatory impulse (p. 167). This progression reminds Poulet of Whitman, Hugo, and Péguy (pp. 169–170); when it expands into disperson and forgetfulness it recalls Lamartine (p. 183), and when it ends in poetized ruins it brings to mind Volney and Chateaubriand (p. 184). Again like Chateaubriand, Reverdy feels an initial lack, but he does not have Chateaubriand's "superabundance of life" (p. 187). He has instead Poe's horror of narrow, enclosed spaces, but not Poe's ultimate fulfilment inside them (p. 194). In this way he is like Mallarmé, but not Rimbaud (p. 196). Ungaretti is like Leopardi, Mallarmé, Rilke, Ossian (p. 211), Hölderlin and Rimbaud (p. 214). All these comparisons (which are themselves only a selection) may be perfectly valid in context, but out of context they give the unfortunate impression of a half-finished argument. Poulet's aim is obviously to suggest some provocative comparisons consistent with his existential perspective, and to propose areas for future analysis inside an existential literary history.

These comparisons are most effective when they are drawn into the thread of the argument. The essay on Sartre is a good example of efficient comparison, for Poulet establishes his definition of Sartre's modern existential *cogito* by reference to a number of preceding *co-*

gito's. This essay begins and ends with a comparison of Sartre and Descartes, whose experiences are similar until they reach opposite conclusions.

Descartes, like Sartre, begins with "hyperbolic doubt," or the abolition of all previous sense of existence. The immediate feeling of life which he then acquires is temporary, insecure, solitary, and lacking any perceivable cause. Up to this point his experience is that of Sartre, who has suddenly "fallen into existence" (p. 226) out of a previous unthinking slumber. However, the feeling of insufficient personal cause leads Descartes to conclude that there must be a sufficient extrinsic cause— God—and Sartre reaches no such comforting conclusion. To this original contrast Poulet adds a number of lesser examples: a sensualist or "felt *cogito*" (p. 220), a romantic *cogito* (Maine de Biran), a symbolist *cogito* (Mallarmé p. 222), and Camus' existential *cogito* leading to feelings of brotherhood among men (p. 227). The most comparable experience remains that of Descartes, and yet it leads in Sartre to nausea and the rejection of existence.

Sartre's "nausea" is the concrete literary expression of the modern existential *cogito*, and for this reason it interests Poulet. If Poulet were simply an historian of philosophical ideas, he would (as he says) draw upon Husserl or Heidegger. Instead, he looks to the literary demonstration of this *cogito* to discover its total significance—emotional as well as intellectual. In *La Nausée*, says Poulet, Sartre first rejects Descartes' *cogito*, after which the word itself "can no longer be pronounced without a tone of derision" (p. 228). Sartre then defines his own *cogito*, which is inverted and sensual, for he feels himself exist as one of an amorphous variety of unstable sensations. He wallows in a sticky glue: "Air and sky are lacking. Thought sticks to itself, becomes heavy and sluggish, drags and sinks into an 'ignoble marmalade,' 'the thick jam sticking to everything' which covers everything and is everything" (p. 230). Mind has become matter: a viscous, disgusting matter that seems to be more the subject of a bad dream than of philosophy. In fact, this nausea is both philosophical and emotional, and calls up both philosophical and poetic comparisons. Poulet identifies here an essential theme of poetry and dreams: "man captured by things, becoming a thing, losing in this contact with matter whatever makes him a free and intelligent being" (p. 231). Poulet's comparisons are now poetic rather than philosophical: Baudelaire and Mallarmé, he says, translate these fears "with the image of ship or swan eternally prisoned in ice," and Poe describes "the horror of the pool which swallows up the house of Usher and its inhabitants" (p. 231). All these comparisons are appropriate to the arguments in which they are found, and they are sufficiently developed to illuminate Poulet's main theme.

In the end, Sartre finds a way out of the glue of existence (the "absurd" *cogito*) to a transcendent melody which represents the human organization of perception (the *"cogito* of liberty"). Instead of passing to the hypothesis of divine creation, like Descartes, he escapes from existence into an emptiness that must be filled with free acts. Poulet's essay ends on this comparison of Descartes with Sartre, to which he gives a somewhat moral turn. "Sartre's existentialism can end only in an ethic which tries to prove that *good* can be created from *nothing.*" By ignoring any "fundamental relationship" with an extrinsic creative principle, Poulet says, man is forced to ricochet "from a full but inert material world to the dizzy void of the self" (p. 236). These images openly represent an unsatisfactory conclusion to the existential experience, and suggest that a successful conclusion involves recognizing an exterior creative impulse.

It is not at all unusual for Poulet to phrase his conclusions in terms of images. If there is any technical form which stands out in *Le Point de départ*, it is the abundance of images used to convey philosophical or critical thought. This technique reflects Poulet's desire to make criticism a reliving of the original impulse, and to provide the reader with transferred sensations rather than with an abstract argument. He has always admired Richard's ability to relate physical images to existential situations, and most of his emphasis on sensuous phenomena is reminiscent of Richard. In Richard and in Poulet, these images run the risk of all analogies: if they permit colorful and dynamic explanations, they also open the way for inexact and unnecessary connotations. Poulet points to the image of a lake of mud in Bernanos as a conscious visual equivalent of sin and inertia, and is able to ring many provocative and illuminating changes upon this basic equivalence. This mud lake is "the *place* and the *time* of evil . . . a fetid reservoir" of evil acts (p. 57). Its flaccid and semiliquid texture makes it the perfect representation of despair, soulless boredom, loss of character, and the stagnation of all physical and moral activity. Unless a supernatural impulse comes, man is petrified in this mud like a fossil—or like the hollow image left when the fossil disappears. As long as images like these develop and accompany the argument, or synthesize separate observations of the author, they fill a useful function.

Instances occur, however, to make analogies seem unnecessary distractions. The casual use of analogy brings with it confusing, and occasionally amusing, overtones. A poem by Char is "a coiled spring . . . which has coiled itself" (p. 102). Supervielle, "like a bull led to slaughter" (p. 111), does not know where he is going. Sometimes the image speaks for itself, as when Perse's time is a "snowball" time (p. 168). Sometimes it is an arbitrary analogy which itself needs explanation in context. Poulet uses the same image of the hole left by a fossil for both Bernanos and Reverdy. For Reverdy the explanation is that his consciousness is "a central hollow surrounded by a peripheral inaccessible zone": an empty thought which can perceive things only as existing outside it (p. 189). The fossil image has no direct explanatory significance, and needs a fairly abstract interpretation itself before it can shed light on the original text. These evocations may lend color to an abstract analysis, but they risk obscuring the original text for a hybrid creation in which literature and criticism compete to express a common experience.

This common experience is the goal of Poulet's analysis, and all analogies and historical comparisons exist only to focus on its initial act or "starting point." Poulet wishes to see this starting point lead to a coherent existence, and *Le Point de départ* follows the attempts of modern authors to create such an existence. The third of the *Etudes sur le temps humain* seems also to represent a decisive point in the history of Poulet's personal philosophy: a metaphysical quest that can be traced throughout his books, but which reaches at this juncture a contemporary and personal assessment.

In Poulet's early works he concentrates on literature's expression of authentic human feeling. Later he looks for a way in which to weave these feelings into a consistent web of existence: a total human identity. This identity is total only if it is integrated with the universe, if (as he says for Perse) there is a "double homogeneity of the world and the poem" (p. 174). Such homogeneity is necessary if the individual author wants to establish a complete feeling of self, but it has larger implications. As the author represents human feeling and self-recognition at its highest, he (again like Perse) can dream of representing man in the universe. "Perse . . . has dreamed, or should we say: has understood? that space and time have as their sole mission to lay bare their secrets before him, so that, revealing them in his turn, the poet may give them a greater meaning and confer upon them a greater splendor" (p. 177). In this role the poet is the universe's consciousness of itself: a subjective literary adaptation of existential perceptions which is nonetheless not Poulet's last word upon the subject. This last (or latest) word appears in the essay on Sartre, whose attempt at pure self-creation seems to Poulet an illusion: "I cannot conceive myself without discovering and recognizing my dependence in regard to a creative principle" (p. 236). Such a "fundamental relation" is not recognized by Sartre, who therefore falls short of being truly integrated into the universe. It would be impertinent to suggest that Poulet has used his analyses to establish a personal philosophy, but these analyses do show an unmistakable growth and development of his personal existential perspective applied to literature.

In 1966 Poulet published *Trois Essais de mythologie romantique*: "Sylvie ou la pensée de Nerval" (published in almost identical form in the *Cahiers du Sud* in 1938), "Nerval, Gautier, et la blonde aux yeux noirs," and "Piranèse et les poètes romantiques français." A short introduction describes these essays as exercises in "thematic criticism," a term that Poulet seems increasingly to be adopting for his own. A certain manner of experiencing space or time, a particular vision or "myth," persists in any writer and becomes a theme for critical analysis. This "thematic" criticism is in fact the same as the "genetic" criticism of *Le Point de départ*, with the critic's attention focused a little farther along the creative process. Poulet is speaking with increasing ease now of the *forms* taken by creative consciousness, and his essay on Piranesi combines the analysis of forms reflecting experience with the *Geistesgeschichte* implied ever since the *Etudes sur le temps humain I*.

If it was necessary for Poulet to distinguish his work from objective or historical criticism when he first began, it is now useful for him to distinguish it from a psychoanalytical or structural analysis which would go beyond the artistic text to previous, noncreative states. Here there is a narrow line to draw, mainly because the Geneva critics are like the structuralists in that they do form patterns of experience, do relate the work to a history of ideas, and do speak of a pre-verbal experience at the base of literature. Poulet, however, will not admit that significant themes "refer to some state which is before the act of consciousness." [12] Social and physiological data serve only to allow the writer to create his own unique experience, and this experience is gradually created only in the literary work. Poulet's text, although a formalist might read it as a biographical portrait, is in fact totally divorced from the writer as historical being. A new personality is created in the course of a work, a personality that exists only in and because of that work. Nerval, in *Sylvie*, seems to "create the labyrinth which imprisons him as he goes along" (p. 10). The text for Poulet is neither an unconscious statement of an historical being nor a conscious message phrased in semiological terms. It is an act of consciousness, a creative choice "relating the mind to an ensemble of set configurations," which work themselves out not in structural reflections of the real world, but in the unique, individually discovered and executed "imaginary universes" of literature.

The text of "Sylvie" is not substantially different from that published in 1938, but the essay "Nerval, Gautier, et la blonde aux yeux noirs" is a cogent example of what Poulet calls a "thematic" criticism. The subject is the "dark-eyed blonde" who fascinated Byron, Musset, and Gautier, and who has become a traditional literary type by the time she appears in Nerval. Poulet stresses the fact that the dark-eyed blonde is a literary rather than an actual figure, and that Nerval's creation is thus a wholly imagined variation on a literary theme—not someone he knew (p. 86). Even her setting is borrowed, for Poulet shows that the scene of Nerval's "Fantaisie" is in fact Gautier's invention, and that Nerval often seems content to use his colleague's vision (pp. 89–93). What remains after this borrowed vision is pared away establishes the true individuality of the poet, and is the subject of Poulet's "thematic" (or genetic) criticism.

Poulet compares two versions of the theme of the dark-eyed blonde: Gautier's, which seeks to incarnate and specify her ideal beauty, and Nerval's, which pursues a still-ephemeral ideal through a number of transformations. Gautier has "an extraordinary will to give his dream a material, even carnal form" (p. 97), but this project results in a de-

---

12. Poulet, *Trois Essais de mythologie romantique* (Paris: Corti, 1966), p. 9.

humanizing of her too-literal portrait. "Clarity suppresses the shadows and removes depth" (p. 111), so that Gautier ends by making his ideal woman a precisely described but inhuman *type*. Nevertheless, Nerval adopts much of Gautier, including his vision of the ideal woman as *bionda e grassota* after Gozzi, his settings, even certain expressions (p. 116). However, Nerval's heroine appears throughout in a series of incomplete and tantalizing aspects which are unclear but give glimpses of an ideal unity. There is an abrupt contrast in perspective on this same type: for Gautier "the type tends to harden, to lose all depth, to be reduced to its pure appearances, but for Nerval, even while nothing in its exterior aspect is altered, the type tends to take on an ensemble of increasingly secret and profound meanings, to be burdened with an esoteric significance" (p. 124). This ensemble of meanings ends as unhappily as did Gautier's "petrification and dehumanization of being" (p. 112), for it loses the ideal image of beauty in an ever-expanding series of its aspects. The last stage of the dark-eyed blonde in Nerval is a "violent disintegration of the central image, an inability to join the pieces of a single thought, the consciousness of having only the debris of his dream before him" (p. 134). Both Gautier and Nerval use the same "primitive form," but their thematic developments of this form reflect entirely opposite manners of vision. The uniqueness of each poet's myth lies not in the image of a dark-eyed blonde dressed in the style of Louis XIII and seated at a window in the Place Royale, but in the transformations this image undergoes with each poet. These transformations incarnate a progressive investigation of the ideal of beauty, and also reflect the seekers' divergent existential adventures.

In "Piranèse et les poètes romantiques français," Poulet discusses the influence of a picture by Piranesi in which the painter seems to be climbing an endless series of staircases. The image of this perpetual climb and search struck a responsive chord in Coleridge and De Quincey, echoed again in Beckford, Musset, Gautier, Hugo, and Baudelaire.[13] Once again there is a common image with many individual variations, a single theme which Poulet can use to examine and compare a series of existential adventures.

13. Poulet also compares Henri Michaux, and could have added Maurice Blanchot, whose "vestibulary universe" he describes in "Maurice Blanchot, critique et romancier," *Critique*, June 1966, p. 491.

The critical approach in the essay "Piranèse" resembles Poulet's earlier views, although he continues to stress the term "thematic criticism." His introduction to the essay gives a double role to thematic criticism: it reveals personal obsessions, the "starting points of a thousand ideas . . . from a single center of thought," and it also shows "what is transmitted from one thought to others . . . their principle or common base" (p. 135). These statements, although newly applied to "thematic" criticism, are no more than what Poulet has been proposing all along: the individual analysis at the "starting point" of thought, and the "history of the mind incarnate in forms." [14] Familiar too is his use of categories of space and time to focus the artist's experience. Piranesi's space is "an inverted space, a space stressing distances," whose expansion makes man appear all the more lost and vulnerable. Similarly, there is a "monstrous dilation of time" (p. 143) oppressing man. The picture of the endless, inescapable climb calls upon both of Poulet's "two great principles for representing reality: space and time" (p. 148). Moreover, he continues to analyze a total experience by means of these predominant existential coordinates.

This common theme of the endless, frustrated climb is evoked in prison-like surroundings that seem to deny the very space they so hopelessly evoke. In later writers space becomes a labyrinth, leading either to a blank wall, an immovable trapdoor, or emptiness. Although each author shapes his own experience in an individual way, they all share the feeling of man as a blind prisoner of himself and his surroundings, "condemned to reproduce indefinitely one fundamental identity" (p. 150) and "deprived of all connections with the external world" (p. 167). This is the drama of thought penetrating its own mystery, "a thought which . . . descends step by step toward a stricter consciousness of itself . . . pure consciousness" (p. 186). Thought conscious of itself is one of the most prevalent modern themes, be it in literature, art, or psychology. Poulet's study focused from the very beginning on this modernity, for he planned to "reproduce the mental echo awakened in the modern reader" (p. 137) by Piranesi's climb. If Poulet studies a "Romantic mythology,"

14. Poulet mentions as examples of this literary history Paul Hazard's *Crise de la conscience européenne*, Arthur Lovejoy's *Great Chain of Being*, Raymond's *De Baudelaire au surréalisme*, Béguin's *L'Ame romantique et le rêve*, Rousset's *La Littérature de l'âge baroque en France*, and Starobinski's *L'Invention de la liberté* (*Trois essais*, p. 136).

then he does so in order to illustrate certain ancestors of modern thought and to prepare the background of a *Geistesgeschichte* for which contemporary literature is but the latest chapter.

Poulet's interest is not confined to works of literature. He is concerned with critical writings as well. Now, in fact, he is preparing a volume to be called *Essai sur la pensée critique de notre temps*. His analysis of criticism resembles his analysis of literature in that he looks for the main themes and fundamental types of experience that shape his subject's critical perspective. Indeed, for Poulet there is no real distinction between imaginative literature and criticism, for both employ a thinking, feeling author who chooses to examine himself, the world, or another's experience. Because the critic is "subjectivity and objectivity grasping himself and grasping things," he behaves "not very differently from his rival, the poet or novelist." [15] Poulet's main concern is an author's characteristic vision. Moreover, he analyzes this vision separate from its object,[16] so that it makes no logical difference whether the writer creates literature (a work focused on the world) or criticism (a work focused on literature).

Thus far, and with few exceptions, Poulet has written about critics with whom he feels some natural sympathy: Raymond, Béguin, Starobinski, Du Bos, Bachelard, and Blanchot. Moreover, he tends to discover a familiar common theme in their work: the initial sense of

15. Poulet, "Maurice Blanchot, critique et romancier," p. 485.
16. In a letter to J. Hillis Miller, Poulet describes his approach as "Cartesian" rather than phenomenological. He also sets himself off from the aims of contemporary "structural" criticism. Poulet is not concerned with systems inspired by the exterior world, but with the author's manner of perception when all conditions and objects are stripped away—with pure consciousness.

> I should readily consider that the most important form of subjectivity is not that of the mind overwhelmed, filled, and so to speak stuffed with its objects, but that there is another [kind of consciousness] which sometimes reveals itself on this side of, at a distance from, and protected from, any object, a subjectivity which exists in itself, withdrawn from any power which might determine it from the outside, and possessing itself by a direct intuition, infinitely different from the self-knowledge which is the indirect result of our relations with the world . . . this double consciousness appears less in its multiplicity of sensuous relations with things, than prior to and separate from any object, as self-consciousness or pure consciousness . . . As you have seen, in this I remain faithful to the Cartesian tradition.

Quoted by Miller in "The Geneva School,"
Critical Quarterly, Winter 1966, p. 315.

distance from reality that they as critics and men must overcome. Such a theme echoes Poulet's own analysis of a *cogito* in literature, as well as the Geneva School's insistence on a growing self-consciousness in modern man. Poulet will undoubtedly discuss other critics, as he is not limited to those who sympathize with his position, but he will probably continue to support his own empathetic, literary-historical perspective.

Poulet's essay on Bachelard functions in two ways: it analyzes a philosophical thought close to his own, and reasserts his definition of literary criticism as empathy. In "Gaston Bachelard et la conscience de soi," he traces a philosophical *cogito* which proceeds from an original rejection of subjectivity to a mind exploring itself by means of its relation to objects. Bachelard's early work betrays a scientific idealism reaching for absolute objective truth. Such objectivity is abstract, however, and can never reach its object: it is "deprived of the very object which should be its center" [17] because it must avoid the taint of a subjective grasp. For Bachelard, "scientific knowledge . . . is what thought always pursues ahead of itself" (p. 3). In seeking to distill and refine a true sense of objects, he is forced to analyze his sense of perception and ultimately to recognize the contours of his own personality. "Psychoanalyzing objective life is also psychoanalyzing subjective life" (p. 10), and Bachelard reverses the focus of his perceptive experience in order to explore his own subjective reality. A philosopher who began as a purist in search of absolute knowledge, he comes to recognize two ideals and ways of thought: "an existential duality . . . a double existence with divergent principles to both of which the protagonist remains faithful" (p. 8). His single experience of reality can be analyzed both in terms of the object and the subject, and Bachelard continues to recognize and to separate this dual possibility.

Poulet consistently stresses the irreconcilable nature of Bachelard's two ideals, but he himself evidently favors the later, subjective attitude which is so much closer to his own. Bachelard, he says, could "ultimately only reject a psychoanalytical method which looks for an *objective presence* in subjectivity itself" (p. 25), and the philosopher tends now to identify a subjective *cogito* which would imply connections between two thinking (if nonobjective) beings. Bachelard's *cogito*, "precisely

17. Poulet, "Gaston Bachelard et la conscience de soi," *Revue de Métaphysique et de morale,* 70 (January-March 1965), p. 2.

because it is a *cogito,* or act of consciousness," leads him from the study of pure perception to a willed existence (p. 18), from his earlier psycho-analytical perspective to phenomenology (p. 24) and the subjective creation of an interior universe (p. 25). Here, with the mention of mental universes and their subjective communication, enters an echo of Poulet's own philosophy and "a marvelous application of phenomenology to literature" (p. 26). "Literature in perhaps its most important sense is just what Bachelard's method touches on and explores: an ensemble of images that must be seized in the very act in which the imagining consciousness begets them." This ensemble can be grasped only by "*assuming* the imagination of another," by identifying oneself with the author's imaginary world and passing "from one *cogito* to another *cogito.*" Here Poulet actually defines his own notion of criticism: a movement of sympathy between two subjects, a literary empathy in which a reader takes on or "assumes" the author's exploration of his universe.

Such an empathetic communication between subject and reality, or subject and subject, is Poulet's main concern in "La Pensée critique d'Albert Béguin," where he proposes that all Béguin's work stems from a single attempt to establish some kind of communication with a reality outside himself. Béguin is unable to attain any sense of material reality or sensuous experience, so that "his look remains inexorably directed within." [18] Because his thought is "never directly related to things, but only to the ideal of things" (p. 181), he favors a literature that will mediate between himself and outside reality. Indeed, his preference for a literature that incarnates physical reality is decided by (although in contrast to) his own inability to experience reality. This preference, according to Poulet, becomes a "theme of presence . . . *being* in its concrete presence, in the self-evidence it displays" (p. 180). The search for presence leads Béguin to seek divine presence in earthly reality, and to favor writers who seem to provide this revelation. He looks past the work's material incarnations to a "sort of transcendence of the work as the symbol it expresses . . . two essential operations . . . the contemplation of things and the creation of symbols" (p. 191). In his latest work, when Béguin seems far removed from the broad humanism of his

18. Poulet, "La Pensée critique d'Albert Béguin," *Cahiers du Sud,* no. 360 (April-May 1961), p. 178.

beginnings, he is actually at the last step in a series of investigations of presence: "presence of things, presence of God in things, presence of time and men, presence in time and among men . . . presence of God in the communion of saints" (p. 197). Poulet thus uses a single metaphysical stance—the search for presence after an initial feeling of absence—to explain the successive stages in a critical thought leading from *L'Ame romantique et le rêve* to *Poésie de la présence*.

In "La Pensée critique de Jean Starobinski," Poulet discusses the problem of absence in some detail. Starobinski's first thought "discovers the distance that separates it from a universe that, as it well knows, controls its destiny." [19] Poulet then speaks of Starobinski's early work on Kafka and Mallarmé, tacitly compares him to these exiled consciousnesses, and concludes that he is tempted into the sin of "angelism" by being "avid of a perfection and completion which can only be outside" (p. 388). Early in his career, Starobinski wants to spiritualize reality in order to attain the harmony of an isolated, purified universe (p. 397). His intellectualized thought sees only aspects and not real being, so that he comes to realize that his vision is "seeing and not seeing . . . He must resign himself to being at least temporarily blind" (p. 402). His ideas change, however, when he begins to study medicine; for he now applies to literary analysis a new awareness of the human body. "Jean Starobinski is one who, after having clearly rejected material reality, little by little comes to accept and even to profit by his fleshly condition . . . an adolescent thought becomes adult" (p. 404). His thought is no longer excluded from material reality. He even attains "a real continuity of exchanges" between himself and the reality outside. Starobinski's later criticism reflects this exchange: it alternates between an involved and a detached attitude to reflect the literary work in a series of interrelated visions (p. 409). Although Poulet's essay on Starobinski is the first in a series not yet completed, it already outlines the critic's metaphysical development from 1943 to 1961.

In one passage on Starobinski, Poulet discusses a type of criticism typical of Marcel Raymond and perhaps of the whole Geneva School. This criticism dominates Starobinski's early work and represents one side of his later dual approach. Here there is a fusion of the reader and

19. Poulet, "La Pensée critique de Jean Starobinski (I)," *Critique*, May 1963, p. 387.

his subject: "Criticism exists in a disavowal of self analogous to that required by mystic thought: by suppressing the distinction between subject and object, by becoming the being of another being, and by alienating one's own being" (p. 407). Such a "hope of fusion" is mentioned again in the essay on Blanchot. For Rivière, Du Bos, Raymond, Béguin, Bachelard, Rousset, and Richard, the goal is "to find in literature, thanks to literature, this unique point and moment of existence where thought and being see all distance effaced, where subject and object shudder in asserting their proximity." [20] Such an empathetic experience is shared by all the Geneva critics, including Poulet (although he returns from it to consider subjective patterns), but it is not one which can be associated with Maurice Blanchot.

Blanchot's criticism attacks this identification of subject with object and tries to establish only the presence of distance. "With Blanchot, everything begins with absence," says Poulet; he reinforces absence; he does not want to overcome it; he describes it in order to approximate the human condition; he wants to measure our fragile sense of reality against an intangible neverneverland where subject and object do unite —although we never see them. Blanchot's thought aims at this final "place of unity . . . toward which it never ceases to aim and aspire," a "unique place, a point with neither space nor time" (p. 494).[21] The positive aspect of Blanchot's negative criticism is that it transmits "the experience of stark existence" and demonstrates "the zone of absolute solitude which surrounds all human life" (p. 488). His studies themselves, says Poulet, "begin actually by being criticism, but become less and less so." They express "the act in which the critic passes from another's mental world to another world, completely inside himself, which he alone conceives and explores" (p. 489). Blanchot not only reasserts the absence represented by literature, but reinforces this feeling of distance by transposing it into his own world—exploring isolation in the midst of solitude. Poulet ends by placing Blanchot in the tradition of metaphysical writers like Mme de Lafayette, Constant, and Sartre, as an explorer of human consciousness. This consciousness is dominated by an

20. Poulet, "Maurice Blanchot, critique et romancier," p. 486.
21. Here Poulet is perhaps too greatly influenced by his own school's positive attitude: the "outside" referred to by Blanchot is probably only a metaphorical point from which to make vivid the distance of knowledge and the impossibility of systematic consciousness.

experience of absence which (unlike the experiences of Béguin and Starobinski) does not seek to emerge from its solitude.

Opposed to Blanchot's negative views are those of Charles Du Bos, whose subjective intuition is closer to the Geneva school than is Blanchot's attempt to maintain distances. The very idea of a starting point in self-discovery comes from Du Bos, as Poulet remarks in "La Pensée critique de Charles du Bos." Also from Du Bos comes the notion of a passive, empathetic reading, a "renewing of the creative gesture," and a "profound tendency to identification" which has influenced a whole body of modern critics (Poulet mentions Raymond and Richard).[22] When Poulet writes about Du Bos, then, he is paying homage to a predecessor as well as analyzing an important twentieth-century critic.

Du Bos' characteristic starting point is both a critical method and an essential manner of being. Unable to conceive any action or cause in himself, and unable to create any initial impulse, he is forced to rely upon repeated "spiritual gifts" from outside. As a critic he finds inspiration in texts and makes himself the passive receptacle of their consciousness. He "interprets" literature as a musician interprets a piece of music, by letting the original conscious gesture repeat itself in a new creation. "I begin by letting thought begin all over again inside me," paraphrases Poulet (p. 499). Du Bos' criticism is not the re-creation of Raymond or Richard, however, for his empathy is pure acceptance and not a reciprocal mental play in which text and critic seek each other out. Rather, his is a "dialogue of self with self" (p. 503), a self-contained relationship between active giver and passive receiver. The essential peculiarity of this position, according to Poulet, is that it reflects an "intuitive certainty that spiritual life consists in the vertical connection of two planes" (p. 513). Both artist and critic receive their inspiration from outside and exist as the lesser, receptive partner of an active, transcendental impulse. When Du Bos leaves himself open to the "essence" of Pascal, Wordsworth, or Novalis, he perceives through them the "essential duplication" of all inner life (p. 504). This duplication reassures him that in coinciding with the artist's inner self he is coinciding with the same ultimate source of inspiration that is his own.

This feeling of duplication or "double interiority" leads Du Bos to

22. Poulet, "La Pensée critique de Charles du Bos," *Critique,* June 1965, pp. 495–496, 512.

practice an extended, interpretative criticism which tries to raise itself to the level of the original creation. Such a criticism is an "exaltation" or an "elevation," for it uses the author's own starting point "as a springboard for its own inventions" (pp. 513–514). Threatened sometimes by the abundance of its own inventions, and bordering on critical incoherence, it surpasses this "secondary failure" to reveal the very quality of thought itself. The primary goal of Du Bos' criticism is to display "in his authors as in himself, a thought which is truly nonobjective: the free play of interior life" (p. 515). In this setting, both authors and critic appear as the purely receptive artificers of a given inspiration. This inspiration sits at the center of Du Bos' argument, provides him and Poulet with an extrinsically based creative theory, and allows both men "to place in the center of this intimate space He who is more ourselves than we" (p. 516).

The almost doctrinal ending to the essay on Du Bos recalls Poulet's implied rejection of Sartre's "dizzy void" and indicates the metaphysical terminus of Poulet's entire theory of creation. The introduction to *Les Etudes sur le temps humain I* revolves around a history of theories of creation viewed from a framework of time and space perceptions. Later works analyze the existence and interaction of these perceptions, with more or less emphasis on the creative principle governing the whole. Literature enters this argument only as the highest expression of human existence, and it enters always as a whole—never in fragments or as separately valuable texts. With *L'Espace proustien,* Poulet again emphasizes the individual creative impulse that stamps each author's production, and his relative position is assessed in a panorama of creative consciousness. Literature thus defined has always been the central referent of Poulet's criticism, so that with all its variations his work can continue to appear what it has always claimed to be, a *literary* criticism.

It is one thing to point out the influence of Poulet's personal beliefs on his criticism and another to assume that such a subjective bias makes his work purely metaphysical, or invalidates it as literary criticism. Given the existential definition of literature, which Poulet in no way contradicts when he presupposes that existence has a divine coordinator, his criticism still stands as an attempt to view literature in terms of existential philosophy. This proposed central existence (whether or not divine) even sets up a hitherto lacking standard of progression, and hence an ideal coherence against which to measure literary expression. Poulet has been working toward an open statement of this central existence throughout all his implied earlier measurements of psychic coherence, profundity, sincerity, and humanity: he has carefully avoided assimilating his method to any one religious doctrine, and now proposes this central source of inspiration as a way to give meaning and coherence to the whole existential view. In this respect his conclusion is no different from the hypothesis of familiar Christian existentialism, but it is reached here as a conclusion and the last segment of an analytical structure. As the essay on Sartre shows, a reader need not adopt the supra-literary values of this creative theory to be able to analyze an author. The method of analysis is independent of any external values, and as such may logically claim to speak as an existential literary criticism.

The formal critic, to be sure, wants to label this approach "extra-literary" and to dismiss it from the realm of literary speculation; but he is not willing to accept Poulet's openly unaesthetic concept of literature. In a letter to Professor René Wellek (written October 6, 1956) [23] Poulet discusses the difference between his definition of literature and that of a more objective, formal critic. Poulet is not willing to be relegated to the category of extra-literary theorist, nor will he forego what he calls "the only title I would dare give myself, which is that of critic." In fact, says he, all real criticism must be subjective "if criticism has for its primordial goal our comprehension of a work, that is to say to situate us in a thinking and feeling consciousness, a subject in connection with its objects." For the formal critic the work of art is an independent, structurally identifiable and analyzable object. For Poulet it is an activity and not a result—it is the human activity that expresses itself via the result. "Every work is not only the formal result of a mental activity, it is that activity itself . . . the literary work is not a flower or a fruit. It is the creature smelling the flower and tasting the fruit." When art is defined in such fashion, it follows that the critic must analyze the thought behind form. Literary forms disappear, and in place of "the poem, the novel, the essay, the play," we find a "consciousness that is substituted for our own." Poulet's approach does not so much

23. Letter quoted by permission of the author.

contradict the formal approach as ignore it, or deny it any real importance.

Poulet's views seem to have developed since this letter of 1956. In the letter he is convinced of the futility of any "criticism" beyond the private act of reading. Any judgment or synthesis is false, for "to criticize is thus to make oneself interior, and to make oneself interior is to situate oneself in such conditions that a judgment (necessarily exterior) is for the moment impossible." All a critic can do "inside" a work is to discover the major themes and spiritual coordinates of this new consciousness. "All that we can do, plunged as we are inside a mental reality which has become our own thought, is to trace itineraries and follow currents." By concentrating on themes and itineraries, Poulet is able to avoid the traditional terms of technical analysis. These themes, however, still allow for implied judgments of depth, sincerity, authenticity, and coherence, and thus reintroduce notions of evaluation and technical competence. Poulet comes to stress especially the idea of coherence, which has for so long been the main criterion of formal analysis. He does not actually condemn inconsistency, but measures all his existential analyses against the perfect coherence of a complete existential (perhaps by extension *divine*) perspective.

In spite of this tendency toward existential evaluations, Poulet's practice is remarkably consistent in its methods and area of application. He still holds, as his letter states, that existential criticism must limit itself to a peculiar region between aesthetics and philosophy: "this does not have to do with philosophical speculation, but with lived experience." There is no interest in the aesthetic or formal structure of a work. He is not concerned with technical uniqueness, verbal manipulation of themes, or any aspect of art that may be called *craftsmanship*. What is more, he recognizes these limitations, all of which tend, as he says, not only to obviate value judgments but "to destroy or to neglect the formal aspect of works."

> In our studies it is as if there were no poems, novels, or plays with their particular meaning; everything becomes a continuous medium in which forms have only an indicative role like everything else. Such is the most serious limitation of such criticism, and the one which, at the same time, makes it differ the most from criticism as it is understood in Anglo-Saxon countries today.

He then goes on, however, to defend the existential against the formal approach. In Anglo-Saxon countries, he maintains, criticism is *merely* objective.

> In these countries, what is most important is the structural—and consequently objective—reality of isolated works. While in France (with Du Bos, Marcel Raymond, Béguin, Bachelard, the early Sartre, Blanchot, Richard, Jean Wahl and myself), as also, I believe, in Germany, in the schools sprung from Dilthey, what is most important is the organizing consciousness which can only be attained by lifting the mask of structures.

Although there may be some truth in what he says, Poulet clearly exaggerates the difference between French and Anglo-Saxon critics. Cleanth Brooks, for example, is not a bloodless critic; and G. W. Knight spoke of nonjudging sympathetic interpretations as early as 1930. But such overstatement is to be expected in any attempt to introduce a new perspective and overturn existing values. Poulet realizes that his approach is limited, especially when art is evaluated from a technical point of view; he simply wants to single out another area of investigation and value.

Poulet is the most ambitious and sophisticated of the French existential critics, and the only one who has consciously tried to work out a system and practice for the existential perspective on literature. He has gradually clarified and systematized beliefs that were merely implied in the works of his predecessors. Moreover, he has shown the courage to experiment with various ways of carrying out an existential reading. Because he is also a literary theorist, he is more concerned than are his colleagues with philosophical hypotheses. Poulet's work presents the most complete system in the Geneva School, and is thus the most useful example for those who wish to acquaint themselves with the nature and scope of contemporary existential criticism.

One possible objection to Poulet's method is that it is so theoretical —that it creates a second work which is abstract, general, and too far removed from the impact of the original text. This first impact is the existentialists' very proof of literature as the highest human expression, and its reconstruction as creation in the mind is the whole goal of their criticism. This goal is destroyed when a critical reconstruction of a whole artistic consciousness becomes only a monolinear, scaled-down version of a thought: and yet Poulet's theoretical reconstructions, patterns, analogies, and parallel images do create a second universe, which has none of the immediacy of the first. There is some disproportion here, when an originally rich work of art is reconstructed as a palely intellectualized version of itself. This disproportion is all the more striking when it reflects a method that claims to combat overintellectualized analyses.

This dichotomy between the work and its re-creation stems from the extreme selectivity of the existential method. However brilliantly the focal aspect of each critique may be presented (as itinerary, pattern, image, or starting point), the original consciousness is narrowed down from a rounded, universal, comprehensive structure (the work) and funneled into the single voice hypothesized behind it. The argument leads only one way, and to a single explicable cause. It is presupposed that the author has embodied his own unique experience in the work, and that it is the critic's task to ferret it out. Once on the right track, the critic may even round out the "discovered" experience by reading between lines, going past the written text, and drawing implications from attitudes he merely perceives. Poulet's own practice is characterized by much restraint, but there is in fact no real restraint upon this procedure when it allows the critic to discover a preverbal human experience. This experience is assumed to be the same as the author's personal experience in creating his work, and the whole procedure is justified by such a quasi-biographical method. In pure existential criticism, however, there are no such visible links that connect the original creative act to the author himself. In general, existential criticism presupposes an act or "creative explosion" as the real work, but the creator of this work has no separate existence apart from the text. This truly "incarnate" author is by definition embodied in the text, and is the universe of its perceptions. Indeed, if the work's act or experience is ideally coherent, then this "author" might be described more accurately as the synthesis of all separate existential analyses of the work.

If we search for the kind of author whose experience parallels our own, we pursue a being who does not exist. Such an investigation is limited to one element; it is monolinear and assumes that the reader can discover a single hidden creator by following "his" traces throughout the work. But if the reader, or critic, does concentrate on finding such a single figure, the work as a whole will suffer. He has analyzed only one aspect of the potential human universe in a work of art. We may accept that an author re-creates a microcosm of the universe in his work, but we still need not assume that this microcosm is confined to one aspect of his complete production. It may exist in separate works, or it may be found in separate characters. Poulet's approach as it stands is particularly appropriate for voluminous works dominated by the author's personality (such as Balzac), and these are the works he prefers. Here the apparently personal stamp of the text allows him to perceive the author's universe. However, this monolinear view, directed only toward the author, seems unable to grasp other qualities that are potentially just as "existential." All literature is not monothematic; not every author expresses himself with a single voice; and a "universe" may exist equally as well in a play or novel with many interacting "existential" characters. Poulet ignores or simplifies any complexity that cannot be assimilated to a central theme. Ultimately, therefore, he seems to destroy what he seeks: the uniqueness of a work of literature.

Because Poulet limits his existential analysis to a single figure, the incarnate author, he simplifies and at times distorts the text. He fails to see that a critic may take into account the author's personality behind the text without having to restrict his analysis of the text to this subject alone. Such a restriction is not necessary to Poulet's theory, and he seems to distort the possibilities of his own approach by limiting it to only one world of a total mental universe. In order to re-create the total existential identity of Molière's plays, for example, he need not be concerned solely with Molière's persistent themes and significant images; he should also be concerned with the existential situation of each character. If he concentrates on the imagined figure of the author, he may shift the emphasis of the whole creation through which this presumed figure is actually expressing himself. In short, the critic must analyze all aspects of the author's expression if he is to represent adequately the author's existential identity. The critic is left with an analysis whose effort to represent a mental universe requires the complexity of a game of three-dimensional chess. Analytical moves on one plane are not enough, for the total game consists in a series of images related also in depth. Perhaps the game—or the analysis—can never be finished; an attempt to execute all the necessary moves, however, would have to involve more than one level. Such an attempt, in criticism, would preserve more of the work's total impact and possibly even come to terms with what Poulet regrets as "the formal aspect of works."

This "formal aspect" is ignored but not contradicted by existential criticism. Poulet has had to prove that his view of literature differs in a valid way from the prevailing formal approach; he therefore stresses these differences. However, he does not deny that formal aspects exist, and his own approach could possibly be completed by admitting forms on an existential plane. Even if a criticism of consciousness must be independent of formal standards of judgment, it would limit itself seriously by being blind to those formal aspects of a work that the author himself chose. Forms have a separate identity in objective criticism, but they possess another in existential criticism—as the units that contain existential universes. When the existential critic recognizes the formal aspects of a work, a series of works, or of a genre, he places himself even more in the author's mind and enriches his analysis as a whole.

Poulet maintains that literature is important because it is the best reflection of human experience, but he ignores the fact that the artistic author (he who creates literature instead of mathematics) finds some special connection between his original impulse and its formal incarnation. The working out into forms is an indispensable part of the author's creative act and inseparable from his creating consciousness. The analysis of form, therefore, should be a part not only of an "objective" analysis but of a properly existential one.

Poulet himself defines the creative act as "consciousness taking form," and outlines forms and patterns to represent his author's universe; he seems, therefore, oddly unambitious when he does not adapt existing formal dimensions as part of an existential critique. He rejects forms partly because he has always opposed formal values; but perhaps also because he distrusts verbal structures. This distrust weakens the appeal of his perspective as a tool for literary analysis.

By ignoring verbal structure and technique, he rejects the distinguishing characteristics of art—whether or not they are the most important characteristics. This rejection, moreover, makes his approach less complete than it should be and less complete than it need be.

Poulet is a philosopher-critic, interested in discovering new approaches to literature and in establishing a viable method of existential analysis.

More than any other critic, he speaks for the present state of existential literary criticism. His view is not limited to specific authors or periods (although his *cogito* is a conception of the Christian era), and his work constantly reassesses the reciprocal duties of a theory that points the way and a criticism that tests and gives the example. Although his colleagues may go farther in analyzing separate aspects of literature, it is Poulet who provides the synthesis of view and the impetus towards self-interrogation from which any further developments of the existential approach are to be expected.

PART II | THE LATER GENEVA SCHOOL

Georges Poulet, the first of the Geneva School to express a fully existential point of view, has been followed by other Geneva critics who recognize his example while developing their own critiques. Jean-Pierre Richard, Jean Rousset, Jean Starobinski, and Joseph Hillis Miller each develop a particular aspect of the criticism of consciousness. All four are personal friends of Poulet, and three, Richard, Rousset, and Miller, have dedicated books to him. Within this group, Richard and Starobinski emphasize the perceptions and development of the incarnate "author," while Rousset and Miller are mainly concerned with his formal incarnation. All agree, however, that the act of creating literature is confined to a special realm of the mind: the interior distance of human perceptions, where alone exists any experience of reality.

Both Richard and Starobinski are close to Poulet in that both examine a literary being [1] who surpasses the text. Richard tends to explain a work as a spiritual career, the development of an author's integrated sensuous experience. His concept of "interior distance" emphasizes the *interior* impact of man's *exterior* surroundings. Richard argues, in general, by analogy and extended sequences of perception. Starobinski discusses the same existential integration on a still more interior plane. He examines the author's mental organization and subjective feelings. Starobinski's criticism is guided by a metaphor of vision, a "look" that perceives

---

1. This nominative use of *être, being,* is not an accepted English usage. However, it is a frequent term in Geneva criticism, where it refers to the figure of the "author" as expressed in the text. The "literary being" is the "incarnate" author: not the historical author who writes the text, but the new human being whose portrait is drawn in the course of the work. Probably these critics use a neutral term such as "being" to avoid identifying the existential with the historical author, and to focus the reader's attention on purely existential traits. A term that fulfils a similar function is *cogito,* used both in the singular and plural to describe the literary being's consciousness of his existence.

on one level the author's attitude toward himself and others, on another level his perception of structures of attitudes, and on a third level the author's development of these perceptions into a coherent mental perspective. Richard and Starobinski both describe literary beings who organize their perceptions into individual forms of consciousness.

Rousset and Miller give more attention to the formal existence of literature, although Miller's definition of form is more technical and Rousset's is more existential. Rousset considers a preverbal "form" in which "themes" and "structures" correspond. The composition of a work, in his view, involves interrelationships of words, images, and characters that symbolize parallel relationships of sensations in the author's mind. Rousset also studies the various forms in which man has expressed himself, and then deduces the attitude of an age by interpreting its prevailing literary images. He emphasizes form, for example, in his studies of baroque literature and in the analogies he draws with baroque art. Such an approach lends itself to existential histories of literature, and thus falls directly within the tradition of Raymond and Poulet. Miller, however, works more closely with the form of the written text. He is more concerned with separate authors than with a history of human consciousness, although he firmly relates his authors to a background of historical consciousness. Miller looks upon an author's work as an autonomous creation that expresses, in terms that can be formally analyzed, a personal adventure and incomparable universe. This critic, perhaps because of his American background, uses existential perspectives to guide a method which is more technical than that of the other critics in the Geneva School.

JEAN-PIERRE RICHARD

Jean-Pierre Richard first gained wide recognition with two volumes of essays on literature as organized experience: *Littérature et sensation* (1954) and *Poésie et profondeur* (1955). In 1961 he developed the critical method of the first two books to outline a single experience in *L'Univers imaginaire de Mallarmé*. *L'Univers imaginaire* is dedicated to Poulet, whose earlier preface to *Littérature et sensation* placed Richard in the critical tradition of Raymond and Béguin, with additional indebtedness to Gaston Bachelard, Jean Wahl, and Maurice Merleau-Ponty. In a third collection of essays, *Onze Etudes sur la poésie moderne* (1964), Richard used categories of experience to develop his thematic criticism into a progressive analysis by categories of experience. While experimenting for the first time with the analysis of verbal sounds and

signs, he refined his thematic approach into a paradigm of phenomenological analysis that is both historical and comparative.

Richard's prefaces to his first two books outline a system of existential
interpretation that is close to Poulet's, but emphasize the role exterior
reality plays in shaping the author's experience. In his third volume he
shows how a series of pervasive images represent the pattern of Mallarmé's existence, and then interprets these images and existence along
the lines of several basic themes. This thematic criticism is pushed to an
extreme in his next book, where he establishes a series of categories of
experience that define the existential patterns of eleven modern poets.
Like Poulet, he sees in literature the expressed part of a whole experience and looks for self-development in the incarnate author. Their difference is one of emphasis: Richard dwells more than does Poulet on the
exterior elements of an author's metaphysical perception, and traces patterns of experience in a more impersonal and technical fashion.

Richard focuses upon a "moment" of creation that is "precritical" in
the sense described by Béguin and Poulet. He scarcely considers the
text at all except as the necessary and indicative result of the experience
he wants to analyze. "Here again I have tried to situate my effort at comprehension and sympathy in a sort of first moment of literary creation:
a moment when the work . . . is created from a human experience." [1]
Literature is a self-creation, "an exercise by which a writer both apprehends and creates himself," "an adventure in being" [2] or "a search
for being." [3] Consequently, literary criticism must go beyond written
technique to capture a creative impulse. In most of Richard's work,
especially before *Onze Etudes*, he does not seem to feel that standard
formal analysis is at all related to this precritical moment. In *Onze
Etudes*, however, he begins to consider a theory of structural linguistics, a "semiology" that allows him to relate human experience to the
most minute, phonemic parts of literary language. In keeping with his
goals, Richard analyzes the manner in which the sounds of words help
give substance to their latent experience. Here, as always, literary technique is subordinated to the themes it serves to convey.

Richard, in his approach to literature, uses a series of orientations and

1. Jean-Pierre Richard, *Poésie et profondeur* (Paris: Le Seuil, 1955), p. 9.
2. Richard, *Littérature et sensation* (Paris: Le Seuil, 1954), p. 14.
3. Richard, *Onze Etudes sur la poésie moderne* (Paris: Le Seuil, 1964), p. 7.

essential themes to describe the author's experience of reality. Each author appears in search of interior solutions, of "certain interior structures, certain attitudes of existence that define and qualify his originality." [4] Such structures and attitudes are most clearly visible in the author's relationship to the outside world, "in things, among men, or at the very core of feeling, of desire or its fulfilment." The task of criticism is clerical or scientific: from the "diverse data furnished by the text and life," Richard creates a "unified perspective" and elucidates a pattern indicating "the superior unity of an existence finally delivered of all mischances and returned to its single coherence" (p. 14). After investigating the patterns of existence that result from human struggle and development, Richard comes to believe in the success or failure of the poetic experience. He then adds a sense of patterning and resolution to what was originally a neutral, quasi-scientific inquiry.

Richard's patterns represent the existential substructure of literature and give a transcription of literature's human "profundity." In *Poésie et profondeur* he evokes the "profundity" of Nerval, Baudelaire, Verlaine, and Rimbaud as their poetry emerges from the very origins of human experience. "Their poetic adventure consisted in a certain experience of the abyss: abyss of the object, of consciousness, of another being, of feeling or of language." [5] These depths must be encountered and tamed. It is the depth of his experience, says Richard, which allows a poet to gain true contact with the universe and communicate "from consciousness to consciousness" (p. 12). Profound experience is both the prerequisite and the mark of profound expression.

This sense of the profound origins of a work appears widely in contemporary thought, both in genetic criticism and in nonliterary studies. Richard is particularly close to Poulet and to a "genetic" theory that deals with literature, but he is also indebted to the phenomenological philosopher Gaston Bachelard. Inside the existential tradition, Richard develops a criticism of the assimilated *object,* or of the manner in which the mind absorbs what it perceives. This perspective is especially associated with Bachelard, whose study of concrete physical references in human experience progresses from *L'Eau et les rêves* and *La Psychanalyse du feu* to *La Poétique de l'espace* and *La Poétique de la rêverie.*

4. Richard, *Littérature et sensation*, p. 13.
5. Richard, *Poésie et profondeur*, p. 10.

Both Bachelard and Richard also recognize the need for constant checking and self-correction in "sympathetic" interpretations, although Richard does not adopt Bachelard's methods. Bachelard is likely to concentrate upon a given series of symbols which he explicates with literary examples. His system is to draw upon heterogeneous texts in order to confirm his interpretation of a single symbol, so that he actually uses literature as supporting evidence for extra-literary ends. In contrast, Richard concentrates upon a selected author whose texts reveal a single personal experience. If his analysis goes beyond the text, it is still bound to the metaphysical vision of its author. Richard's fusion of these two techniques results in a personal system of analysis, which interprets a pattern of concrete images and physical references to determine an author's existential career.

Richard's first collection of essays, *Littérature et sensation,* begins with a study of Stendhal. He describes the novelist's experience in terms of two opposing, coexisting movements, "the two essential climates of *dryness* and *tenderness*." [6] Stendhal integrates both tendencies into a comprehensive pattern aimed at rationalizing the original experience of "ardor." In this essay, Richard attempts to trace Stendhal's fundamental attitudes, the forms and structures of his experience. As he says of his own goals, "the essential thing was to rediscover, in every instance, the presence of certain abstract structures which appeared to us to govern this living experience" (p. 115). In examining these dominant structures, Richard uses an inductive technique that mounts quickly to supra-textual discoveries.

The chapter on Rimbaud uncovers other patterns of opposed but integrated movements. In Rimbaud's poetry, says Richard, various forms of flight express contrasting impulses: "Directly opposed to the dynamic theme of winged explosion appears the passive, unsatisfied one of the *swarm*, or halted flight—moving, but condemned to move around an immobile center and never to break out on its own." [7] Rimbaud's experience focuses on an effort to cope with the feeling of space: his "true salvation . . . mimics the movement of a cosmic expansion" (p. 210). There is "no sense of a central source or of distance, for him: Rimbaud refuses all perceptible forms of profundity" (p. 240). He wishes to

6. Richard, *Littérature et sensation,* p. 17.
7. Richard, *Poésie et profondeur,* p. 192.

destroy ordinary aspects of space and to invert the accustomed perspectives of human experience. This attempt to comprehend experience emerges in the poet's works from a series of concrete descriptions which reveal attitudes toward his environment.

In both instances, Richard's analysis of experience leads to a discussion of perceptive patterns, and so recalls the essays of Georges Poulet. The two approaches must be distinguished, however, by Richard's emphasis upon the concretely sensuous forms that create patterns. Much of this analysis involves an existential evaluation of separate objects as they appear in the text: the meaning of pomade, a drop of water, fire, earth, mud, crystal, or vegetable existence for the person who consistently uses these images. The sensuous contact of Flaubert's characters evokes the image of a pasty consistency: as mustache wax, rouge, or cold cream, it "represents a sugared state of being where liquefaction coagulates and stops in self-enjoyment even while it keeps enough solidity to stream towards another being." [8] For Flaubert, a drop of water represents various states of existence: "thus it falls in all the scenes of desire, boredom, and death, at all the moments when a half-undone being needs to assemble itself into ultimate unity, either liquid or ephemeral, before giving in to nothingness" (p. 138). For Rimbaud, it is still the "*drop* which best incarnates this dream of liquid fulfilment: fully satisfying, because it creates from the beginning a whole, a microcosm, a tiny, closed, yet full-fledged world." [9] This emphasis on material forms becomes a kind of psychological-metaphysical symbolism. Objects with a particular psychological interest for an author become endowed, through his inner development, with the metaphysical meaning and coherence of his eventual world view.

This symbolic life of images, says Richard, can be seen in the poetic use of greenery. For both Nerval and Rimbaud, "what is vegetal constitutes the unequivocal sign of a vital impulse, an emergence of being" (p. 39). For Nerval, in particular, the flourishing of vegetable existence culminates a whole mythology of earth, water, fire, and mud. In the myth itself, basic dry earth needs to be fertilized, for "deprived of a true contact with depth, men and things can only languish on the parched surfaces of the world" (p. 50). Dust must be penetrated by water "to

8. Richard, *Littérature et sensation*, p. 130.
9. Richard, *Poésie et profondeur*, p. 212.

become human and beneficial" (p. 51), and "muddy existence" takes on the aspect of a natural miracle. "It creates a substantial interpenetration of things throughout matter, and also constitutes a marvelous promiscuity of being with itself" (p. 52). In this instance, a coherent series of interrelated material objects combines to create a symbolic pattern.

Richard examines Baudelaire's feeling of life on many levels. Baudelaire's universe runs the gamut from vaporized to crystallized expression, from a "nebulous" to a "rocky obsession" (p. 110). Scintillating atoms of light embody the same phenomenon as does the vaporization of molecules of perfume, in which "the object exists in its entirety with each odoriferous particle, but this presence is felt as an absence. Perfume is a rustling of being" (p. 107). Fog, Baudelaire's familiar *brouillard,* mediates the sun's rays but becomes in itself a sort of opaque and "airy mud" (p. 110) that cannot transmit light. In its place arises the image of the window pane, the *vitre* that "does not disguise the abyss, but does better: it points it out and forbids it" (p. 112). The problem of a coherent pattern of existence thus finds its resolution in the image of a hard transparency: "in the forbidden limpidity of the pane of glass, Baudelaire discovers a living and mediating element, a creative thickness" (p. 113). To Richard, these images reveal the spiritual struggle of a literary being. They parallel, insofar as they symbolize, his succeeding attitudes toward reality. When successful, an image can be interpreted in all its aspects as a coherent metaphysical symbol.

The perception of concrete images, and their arrangement in spiritual coordinates, represents only part of Richard's method. Patterns of objects imply a further and complementary pattern of a perceiving subject. Richard investigates authors (or their literary figures) as so many "consumers" of outer phenomena. Their manner of being is to be perceived as a manner of consumption, or integration. In discussing the perceiving subject from such a perspective, Richard maintains his previous emphasis on outer perspectives.

Authors use their environment as a foil upon which to test their own existence. Flaubert's existence adopts an attitude of voraciousness: here "perceiving, thinking, and loving, in a sense, are all ways of devouring." [10] Richard comments on the ubiquity of alimentary images in

10. Richard, *Littérature et sensation,* p. 122.

Flaubert and induces from them a certain attitude of absorbing existence: "Digestion and rumination: these alimentary metaphors evoke a process of interior transformation in which feeling is no longer just mine, but is myself" (p. 123). The existential explanation of Flaubert's indiscriminate appetite is that he is seeking to establish his own identity after an exhaustive experience of the outside universe. It is a "haggard race throughout the totality of things in order to go beyond them, to emerge in an empty state so as to recognize and take possession of oneself alone" (p. 166). Flaubert's quest is futile. He can never emerge beyond other things and beings, and so his effort changes shape. Fixed in the "sensuous mass," he no longer attempts to pierce it; rather, he wants to "peel off one form from another in order to separate out his own being" (p. 175). His search for identity underlies his literary creation, and this search—or self-creation—gives birth and duration to the work of art.

Each author presents a particular self, one that reacts to outside objects and impulses and that arrives, in Richard's composition, at a pattern uniquely its own. Nerval's self remains always the same, for "everywhere Gérard projects and rediscovers his own image." In contrast, Rimbaud's self is a *je* which *"becomes,"* Verlaine's is one which "fades away," and Baudelaire's *je* "exposes itself" to a "metaphorical enlargement." [11] These characterizations remain constant throughout Richard's work: in the later *L'Univers imaginaire de Mallarmé*, Mallarmé's speech "has an insular essence, an original pride . . . contrasting with Verlaine's speech, which tries to diffuse an emptiness, or even Baudelaire's speech, which would universally irradiate the intimacy of a substance." [12] The various patternings of existence in Richard's authors reflect complementary impulses of the self and of the concrete universe with which it must come to terms. Such an analysis, then, is completely phenomenological, leaving no room for any interpretation of style unless this style indicates an underlying attitude toward the universe.

Style, however, is not entirely neglected, as Richard's patterns of existence eventually become patterns of language; and language becomes a tool with which to work toward a given existential end. Thus, Stendhal used a legally precise vocabulary because he trusted in its bor-

11. Richard, *Poésie et profondeur*, p. 55.
12. Richard, *L'Univers imaginaire de Mallarmé* (Paris: Le Seuil, 1961), p. 380.

rowed exactitude to codify fleeting reality. He used exact language in order to create a knowledgeable work, a "perfect expression in which words coincide with what is behind them." [13] Flaubert's style is the formal "crust" that covers subterranean movements. For him, Richard maintains, "writing is digging oneself into these depths . . . this mud of existence, then coming back up to the surface with it and letting it dry itself out into a crust which will constitute perfect form. Writing . . . is a recuperation of being" (p. 208). Here the notion of style is clearly rooted in its supposed metaphysical origins; it is not the verbal patterns found on the surface. Literary composition is everywhere a human composition in which the author's energies explore his condition to shape it toward some harmonious pattern of existence. Richard finds that Baudelaire's success depends upon the close relationship between the "rhetoric" he employs and the interior necessity of his being: "It was his great fortune, or rather his genius, that the ontological structure of this language corresponded so exactly, so spontaneously, to the interior architecture of his being." [14] Style, properly conceived, is only the verbal equivalent of an experience. Consequently, a writer must examine himself in order to write, and a critic must look (through style) for preliterary prototypes.

Richard gives the fullest exposition of his stylistic theories in the introduction to *L'Univers imaginaire de Mallarmé*. (The book itself serves as an example of this stylistic criticism.) Every important body of works, says Richard, "communicates a unique manner of existing and expressing itself." Any group of works by a single author possesses an existential structure (not a formal one) which represents his unique manner of existing. Formal structures function simply as objective patterns for the themes that organize a mental universe; they cannot claim any independent value because they are well arranged. Each formal structure represents, on an existential plane, a significant theme: "a concrete principle of organization . . . around which a world would tend to be constituted and deployed." [15] Richard defines themes in existential rather than formal terms; themes organize a mental universe, not a formal pattern.

13. Richard, *Littérature et sensation,* p. 98.
14. Richard, *Poésie et profondeur,* p. 161.
15. Richard, *L'Univers imaginaire,* p. 24.

This interpretation of themes allows Richard to devise a means for measuring the "profundity" in literature, and thus to examine a quality constantly mentioned but rarely analyzed by the other critics of consciousness. He applies to the text, perhaps for the first time in this criticism, a system of objective standards which he believes must accompany the difficult analysis of "profundity." Heretofore (and especially in Poulet) the frequency with which particular words appear has been taken as sufficient evidence of their importance in the writer's universe. Now Richard distinguishes between the mere repetition of a word and its use in a widely significant context. A word's importance must be gauged not merely by its frequency, but by its use in connection with important events. This evaluation by context leads Richard to emphasize the "strategic" or "topological" value of a word or theme. In his work on Mallarmé he shows how the topological value increases as a word gathers associations: any expression accumulates "profundity" as it relates itself to other meanings and symbols.

This examination of the contexts and frequency of words resembles some formal criticism. Richard's perspective, however, remains completely antiformal. He recognizes the strategic importance of themes in establishing a mental universe, but will not discuss them as independent formal entities. For him, these themes are "internal" and not "formal." He maintains that his way of reading is superior to what he calls "Anglo-Saxon criticism," where a specious external order overshadows a true, or interior meaning. For "profound understanding" (p. 31), Richard chooses to read the work on an interior, creative plane, where "the work takes hold and forgets the schemas by which it had, nonetheless, chosen to form itself" (pp. 36–37). Existential style looks to formal style merely as a point of departure, as an incomplete expression. The existential interpretation of style, says Richard, gives forms a "new dignity, by reintegrating them into the line of a human project . . . they appear as the ideal molds in which existence attains its true perfection. From data, they have become solutions" (p. 32).

This emphasis upon solutions, and upon psychic patterns that lead to failure or solution, is not new in Richard. His lengthy study of Mallarmé, however, represents his first attempt to diagram a complete literary career, and goes beyond the range of his earlier separate, short, and appreciative essays. The study itself is impressive and always intelligent: it suffers only from an excessive dedication to the "pattern" developing before the critic's eyes. In this study Richard abandons the purely concrete scale of references found in his earlier essays: although material phenomena are noticed and interpreted, the shapes of reality in Mallarmé's universe acquire significance mainly from their being related to one another. The poet's "adventure in being" is seen more abstractly, in this respect, than were the careers of Flaubert and Nerval. Richard discovers the beginning of Mallarmé's quest for "ontological integrity" (p. 112) even in early "imperfect" verse. "Let us forget the prettiness, banality, or naïveté of these infantile imaginings, and retain only their profound intent" (p. 42). Through the development and relating of various image types, Mallarmé is striving to "harmonize an outside and inside," and to acquire "proofs" of selfhood by the contemporaneous transmutation of "the self, others, and the world" (p. 376).

Mallarmé is led by an "existential refusal of *matter*" to create a world of essences. If there is a source of being in his universe, "this source is dug out of infinite void . . . no difference here between inside and outside, high and low" (p. 599). Thus Mallarmé's career deals in abstract essences as manners of being—not, Richard rightly observes, as so many tragic disappearances, but as "a life which enjoys, in all consciousness and knowledge, the only grace it is indisputably given, that of living" (p. 601). This career reaches a kind of resolution in an immense structure of relationships, a system of transitory experiences lived by a central being. In theory, this resolution is a dynamic equilibrium; in practice, an ambitious paralysis. The poet's "failure," says Richard, comes from the "excessive power of his structural intuition. He wants to hold both center and periphery and to set down at the same time, as he saw them in himself, convergence and divergence" (p. 435). The scope of this ambition is enough to preclude any beginning, any sense of a creative base in reality: therefore, to an existential critic, it provides the perfect example of literary "failure."

Richard's analysis of creative style in Mallarmé is both sympathetic and lucid. According to him, Mallarmé's style begins with a "planar and linear rhetoric" that soon gives way to a "deep" and later "disarticulated" mode of expression. All levels of style reproduce the poet's metaphysical experience in a significant arrangement of words (p. 72). Each line of Mallarmé's poetry achieves a temporary "explosion" into a special meaning when its imaginative combination of words surpasses their common-place dictionary definitions. Words thus acquire a new sense from their poetic context alone. They are further transformed by their place in the rhyme scheme, for a word that rhymes with another suddenly appears related to it. New comparisons in meaning are suggested by a purely musical comparison of sounds, so that rhyme serves in fact to redefine ordinary words in terms of poetic vision. Many have called Mallarmé's use of rhyme both unimaginative and conservative: to Richard, such a use represents the development of vision inside codes of versification. He argues that Mallarmé finds a sense of solidity in working with formal restrictions, and that this solidity provides a base for the most abstract inventions. Richard examines closely many aspects of Mallarmé's literary form and presents a thoroughly documented description of the poet's mental expression. His analysis, although convincingly based on texts, is nonetheless always tied to his own conception of the poet's mental development. Richard's amazingly perceptive and ingenious interpretation of Mallarmé's *Livre*, in which the critic analyzes mathematical, financial, theatrical, and metaphysical as well as verbal aspects, is possible only because he sees *Le Livre* as the culminating expression of Mallarmé's literary-metaphysical career. Richard is unwilling to explore the "profundities" of pure form unless they are directly related to a mental universe.

L'Univers imaginaire de Mallarmé shows the value and yet limited applicability of Richard's theory. At times his sympathetic interest in the poet's inner development provides valuable clues to many apparently baffling poems. His comprehensive view of involved image systems and his scholarly ability to unite metaphysical, verbal, and psychological concepts in a coherent pattern, may well be the critical *sine qua non* for such a complex poet as Mallarmé. A typically existential desire to analyze the personality of the man in the writer allows Richard to see the "irrepressible vitality" in this poet, who conveys his most nihilist concepts in vivid and sensuous images. The existential feeling for human development and transformation finds a certain kinship with poetic metamorphosis of objects and images: thus Richard is particularly well qualified to follow sequences of meaning in works like *"Igitur,"* "Quand l'ombre menaça," and the notes for *Le Livre*. Existential inquiry has an advantage from the beginning when it deals with Mallarmé, a poet who uses his perpetual meditations on being and consciousness to form the base of a symbolic work. However, the advantages derived from this metaphysical comprehension may turn into disadvantages when the same perspective is turned on all separate works.

Richard sees a master plan behind every poem and tends to over-emphasize the amenable themes and to underinterpret others. Meta-physical patterns screen out much of the light humor, free elaboration, and the unexistential ambiguities which are as true of Mallarmé as are his abstract speculations. Richard unfailingly accepts poetic conceits or imaginative allusions as full statements of the soul: thus Mallarmé's surprise at his daughter's birth makes of her a genuine "Don du Ciel" (p. 58), and his wife, Marie, becomes the "perfect archetype of wilted womanhood" (p. 67). The critic's appreciation of related symbols leads him to interpret any familiar aspect wholly for its symbolism—thus maternal milk, being white, is frigid and sibylline (p. 68). Richard speaks at length on the similarities between Wagner and Mallarmé; yet these similarities are overstated. Mallarmé appreciated music in general because of its abstract or architectonic qualities, and had scarcely heard Wagner when he first wrote about him. Indeed, the poet's interest in Wagner stems from the musician's current popular reputation as a great creative genius.[16] At another point, Richard quotes a passage from L'Etoile des fées to illustrate his argument; this work cannot represent the poet's original inspiration because Mallarmé merely translated on commission the English story by Mrs. W. C. Elphinstone Hope.

Richard's own manner entails further departures from a pure con-sideration of Mallarmé: his is a visual criticism that describes objects, explains by images, and singles out visual aspects as those carrying the sense. Such terms as horizons, periphery, center, transformation, void, focus, irradiate, and profound are all related to the sense of sight as well as to existential theories. Vision becomes the vehicle of Richard's own appreciations: "to the continual voluptuousness of Baudelairean sinuosity . . . Mallarmé opposes the angular caprices of the ara-besque." [17] The visual terminology that he uses to compare poetic im-

16. Stéphane Mallarmé, Oeuvres complètes, ed. Henri Mondor and G. Jean-Aubry (Paris: Gallimard), pp. 1592–1593.
17. Richard, L'Univers imaginaire, p. 550.

pressions gives an evocative illumination, but makes the reader see the poet in Richard's own light alone.

Richard exposes the poet's thought but cannot always retain his individuality in such an abstract outline. When he says that "for Mallarmé the presence of any object exists solely to be surpassed toward the aspect or *manner of being* of that object," and that there is "a perceptible tissue of abstractions that awakens the immediate architecture of a meaning" (p. 561), Richard presents an indisputable statement that is as true of Blanchot's novels as it is of Mallarmé's poetry. He gives a description of existential literature that may be used to explain but not to characterize—individually—any author. The "Conclusion" to *L'Univers imaginaire de Mallarmé* is somewhat disappointing in that it describes a stereotyped "adventure in being," generically existential and without any of the specific qualities that create the "Mallarmé" of the preceding study. Richard seems to have succumbed to a difficulty which he himself points out earlier in the book: that the deciphering of a work "only has value if it also includes, in the protocol of its clarification, everything that is bizarre in the poem, that is to say the very resistance which it opposes to our deciphering" (p. 419). In discovering a metaphysical attitude, he has eliminated some of the peculiar human qualities of the literary being.

Richard's later publications demonstrate a more ambitious use of metaphysical perspectives and attempt to discipline the reader's technique of "sympathy" into a scientific appreciation. His empathy is used to fill out given categories of experience and to combine these categories into literary portraits. Up through *L'Univers imaginaire de Mallarmé*, and somewhat thereafter, Richard uses a plainly implied value system that occasionally works against his ideal attitude of complete sympathy. His portraits of authors are often stories of success or failure in the existential world, and take their place in a literary history of compared consciousnesses.

The idea of a new kind of literary history comes naturally to theoreticians who hold a new concept of literature. Just as Poulet wants to initiate a "history of the human consciousness," so Richard suggests a "study of sensitivities or *collective* imaginations" (p. 30, n. 27). His own literary studies make up separate parts of a larger history of the human mind, a history that is supra-literary in both aims and method. Such a history implies a perspective which Richard can attribute to Mallarmé, but which is indistinguishable from his own as well. "Literature, thus, can be the object of a double look: the look of the poet who comprehends the world and the look of the critic who comprehends the poet's manner of vision. Why not dream of a history of literatures which would be reduced to a series of illuminating and illuminated visions?" (p. 505). In this literary history, a poem is merely the expression of a human attitude. *Qua* attitude, it need not even be written down, and brings about the philosophical equivalent of Musset's "pur sanglot": "The most abstract theories of a poet are so many unavowed poems" (p. 22). It is only natural that an approach which deduces so much from and beyond the work of art should result in an increasingly deductive form, the history of literature.

This history of literature deals in existential silhouettes of authors and their works. Authors are defined and compared according to their fulness of experience, a criterion which is neither so sympathetic nor so impartial as its original ideal of empathetic analysis. When a sense of life becomes the exclusive standard of measurement, it is not far from being a standard of judgment. This judgment may remain finely drawn, but it nonetheless comprises an objective hierarchy of works.

Richard ventures into this objective hierarchy from time to time and feels no hesitation in qualifying an artist's "perceptive experience" as a success or failure. His system itself provides for such evaluation. When he speaks of the "perceptive failure" of Rimbaud, this judgment is not the same as Sartre's more social condemnation of Baudelaire. It is the logical result of the critic's existential method of investigation. "We must, then, conclude that there is a perceptive failure in Rimbaud . . . he does not succeed in creating a reality that is both natural and human . . . doubtless it is for this reason that he is finally silent." [18] Existential failure may also be found in Fromentin. "What, then, were the causes of this failure? Essentially, a certain lack of coordination, something like a lack of balance between the diverse movements of his interior being . . . they are always separated by a difference of *tempo* and, so to speak, of existential density." [19] This failure does not

18. Richard, *Poésie et profondeur*, p. 248.
19. Richard, *Littérature et sensation*, p. 230.

denigrate Fromentin as an artist. It does, however, declare that the existential experience that underlies his writing never managed to reach a successful resolution. Richard sees an existential defeat rather than a simple "failure" in Verlaine's late expression. The "faded" aspect of Verlaine's universe, which embodied his peculiar sensitivity to the passing quality of objects, is renounced for a foreign sense of religious security. The result is the destruction of Verlaine's particular individuality: "This originality was entirely situated on the plane of feeling, and now, feeling itself has become suspect . . . Tragedy of a being who, at a certain moment, refused the perceptive experience, and who knew nonetheless that everything else is literature." [20] In the first two instances the author was able to integrate his modes of perception into a unique existence; in the third the poet renounces the implications of his own individuality.[21]

In an essay of 1962, "La Nausée de Céline," Céline's misfortune is defined as his refusal to accept his own sense of existence, which is a feeling of "contingency lived physiologically as dissolution and rotting." [22] Richard's essay describes, for the most part, Céline's nausea as an existence in which "flesh is really only meat" [23] and where all being heads into flaccid and diarrhetic death. The critic juxtaposes numerous expressions of constriction and deliquescence, of lethargy and effusion, and establishes valuable coordinates for Céline's moral universe. He compares this universe with other literary worlds: its "antiverve" is the opposite of Rabelaisian vigor (p. 37), and the dispersion of its odors is the opposite of permeating essences in Baudelaire. Céline's expressions of moral choice fall into a coherent pattern, but

20. Richard, *Poésie et profondeur*, p. 185.
21. Richard and Poulet do not, of course, wish to condemn any human experience; nor do they deal in ordinary aesthetic terms of "good" and "bad" whereby "failure" implies inferior artistic quality. However, there is in fact a hierarchy of experiences drawn up by these critics, a hierarchy in which a "successful" experience exists and is more admirable than a "failure." Poulet and Richard do appreciate the unique quality of each writer's experience, be it "success" or an authentic "failure," but they also recognize a scale on which some experiences are more successfully executed or coordinated than others. Hence they arrive at a hierarchy of existential, if not moral, values—and it lacks only the guiding religious belief of a Béguin or a Du Bos to apply moral significance to such a hierarchy.
22. Richard, "La Nausée de Céline," *Nouvelle Revue française*, August 1962, p. 251.
23. *Ibid.*, July 1962, p. 34.

a pattern of "truth" in which his last two books are "as authentic as the first two," even if "a bit less pure and profound." [24]

Each of these failures is a human failure; as such, each remains within the scope of an existential inquiry. Céline's failure is only temporary, for he returns to his early and characteristic sense of abandon. Mallarmé's "failure" is an inability to create what he conceives rather than an inability to imagine or comprehend: the intuited and reasoned possibilities of his literature outstrip human capabilities and leave him without a starting point from which to achieve a "candid contact with being." [25] Richard's system at this point opens a framework of existential evaluation to familiar thematic and phenomenological analysis. The coherence and profundity of human experience, expressed and analyzed in literature, is now an openly evaluative standard.

With *Onze Etudes sur la poésie moderne* (1964), Richard is able to push into the background this system of evaluation. Similar criteria are implied, but here they lead only to a positive appreciation of the contemporary poet's sense of being. In the essay on Reverdy, a poem "orients us toward our most profound truth." [26] Char's "optimistic uncertainty" is "truer, at least more moving, than many loud affirmations" (pp. 102–103), and in an anticipatory "dimension of the *future*" Eluard can "rediscover the vitality of being" (pp. 138–139). Ponge sends us back to "the limpidity of a true world" (p. 180), and Bonnefoy establishes a perfect and continuous cycle of "existence itself," where the force called time is "saved and somehow eternal" (p. 232). Richard's phenomenological idealism is able to accept the metaphysical stance of these contemporary poets; he therefore concentrates upon refining an objective and systematic method of thematic criticism and casts glances toward its possible enrichment by structural linguistic analysis.

Onze Etudes could be taken as an example of thematic analysis applied to physical perceptions. Richard takes eleven poets to show how "in each of them the primitive elements furnished by feeling or meditation . . . are linked to each other in the global perspective of a project, a search for being" (p. 7). His approach is more detailed than ever before: the table of contents is arranged to contain its own index

24. *Ibid.*, August 1962, p. 252.
25. Richard, *L'Univers imaginaire*, p. 602.
26. Richard, *Onze Etudes*, pp. 28–29.

within each chapter, and this index itself is a system of categories and subheadings for physical experience. Such a method is not a chance discovery with one book: Richard has always included a certain index within his table of contents, and the table for *L'Univers imaginaire de Mallarmé* is an index to the steps in Mallarmé's existential career. An essay on Saint-John Perse (dated November 1960 in *Onze Etudes*, but first published in *Les Cahiers du Sud*, 1961–1962) begins to emphasize symbolic objects or experience in a dictionary-like, or encyclopedic approach. In thirty-four paragraph headings (for example, "Palms . . . Happiness . . . Nauseating Elegy . . . Cloacal South . . . Awakened Stone . . . Bird . . . Tender Heart of Lightning"), the critic organizes a progressive concordance of Saint-John Perse into a cumulative definition of "vivacity." Perse's nature is equated with salt, angularity, emptiness, viscosity, and "a fertile dryness and fecund aridity."[27] The essay is printed almost without change in *Onze Etudes*, except that all the paragraph headings are dropped from the text and give way to a more comprehensive (and considerably altered) pattern in the index. In the essay as given in *Onze Etudes*, the technique of category and subheading is even more obvious:

> . . . Return to reality: alternation (51). From empty to full: swarming solitude (51); awakened stone (52); salt (53); love (55); copper (56); bubbles (56). Open cutting edge: ridge (58); quiver, shell (58); grain (59); insect (60). Paradox of instant (61) and lightning flash (62). Continued thunder: flesh (64), sea (65). Final vivacity (66).[28]

With such a system of observation, extraction, and arrangement of evidence, Richard offers in fact a public and "scientific" method for thematic analysis. The choice of specific themes and examples will always depend on each reader's capacity to enter into the original literary experience. Richard has shown how to project and coordinate the lines of that perceived experience.

This extremely systematic method is exclusive: it chooses limited categories of reality; it ignores formal and aesthetic qualities, together

27. Richard, "Saint-John Perse, poète de la vivacité," *Cahiers du Sud*, December 1961-January 1962, p. 274.
28. Richard, *Onze Etudes*, p. 299.

with other categories of experience. Richard recognizes one contingent manner of analysis: a nonaesthetic "study of the structures of language and their connection with the structures of experience" (p. 156, n. 1). He even experiments occasionally with linking word sounds and sentence structure to his thematic observations, but in general he continues to analyze the same carefully limited categories of phenomenological perception.

The preface to *Onze Etudes* reasserts Richard's general definition of literature as an imaginary universe in which individual "problems" or "projects" move toward their "solutions." Again, these projects are not extra-literary: each is "exactly contemporary" with its work, born with it and coexisting "in its writing, in contact with an experience and a language." The eleven projects described in *Onze Etudes* all have a special relevance to Richard's own attitude, mainly because they combine the elements of poetic experience into a global vision—"a meditated problematics of presence" (p. 9). They represent one common project in modern poetry, which is to state, surpass, and reassemble the separate chaotic elements of existence. This modern poetry "tries to create meaning by a violent, sometimes tragic assumption of nonsense" (p. 8). Each poet feels an original dichotomy which he tries to transcend either by synthesis or by maintaining a conscious tension of opposites. Richard borrows from Pico della Mirandola the image of literature as the ladder of Osiris: the poet descends into reality, splits apart the apparent unity of life, and then ascends like Phoebus gathering Osiris' scattered limbs into a new unity. This ladder of Osiris, as a modern poetic project, calls upon the whole range of Richard's thematic criticism. With it he is able once more to discuss the precritical point at which individual poets emerge from "an original contact with things" (p. 7) into a private cosmogony, a thematic restructuring of the world in terms of language.

Richard now gives language a greater part to play in the literary work; he combines a coordinate method of analysis with thematic (or "categorical," p. 10) criticism. "Verbal structures . . . enter into a homological connection with perceptive or meditative structures . . . It is without doubt this isomorphism which distinguishes the properly literary meaning from all others" (p. 9). For the first time, Richard speaks of including various aspects of style in literary analysis—even though these levels all reflect one "search" or "trajectory." "True literature . . . establishes a connection, an immediately felt echo between the forms of its expression (syntactic, rhetorical, melodic) and the shapes (thematic or ideological) of the deep experience it expresses and incarnates" (pp. 9–10). Thematic criticism is valuable because it gives a "certain solidity, a certain objectivity" to our understanding, but it must be coordinated with an analysis of the ways in which words sustain and incarnate themes. For this second analysis, says Richard, the tools are still imperfect; therefore we need "a phonetics of suggestion, a structural stylistics" (p. 11). Because he has sighted a new goal, the linguistic "confirmation" of thematic evidence, he wants "to unite in a single act of comprehension the whole volume of meaning . . . to feel a given fold of language correspond to a given displacement of being." In terms of the ladder, "knowing what separates Osiris from Phoebus, or Osiris from himself, is just as important for us as to grasp what unites them." A comprehensive criticism will end by trying "to hold all the ladder rungs at once."

There are several instances in *Onze Etudes* where Richard discusses or begins to employ a verbal confirmation of his thematic analysis. Word order, rhythm, sounds, distinctions in sense between juxtaposed prepositions, the way in which words symbolize acts and things symbolize words—all find their way into a study of how "verbal invention . . . formally verifies a profound wish" (p. 81). In the essay on Philippe Jaccottet, Richard quotes the following description of the moon at dawn:

> Demeure ainsi suspendue
> sur la balance de l'aube
> entre la braise promise
> et cette perle perdue.
> (Stays thus suspended
> on the edge of dawn
> between the promised embers
> and this lost pearl.)

The critic comments that "this spell of a transparency arrested between two transparencies comes home to us because of the extreme sonorous subtlety of its language" (p. 272). He goes on to discuss the relationship of the separate sounds to the experience taking place in the poem.

The modulation of the *b* and *p*, that is to say their double relationship of nearness and opposition, lets us feel on the other hand all the ambiguity of the connection established between the dying crystalline light (*perle perdue*) and the larger, warmer one which begins (*aube, braise*). More difficult to analyze, vocalism contributes doubtless as well to the expressive success of this suspension of day: if only by the broadening which the deep open vowels (*demeure, suspendue, balance, aube, braise*) bring to the actually very thin instant of dawn, while past and future mark their double absence by the slightly painful sharpness of the *i*'s and *u*'s placed at the rhyme (p. 273).

Although this commentary seems at first to resemble a formal critic's discussion of sonorous echoes or onomatapoeia, it relies upon a different frame of reference. Richard does not speak of sound patterns in isolation, or of sound reflecting sense (*b* does not suggest in itself the warm glow of the rising sun). Rather, he draws an analogy between the relationship of sounds (*b/p; eu/u*) and the developing pattern of experience they incarnate. If this is "imitative harmony," it is a harmony that imitates experience.

In the essay on Georges Schehadé, Richard describes this literary harmony as a meeting point between semantic and semiological coordinates. "Language is meaningful here—as in all poetry—in two ways, which we may call semantic and semiological: through its thematic structure and through its formal structure. These two meanings, however, should make only one—and this is even a standard (perhaps the only one) of literary authenticity" (p. 159). This semiological or thematic structure of a work is a unified whole, but is broken up when poetic language presents it in various aspects. The critic's task is to "expose the convergence existing between two horizons of meaning, to bring out the homologies that connect the (interior) forms of continuity to the (exterior) forms of its breaking up . . . and to define, for each author, the specific quality experienced in this relationship" (p. 160). By returning to the unique experience of each author, Richard integrates the semantic coordinate into a global perspective. The structures of language exist in the same precritical moment as do thematic structures, and interact to incarnate the same moment of creation.

Inside this interaction of thematic and verbal patterns, most of Richard's earlier perspectives find their place: the linear analysis of experience ("The straight line . . . is much preferable . . . to roundness," p. 73); the echoes of Bachelard ("The same protective function actually joins nest and meadow, the rounded wool of the one and the creased velvet of the other," p. 70); and of Poulet ("Being is for Char, as for Descartes, a sort of continued creation," p. 73). Richard, in combining these observations, unites them into a system of quasi-scientific observation which gives what the critic calls the "concrete tissue" of a poem (p. 89), or the poem's "very concrete meditation on matter" (p. 93). It is part of Richard's faith in scientific method that he does not seem to trust words in themselves, as clusters of mental associations (public and private), but prefers to treat them on the level of their relationship with physical experience. In so doing, he is able to extract a meaningful series of perceptive experiences at the price of ignoring other mental overtones in a given text.

Richard's analysis of images follows a familiar pattern which often gives startling insights, but sometimes neglects other aspects or seems to reduce the total poetic experience to a single level of phenomenological perception. He brings his technique to bear on the following selection from Char:

> Fermée comme un volet de buis
> Une extrême chance compacte
> Est notre chaîne de montagnes,
> Notre comprimante splendeur
> (Closed like a boxwood shutter
> An extreme compact fortune
> Is our chain of mountains,
> Our compressing splendor)

He comments rightly that the usually "ill-omened" overtones of a closed shutter take on positive tones from the poet's emphasis on their material—boxwood. Certainly the most unique aspect of this image is the experience of solidity and intensity that emerges from the wood, the mountains, the chain, and the extreme compactness and compression described. Richard calls this experience a "sedimentation of feeling" (p. 93), thus adapting it to his own terminology; but it would perhaps be worth while to mention as well the poet's reversal of an implied landscape. The splendor of the mountain chain seen through an open window is compressed into a room and carried into an inner experience. If the reader accents this interpretation, the outer landscape is negated and yet retained as an image of private splendor. The shutter need not be ill-omened, since it introduces the original image's transformation. In another quotation from Char, "Eclair et rose, en nous, dans leur fugacité, pour notre accomplissement, s'ajoutent" ("Lightning and rose, in us, in their fleetingness, for our accomplishment, are joined"), Richard points out the "ripening and trajectory" of this combination, which waits until the final word to bloom (p. 89). And yet this word, "s'ajoutent," is rather a colorless verbal synonym for what he has just called the "principle of unity" in the copula *et*, an *et* which establishes the trajectory here from the first phrase. Without speaking of the hesitant rhythm, the series of varying prepositions, and the undeveloped association of *fugacité* to *rose*, Richard seems to propose a trajectory which would use the text as springboard for the reader's own phenomenological experience. The reader is completing an experience in his mind, and therefore runs the risk of distorting it, valuing in it those elements which are familiar to him, and perhaps experiencing it only partially.

Richard's system for re-experiencing a poetic text works most effectively when it transcribes sense perceptions into a web of meaning— when it locates and explains them. It works least effectively when it tries to discern the impact of each experience. He shows in a convincing way how René Char's use of *et* and *entre, à la fois* and *tour à tour* develops in his poems and implies a parallel existential development from a sense of being *with, between, at the same time,* and *in turn* (pp. 89–91). He also identifies a series of expressions in Du Bouchet that show the poet immobilized "beside being" (p. 254). Further, he notices that fire is a sudden, blazing experience of dry wood in Bonnefoy and a gradual metamorphosis of green wood through smoke, embers, and ash in Jaccottet (p. 272, n. 1). He astutely units several aspects of Char in showing how themes of wind and rock lead to "this sort of living stone of the sky, the *bird*" (p. 77). In Char's line "Seigneur Temps! folles herbes! marcheurs puissants!" Richard points out the underlying feeling of time that gives meaning to each experience: that of the man advancing through a field of high grass, and of the grass itself delirious with its own rampant growth (p. 92). However, along with these valuable analyses and correlations comes a peculiar unwillingness to comment on the varying novelty, unique impact, or perhaps indeed "authenticity" of given poetic experiences. To say this is not to accuse Richard of refusing to judge, for he and the Geneva critics have no intention of judging aesthetic merit. However, if there is any general weakness in the quasi-scientific approach, it is to be found in its inability to distinguish between various tones of experience—ultimately, perhaps, to single out the specificity and originality of each poetic experience.

There are times when it seems more important for Richard to marshal evidence for an overriding pattern than to record the perceptive impact of separate moments of creation. Two images from Philippe Jaccottet, quoted in the same sentence to prove the same point, show startlingly different degrees of originality.

> Few more exciting feelings than to see, in the spring:
> Abundant waters descend
> Steps of grass or rock
> (Les eaux abondantes descendre
> Aux degrés d'herbe ou de roche)
> or to come upon, during a ramble in Correze, thousands of "thin veins of sparkling water, irregular as the lines on a hand" ("minces veines d'eau étincelante, irrégulières comme les lignes de la main" p. 265).

The rather mechanical and even hackneyed image of water descending steps, and the vital personification of a natural irrigation system seeming at once like the veins and lines in a human hand, are images of such different quality and even spontaneity that it is hard to imagine Richard accepting them both on the same level of poetic perception. There are a few instances (such as at the end of the essay on Char) when Richard attempts to differentiate between authentic and inauthentic tones, but it is more usual for him to subside into an objective description of the presence and use of themes. This technical neutrality can lead into extremely generalized descriptions fitting many a modern writer: when Richard says that "his poems . . . have a sort of absent weight: or a weight, shall we say, which absents them, or which opens them to an absence, to this absence of reality which is, as we know, the very being of reality" (p. 205), it would be a rare reader who thought immediately of Guillevic. The trend of Richard's observations and analysis is often to draw the metaphysical coordinates of a given poet's experience and then to relive them within the framework of his own mind—a step toward human fraternity, perhaps, but a step away from the individualized textual experience.

This extreme tendency of Richard's criticism should not obscure his position as the most important purely phenomenological literary critic. No one else has so thoroughly followed the author's career in its various confrontations with physical reality. No one else has analyzed so carefully, sensitively, and consistently the presence of the material world as it impinges on poetic creation. Richard has gone beyond the mere observation of successive states of mind to propose an architecture of meaning developing within each poet's universe. He has further surpassed this second level of criticism to present a paradigm of phenomenological analysis, and thus made his method public and viable for other readers. Here is a remarkable achievement in phenomenological analysis: a criticism which remains consistently literary, consistently text-centered, and yet exclusively concerned with the literary perception of material reality. Richard is in effect the "scientist" of the Geneva School, as he carries out his analysis with precision and method in a predetermined frame of reference. The other critics may borrow elements of his phenomenological approach from time to time, but none approaches his single-minded dedication to the "concrete tissue" of life reproducing itself in the "concrete meditation" of literature.

5

JEAN STAROBINSKI

With Jean Starobinski, professor at the University of Geneva, emphasis returns to the subjective element in an author's literary career. The key to Starobinski's approach is the idea of subjective *vision*, for he expands the basic existential concept of a naming, characterizing look (*regard*) as a metaphor which offers various critical perspectives. "Vision" corresponds to an author's image of self and the outside world, to the role of language as codified human perception, and to the exterior, synthetic view of the literary critic. This visual motif guides the structure of three books: *Montesquieu par lui-même* (1953), *Jean-Jacques Rousseau: la transparence et l'obstacle* (1957), and *L'Oeil vivant* (1961). It emerges openly as a vehicle of thought when he publishes *L'Invention de la liberté* (1964), a combination of art book and

165

essay on the eighteenth century's change of temperament. In the beginning, this visual technique is a rather simplified schematization for literary analysis, but it soon acquires more complex interpretations.

Starobinski is experimental and eclectic within the general area of existential criticism, as befits a man who has completed both literary and medical degrees, and is a professor of literature and a physician and lecturer in medicine. The author of books and articles on medicine, art, and literature, he looks from various perspectives on the human consciousness creating its world. His approach is close to Raymond's description of individual human adventures, and to Richard's formulation of patterns of existence, but his scope is wider than either. He adopts a limited form of *Geistesgeschichte,* after Poulet, and analyzes the cultural significance of forms in art, like Jean Rousset. Unlike the other members of the Geneva School, who turn naturally toward nineteenth-century literature, he has concentrated on eighteenth-century authors and artists. Where his colleagues derive modern literature largely from Romantic and Symbolist art, Starobinski stresses the Enlightenment and its "invention of freedom." As a theorist, his discussion of the nature of language and of the reader's role leads him close to Blanchot; but unlike Blanchot, he believes that words and physical phenomena have a certain reality supporting literary communication. Starobinski's aim is to describe each author's unique perspective upon existence, and then to evaluate the role taken by this perspective in each author's artistic development. At the same time, he observes his own method of approach and compares it with other critical practices. In a complex, thoughtful prose, he expresses a variety of interests ranging from pure criticism to a mixture of criticism and literary theory. He also has written essays of a purely theoretical nature, such as "Poppaea's Veil" in *L'Oeil vivant.*

In an early book, Starobinski uses a metaphor of vision to describe Montesquieu's characteristic manner of being. Montesquieu's works embody a rationalizing glance that exists apart from and uninvolved in the world it considers. The idea of the *regard,* so frequent in existential accounts of the search for profundity, represents here a rather superficial, intellectual view of the surface of reality. It is a vision from above, which seeks to discern a natural order in the universe and coherent relationships between elements of existence. Starobinski emphasizes the classical and formulaic aspect of this disengaged view of reality, for the author "is preoccupied with a single question: the relationships maintained by things among themselves and according to their natural order." [1] In this respect, Montesquieu's unique problem is to find a mode of vision which makes possible an all-embracing glance. He must reconcile an instantaneous, intuitive vision into basic impulses, with the discursive reasoning which displays cause and effects. If "the pleasure of looking is enough for Montesquieu" (p. 40), this pleasure occurs only in a comprehensive and total vision. "What he seeks is a vantage point from which he can dominate the sequence of phenomena . . . a vision from on high which is also the vision of the linkage of things" (p. 39). His attitude is perennially that of an observer from the outside who considers reality but does not fuse himself with it in any emotional or existential effort.

Starobinski describes the judging look as a symbol developing through Montesquieu's entire work, from the satirical *Lettres persanes* to the philosophical *Esprit des lois*. As early as the *Lettres,* "the indiscreet look on harem mysteries is the counterpart of the free look on French civilization," and the libertine observer himself "has turned into a disillusioned glance which no longer sees anything but objects" (p. 68). Here is the typical classical or antiexistential perspective usually condemned by genetic critics, and Starobinski appears as the first such critic to devote a sympathetic analysis to its "antireal" vision.

Montesquieu's vision renounces any "profound" knowledge of reality for a coherent, logical ordering of apparent phenomena. It is an avowedly superficial comprehension of the universe: "By renouncing any meditation on the secret profundity of things, human knowledge can describe all the phenomena of the universe . . . In no longer seeking to force out the secret of things jealously closed upon their essence, the mind concerns itself only with finding the most rational formula for obvious material relationships" (p. 58). Starobinski points out the difference between this attitude and the experience of involvement ordinarily investigated by existential critics: the author of *L'Esprit des lois* "ignores dizziness . . . Montesquieu does not approach any 'point of no return.' (Something one cannot say of Pascal, or Rousseau, or of

1. Jean Starobinski, *Montesquieu par lui-même* (Paris: Le Seuil, 1953), p. 23.

the greatest Romantics, or of the initiators of modern poetic language)"
(p. 59). The fact that the critic draws such a direct contrast between
Montesquieu and other, more existentially involved authors characterizes
Montesquieu par lui-même as an exercise in the analysis of only one
side of literary vision. Another side, that of literature as an act involving
the author's own experience and spiritual development, is represented
by *Jean-Jacques Rousseau: la transparence et l'obstacle.*

In the preface to this study, Starobinski proposes to analyze the author's character as it reveals a fusion of idea and experience, of theories
and personal destiny. "We are led to analyze the literary creation of
Jean-Jacques as if it represented an imaginary action, and his behavior
as if it constituted an actually-lived tale." [2] The critical method here
turns towards the structures organizing Rousseau's experience, and to
the various symbols which represent his thought. Starobinski maintains
a visual motif throughout which is especially appropriate to the categories of *being* and *seeming* that he analyzes. He also outlines a framework of perceptions, and his analysis of Rousseau is a description of
perceptive structures.

An essay published the year before, entitled *L'Idée d'organisme,*
illuminates certain aspects of this patterning approach. Starobinski uses
a biological analogy here to corroborate the idea of organism in existential literary criticism. All existence arranges itself in certain organic
patterns, he says, and the biological idea of "organism" is now being
adopted for aesthetic investigations. If "the scholar recognizes that he
obtains knowledge of organisms only in projecting patterns," [3] then
the literary critic must likewise view a work as a series of orders. Both
scholar and critic perceive, and "perception always has to do with synthetic structures, global structures or totalities" (p. 6). The fact that
there are organisms to be perceived does not insure that a true perception
always occurs, however. A certain amount of subjective distortion is
inevitable. "The unification of perceptible data depends upon my existence, upon the inescapably implicit basis of my consciousness and my
corporeal existence." Thus the analyst realizes that his perceptions are

2. Starobinski, *Jean-Jacques Rousseau: la transparence et l'obstacle* (Paris: Plon,
1957), p. i.
3. Starobinski, *L'Idée d'organisme* (Paris: Centre de documentation universitaire,
1956), p. 3.

both inescapable (he must perceive significant structures) and false (he cannot disassociate himself from his vision). He is condemned to a partial vision, no matter how he proceeds. Coordinates of time and space, for example, represent a valid choice of method, but valid in their own limited scope: "The organism can respond to such coordinates of space and time only in terms of these same pre-established coordinates" (p. 20). Answers are always given in terms of a question, and "time" and "space" are only convenient approaches to a total reality beyond their horizon. There is "a flight of totality, of this totality which is always *there* before and which however is *not there*, remaining forever out of reach." In *L'Idée d'organisme*, Starobinski admits the partiality of all perception and criticism, and tacitly clears the way for his own among a multitude of limited approaches.

The preface to *Jean-Jacques Rousseau* quickly differentiates Starobinski's approach from one "imposed from outside," which would consider a work's structure in pre-existing formal classifications. "Rather than a restrictive criticism, imposing from without its values, its order, and its pre-established classifications, we have preferred a reading which simply tries to reveal the internal order or disorder of the texts interrogated, and the symbols and ideas organizing the writer's thought." [4] Like Richard, Starobinski wants his study to be "more than an 'interior analysis,'" and to take into account the exterior objects met by each author. However, his approach still emphasizes the writer's transmutation of reality, while Richard gives to exterior reality as much importance as he gives to the perceiving subject. Starobinski says that "evidently Rousseau's work is not to be interpreted without considering the world against which it is written" (p. ii), but he also thinks of this world as social and human. Exterior reality is a world of other subjective beings, not merely of inanimate objects. Rousseau looks for a "transparency" of communicating human hearts, and when frustrated he creates a vision of "obstacle" which forces him back into his own subjective self. In *Jean-Jacques Rousseau: la transparence et l'obstacle*, both the transparency and the obstacle are defined in human terms; they both refer to forms of perception, and become instruments of self-creation by which Rousseau is able to view and grasp his feeling of existence.

4. Starobinski, *Jean-Jacques Rousseau*, pp. i–ii.

Rousseau's first sense of this existential opposition comes when he recognizes a difference between the actual existence and the deceptive appearance of his surroundings. He is also disturbed by a sense of distance that sets him off from material objects and from other human beings. Rousseau feels doubly cut off from reality, for "even before he feels his distance from the world, his *moi* has undergone the experience of his difference from others" (p. 9). This original feeling of isolation leads to a whole series of obstacles set in the way of a transparently integrated existence. "The rupture between being and appearance engenders other conflicts . . . between good and evil . . . nature and society, man and his gods, and man and himself" (pp. 2–3). Rousseau's whole development, both literary and social, springs from this sense of rupture. He tries in a futile way to dominate the chaos of his personal experience by living up to a transparently pure ideal image of himself. Rousseau intends this image to eliminate his earlier troubled feelings, but instead it serves only to impose a rigid form on his spontaneous emotions. Ultimately, this attitude of conscious virtue destroys the underlying coherence of his earlier feelings, and Rousseau comes to be "in conflict with his own empirical nature" (pp. 68–69).

Starobinski subsequently describes Rousseau's extensive literary self-justification as a catharsis which provides the solution for the author's spiritual dilemma. He proposes that Rousseau (having lost his original innocent coherence) must use his bitter knowledge to create a newly consistent being. He "must justify himself, explain himself; he must therefore write or experience the mediation of language and literature." After a coherent but unsatisfactory preverbal experience, Rousseau turns to the cohering structures of language and creates his own image.

At this point, the figure of Rousseau begins to represent the genetic theory of expressive composition. When Rousseau turns to literature as a means of organizing his sense of identity he resembles the generic picture of the existential author who assembles and recreates in literature all the separate, dispersed elements of his personality. "There is no madness or delirium which is not absorbed into the totality of the human being, a totality all of whose aspects are equally contestable and equally illegitimate, and whose synthesis establishes the value and irreducible legitimacy of the subject. That is why everything must be told, confessed and uncovered, so that a unique *being* appears out of the most complete dispersion" (p. 70). Literature becomes a means by which Rousseau or any author can re-create a sense of his total being; literary language takes on special significance because it communicates this inner reality.

Starobinski does not suggest that Rousseau renounces the traditional idea of language as a tool governed by the writer, but he emphasizes that this writer's innovation (followed by the Surrealists) is to let himself be guided by words and emotions. In this theory, language describing a particular state also embodies the gradual development of a writer's *moi*: it is the continuing revelation of his state of mind as he composes. The critic is describing what Raymond early called an interpenetrability of subject and object—of subjective emotion and the language communicating it—in a "new conception of language." "Subject, language, and emotion can no longer be distinguished from each other. Emotion is the subject revealing itself, and language is emotion speaking to itself . . . Certainly speech retains its function of 'mediating' the relationship between the self and others. But it no longer forms an instrument distinct from the subject using it; it is the self incarnate" (p. 244). In this metaphysical sense, literary language actually is the new *moi*. The *moi* or self put down on paper as an immediately felt reality is the only true one—the only reality closely enough recognized and expressed to be humanly valid. Literature, in being allied with an author's existential situation, is thereby endowed with metaphysical authenticity; "the problem of language vanishes as soon as the act of writing is seen no longer as a technical method utilized to reveal truth, but as the revelation itself." When the "immediate truth of language" is guaranteed by the "spontaneous fidelity linking words to emotion" (p. 245), literature becomes the means by which the author pulls his variously felt being into a coherent and visible framework.

The "author" now is a figure who exists on a purely literary level; but the "problem of language" does not vanish—it has been diverted. Starobinski discusses his attitude toward language and reality in "Poppaea's Veil," the introductory essay of his third book, *L'Oeil vivant*. "Poppaea's Veil" describes the relationships between language, literature, and reality in terms that enrich rather than simplify the various "impossibilities" comprising existential literature. Language up to now has been seen as the catharsis of the subject, the author's self-exploratory and self-developing means of expression. Language in a text, however, implies a hidden reality which refers both to the material reality of the objects described and to the spiritual reality of the incarnate "author." Words indicate a preverbal existence just as material objects point to "something they are not." [5] Both throw a "veil" over reality and make visible "the imperious appeal of absence" (p. 9) which fascinates writers and critics.

Starobinski's metaphor of the veil hiding reality allows him to connect two different perspectives, that of writer and that of the critic. Each wants to look beyond appearances, to transcend forms of reality, and to reveal an absolute, universal verity. This "look" is already "an intentional relationship with others and with the experienced horizon" (p. 13). But the "look" itself cannot grasp what it seeks. Moreover, for Starobinski the will to look is a "crime," an "excess" and a "failure." As speech it abandons immediate perception for incomplete reporting. As an actual glance it is superficial and precarious, an inadequate attempt to understand. Nonetheless, it is a unique human endeavor, "assuring our consciousness of an outlet beyond the space occupied by our body" (p. 14). If the human being is so inescapably subjective that he will always miss what he sees, then at least this subjective carry-over provides a key (an "insight") into his own existential pattern.

Out of this failure of vision comes an unexpected opportunity to see into another human being by means of clues which he himself provides. These clues may be described as a pattern of subjective references discovered in the author's reactions to reality. Such reactions make up a "first vision" without which there can be no "second sight." The critic begins by observing these reactions, and then proceeds to look past them to the existential pattern they imply.

Starobinski asserts that the critic, although empathetically "fascinated" by the text, conserves in fact a vantage point of comprehensive vision. "He wants to penetrate still farther; beyond the evident meanings revealed to him, he suspects a latent significance." His search for this latent significance leads back to the actual words and expressions of the text: "to the words themselves, in which the meaning resides" (p. 25), and to an attempt to elucidate their meaning through identifying

5. Starobinski, *L'Oeil vivant* (Paris: Gallimard, 1961), p. 10.

empathy. Complete criticism combines the over-all with the interior look; it does not function using one or the other exclusively, but goes back and forth from one to the other. Like other genetic critics, Starobinski prefers to emphasize the empathetic glance: "In recompense, I will feel a glance arising from the work and directed on me: this glance is not the reflection of my interrogation. It is a foreign consciousness, radically other . . . the work interrogates me" (pp. 27–28). In his criticism he tries to maintain this sense of living interrogation by tracing its development throughout a career framed in vision. *L'Oeil vivant* consciously limits its horizons to the existential patterns of development in Corneille, Racine, Rousseau, and Stendhal.

In speaking of Corneille, Starobinski takes up Poulet's theme of the hero's image of self and treats it in terms of his own visual motif. A character in Corneille clings to his own image as both a willed and a manifest identity. His vision is an eternal standard, an ideal toward which he always moves. In a perpetual act of self-creation, he is a "man of his word": his verbal image of self is forever the source of his acts. Corneille's hero tries "never to lose the power or the will to become the person his speech anticipates" (p. 53). The name he wins is a constant witness to a successful creation of being, and for this reason he may not abandon any particle of his reputation. According to Starobinski, this willed heroic creation recalls a primitive human feeling of "astonishment before sacred things and their light" (p. 33); and a hero of Corneille, in order to take on his full identity, must unite two aspects of this astonishment. "It is not enough for him to be the source of light; he must also be the eye opened to this light . . . must see, be seen, and show forth with no other object than himself" (p. 57). Although he knows he is heroic, he must continually recognize and assert his heroic magnitude.

The essay on Corneille upholds vision as a means of naming and establishing identity in relation to other "seen" parts of the universe. In "Racine et la poétique du regard" (dedicated to Georges Poulet), vision is not so secure an act. Rather, it is an apprehensive, questioning look like the "intentional glance" described in "Poppaea's Veil." Theatrical, biographical, and verbal indications combine to display Racine's obsession with an excessive, prying glance. Scenes in Racine's plays are "interviews" in which responsive gestures lend a further meaning and profundity to the lines spoken on stage. In Racine's own life, Jansenist influence inspired a feeling of weakness and sin in any yearning, questioning look outside the self. Looking is "a worried question plunged into others' souls" (p. 83); it is a pathetic, frustrated act whose "shadowed perspective" into human nature nevertheless provides the "impression of truth" given by his characters. Starobinski's view of Racine relates to a single creator revealed through the technical evidence of his plays. Biographical material helps to explain this creator, mainly because the material itself contributes to the personal focus of the existential analysis. In this essay, Starobinski examines the author's own attitude toward reality, not—as in Corneille—an existential attitude manipulated by the characters themselves.

The chapter on Rousseau carries on, rather than transforms, the earlier analysis of *Jean-Jacques Rousseau: la transparence et l'obstacle*. Starobinski has already discussed Rousseau's perception and assimilation of the "obstacles" in his existence, and now analyzes a sense of being watched, a sense by which the author recognizes his different situations in the world. The essay entitled "Jean-Jacques Rousseau et le péril de la réflexion" (dedicated to Marcel Raymond) identifies, as does the essay on Racine, a repressive feeling of being observed which influences Rousseau's later development. "Puritan terrorism" keeps a suspicious eye on the young Rousseau, so that he sees himself only through the eyes of others. He may attempt to control his image by projecting his own view of it, but the very attempt to do so prevents him from developing a securely anchored personality. Rousseau's frantic desire to know and manipulate the impressions of others, together with his own inability to discover who he is and what he wants to be, frustrate his effort to conceive and create any fixed identity.

Rousseau sees himself in mirrors: literally so, when he recalls a scene where he was reflected in Madame Basile's mirror, and figuratively so when he sees himself, in his own and others' eyes. His literary activity is still another kind of mirrored vision, an attempt to create a unique image of self by the coincidence of his own and his reader's imaginary projections. Starobinski's earlier analysis already spoke of such an aim, an aim which was to be reached in literature, by a perfect coincidence of subject, language, and emotion. Ultimately, however, Rousseau's personal integration surpasses the mirrors and reflections of literary form. His self-portraits are only aspects of a larger, supraliterary self: "Should we not consider, beyond Jean-Jacques' speech, a certain exigence of his soul—an emotional vibration? . . . his true presence is not in his discourse, but in the lively and confused animation which precedes speech, and which uses words and ideas to become manifest" (p. 184). Reflection, as the mirroring of others' opinions or as his own meditation, is a medium Rousseau uses but surpasses in his search for intuitively integrated existence. Once he has convinced himself that instinct (and not rationality) is the key to integrated existence, he is ready to discard conscious reflection. Henceforth, he recognizes only incidental ripples on the surface of a hard-won placidity.

The vision of self against which Rousseau struggles is the very means by which Stendhal (like Corneille) develops his own personality. Stendhal shares Rousseau's basic uncertainty and lack of satisfactory relationships with other human beings, but this insecurity leads the second author to create a new identity as a mask confronting the world. As Henri Beyle, Stendhal's earliest experiences are of awkwardness and shame, so that his passion for pseudonyms, imaginary metamorphoses, and real disguises springs from a desire to create a situation over which he will have total control. Thus his metamorphoses are active, not passive imaginings; they are methods of living, substitutes for an interior truth which is either unsatisfactory or nonexistent. Stendhal recognizes the conflicting claims of immediate feeling and conscious reflection, and uses the latter to create a being who can attain moments of entire, immediate happiness: "instants when consciousness vanishes in an incandescent whiteness" (p. 227). His masks before other people are like his technical manipulation of language, for speech, because of the imperfect coincidence of words and their objects, is already a "masking" of the truth. "Since we are condemned to sham what we think, the important thing is to sham as well as possible" (p. 232), paraphrases Starobinski. It is only by compressing himself into a consciously created fictitious "perfection" that Stendhal can achieve personal harmony.

This visual metaphor, which remained one of several possible approaches as long as the subject was literature, emerges as the full and necessary approach when Starobinski writes an essay on eighteenth-century art for Skira in 1964. Although *L'Invention de la liberté* discusses the "invention of freedom" illustrated in eighteenth-century art, and stays close to the visual arts for its examples, it reveals another probable ancestor for this criticism of the over-all glance. When the Geneva School seeks to define the dominant impression of a literary work, it often falls back upon the eighteenth-century view which gave to art "a psychological function whose dominant values are emotion and intensity." [6] The vision of an all-embracing subjective and sympathetic glance is first of all appropriate to criticism of the visual arts, and Starobinski quotes La Motte in a phrase which gives to art a quality sought by the Geneva critics in literature: "The quicker impression of the painting unites, in a single moment, what poetry says only in succession." This emotive art is "defined by its subjective effect" and its "limitation of an instant" of emotion inspires, "through sympathy, a similar impulse." Elsewhere, Starobinski comments that our modern sense of history and aesthetics is indebted to eighteenth-century thought (p. 9): he could have added that his own criticism is influenced by their calm reflections on artistic irrationality.

L'Invention de la liberté shows another change in Starobinski's method: it moves into the realm of historical analysis in the manner of Poulet (and of A. O. Lovejoy, whom both admire). Starobinski seems to use the historical perspective as a means by which to connect individual observations, and not as an end in itself. His principal concern is to define and relate a series of individual visions rather than to pursue a single all-embracing historical interpretation (p. 10). The critic's choice of illustration and interpretation is necessarily arbitrary, and at times he stands back to let Panofsky, Bosanquet, Addison, Philippe Monnier, and Marjorie Hope Nicolson express views for which he would ordinarily be the sole voice. *L'Invention de la liberté* is selective rather than encyclopedic: if the argument seems less thorough and yet more assertive than those found in Starobinski's other works, the reason may be that the book is a general study aimed at a wide audience. As such, it is a provocative outline for others to take up and explore.

Although Starobinski is not so dedicated an historian as Poulet or Lovejoy, he nonetheless begins to frame his work now in historical and

6. Starobinski, *L'Invention de la liberté* (*Geneva: Ed. Skira*, 1964), p. 11.

"sociological" terms.[7] Works are seen in an historical sequence which they illustrate, and the artistic freedom to create new forms becomes one of several freedoms gained in the eighteenth century. The general "freedom" discovered in the eighteenth century is the freedom to throw off old cultural and intellectual patterns and to develop a new manner of thought which would be both democratic and intensely individual. In society it is the change from monarchy and aristocracy to a republic and new economy—a total change which society reflected in furniture, in ways of setting out one's garden, in the celebration of holidays, and in art and architecture. The first reaction against the strictures of old forms was a kind of libertinism, a desire to feel and act outside of prescribed limits. "Feeling, and feeling strongly, is one way of arriving at the consciousness of our existence." This first freedom appears in social revolution and in the subject matter of art before truly engraining itself in consciousness and becoming a matter of style (p. 72). When the French Revolution tried to resurrect ancient rhetoric, it proved only "the gap between the intellectual situation of the times and the invention of forms" (p. 41). It was only after eighteenth-century society had truly freed itself from inherited ways of thought that it began to envisage creating new forms, new styles. "No century was better aware of the conventional nature of its tastes or more curious about changes which it dared not put into effect . . . Some bold thinkers even assert that man is the author of his history and perhaps also the creator of his values: what he is and what surrounds him can change through an act of his will." At the end of the century men have accepted their situation in a transformed universe. "Earth is no longer the center of the world, and space is infinite. But man, in return, has made himself a sphere whose master

7. Starobinski's use of what he calls "sociological" structures to convey cultural analysis probably reflects movements in contemporary structural criticism (e.g., Goldmann, Mauron, Barthes, Lévi-Strauss). If "structuralism" refers to the analysis of similar existential structures in different arts and sciences, then the Geneva School has already shown "structural" interests in Raymond's translation of Woelfflin and in Rousset's book on baroque art. However, the Geneva critics differ from the "structuralists" in that their studies of man in literature lead back to literature alone. Thus far, the structuralists have been content to go from one or the other art or science (such as sociology or philology) to a composite picture of man in his world. Such a broad perspective may be able to discover new cross-disciplinary methods of examining man as a cultural being and to use literature as one (even the most important) tool of its investigation. For the structuralists, literature remains a tool with new uses; it is not an end in itself, as it is for the Geneva School.

he is" (p. 203). The artist feels this new ability to shape and mold his surroundings. What is more, he creates styles which could not have been created at the beginning of the century.

Starobinski illustrates this transformation in temperament, which he calls an evolution from a "subjectivity of feeling" to a "subjectivity of willing" (p. 207), through the pictures he puts in his book. He interprets these pictures in much the same way that the Geneva School interprets literature: he is concerned with the manner in which artistic structures reveal patterns of human experience. He also adds references to their sociological settings. Baroque art, says Starobinski, is "a world separated by its privileges" and enclosed in an illusionary, narcissistic décor (p. 15). This illusionary, unreal art then becomes solipsistic: it "treats good and evil, suffering and voluptuousness, as the materials of an aesthetic creation" (p. 73) and ends with the artist "a captive of his dream and incapable of making connections with reality" (p. 74). The paintings by Fuessli and Goya that depict scenes of destruction seem also to destroy themselves; they indicate "the search after some outlet from the unreality in which their art is developing" (p. 75). Ordinarily Starobinski is careful to discuss examples of art in which the style incarnates a certain characteristic of the period. However, he chooses in some instances illustrations whose subject matter (but not *necessarily* style) embodies this characteristic. Since his argument rests on the analysis of patterns of style, this is an unfortunate digression toward an analysis of subject matter. For example, when speaking of the eighteenth century's taste for disguises, he illustrates his discussion with a picture by Pietro Longhi which shows people in masks; it is the subject, not the style, which conveys the idea of masked reality.[8] When he reproduces Watteau's "Gilles," he comments that "Gilles represents a dazed

8. Starobinski's preoccupation with masks is connected to his interest in "irony and melancholy," an interest that he develops throughout these years. Man, cut off from a satisfactory or "true" personality, takes on a role in which he can develop a second identity. He may develop this second identity in a social or literary manner (cf. "La Rochefoucauld et les morales substitutives II," *Nouvelle Revue française*, August 1966, pp. 227–229). This role serves the functions of a mask: "Delivered of everything which chains and defines him by birth, condition, or function, the masked figure is reduced to the image he offers at the moment, to the words he invents on the spot. Like an actor, the masked man displays an instantaneous essence, whose short but inexhaustible freedom enjoys the protection of a lie" (*L'Invention de la liberté*, p. 90).

state just before waking up, a consciousness imprisoned in its confusion. The most vigorous men of the century have known and described this stupor or this lethargy: it is the necessary antithesis of the virtuoso intelligence which triumphs in Harlequin or Figaro" (p. 89). Again, this argument may follow from the look in Gilles' face; but it has yet to be substantiated by a stylistic analysis like the one he gives for baroque art. Starobinski speaks occasionally in a casual, intuitive manner that proposes analogies without subjecting them to real analysis. Thus, Bibbiena's theaters are more suited to the music of Haendel, Scarlatti, or Rameau than to "the mediocre tragedies of the time," and although we have the "right" to like Mozart's masterpieces for themselves, this music (even in sonata form) represents "events and affective movements: that is to say that 'spectacular structure' inhabits even the musical language of the time" (p. 106). These rather general appreciations soon yield to an analysis that is closer to Starobinski's concern: the manner in which a new, voluntary, and examining vision prefigures contemporary phenomenological thought.

It is genre painting (especially the painting of Chardin) which gives this close look at objects in themselves and provides one of Starobinski's major comparisons with twentieth-century culture. Although eighteenth-century critics considered genre painting a minor, limited art, Starobinski maintains that this minor art had "happy limits, which led the painter to marvel at the presence of objects and bodies in light!" Chardin does not need to paint people in order to convey the sense of a close look. "With him, things see; a look, coming from them, responds to our look" (p. 127).[9] "Chardin, painter of the mystery of presence, who evokes a sense of being offered simply in the light and substance of objects . . . preserves the opportunities of another poetry, which did not find its *literary* voice in the eighteenth century" (p. 135). This feeling of existence captured in a look is one of many "freedoms" discovered in the eighteenth century that find their echo in our time. The rise of modern historical thought, an attempt at independent aesthetic speculation, the focus upon the senses and intellect by which man structures his en-

9. Compare this passage with that in *L'Oeil vivant* where Starobinski speaks of literary analysis: in a proper sympathetic appreciation of the text "I will feel a look arising from the work and directed on me . . . a foreign consciousness, radically other, which seeks me out, stares at me" (*L'Oeil vivant*, p. 27).

vironment, the value placed upon intensity and authenticity of experience, a new democratic humanism in art and literature, and a sense of
being able to create one's own self and environment: all these are aspects
of eighteenth-century thought that later men may be too eager to claim
for their own invention. Starobinski's aim in *L'Invention de la liberté* is
openly to draw this comparison with modern culture and to provide another parentage besides nineteenth-century literature for the existential
culture and criticism of the present.

Between 1960 and 1964, while he was preparing *L'Invention de la
liberté*, Starobinski began to study "melancholy" as a condition that influences man's social behavior and artistic creativity. His essay on Montaigne (1960) shows that he is still concerned with the perceptive,
self-creating personality, but it also suggests ideas that later appear in
L'Invention de la liberté. Montaigne must separate himself from a world
that offers him no metaphysical support or certainty, and he engages
in a movement of self-analysis to obtain a sense of identity. This "self-
inspection" results only in a "muscular consciousness of the very movement of inspection,"[10] a consciousness that sees itself act and finally
accepts its double nature by simultaneously yielding to and directing
its experience. Montaigne's literary personality is created from a sense
of emptiness—from a paralysis that will be the "melancholic state" of
Starobinski's later essays. "A curious reversal; recognizing emptiness
precedes and provokes the moment when the self becomes a *presence*
for itself. Speaking of oneself is filling an empty space . . . the empty
background calls forth a proliferation of free forms."[11] Such a description could apply to baroque art; it will also be echoed in later essays
on melancholy.

In "La Mélancolie de l'anatomiste" (1962), Starobinski mentions
Montaigne's comparison of his *Essays* with the "grotesques" in contemporary frescoes, and links this aesthetic, with its "ideal of limitless
riches,"[12] to Robert Burton's *Anatomy of Melancholy*. Montaigne's "interminable task of self-description" becomes the impersonal accumula-

10. Starobinski, "Montaigne I," *Nouvelle Revue française*, January 1960, p. 22.
11. Starobinski, "Montaigne (fin)," *Nouvelle Revue française*, February 1960, p.
259.
12. Starobinski, "La Mélancolie de l'anatomiste," *Tel Quel*, Summer 1962, p. 21.

tion of statements on melancholy which Burton creates to express his own melancholic "depersonalization" (p. 23). "To fill up his own emptiness, the author of the *Anatomy of Melancholy* collects other peoples' sayings . . . crams himself full of foreign substance." The preface to the *Anatomy of Melancholy* has as its theme a sense of theater, of the masks and unreality that Starobinski finds typical of a melancholic mind. Jaques, from "As You Like It," is the "perfect melancholic type" (p. 24); he expresses perfectly the melancholic's feeling that he lives at a slow pace, set apart from the dizzy and incomprehensible world. This separation of mental worlds explains the historical position of melancholic "fools," set apart in society and tolerated as outcasts. Society inflicts on them a special role, and in fact stylizes them insofar as they accept this role. "Thus a certain *style*, which is a product of culture, takes up, exploits, and organizes the confused *no* which melancholia utters" (p. 28). Starobinski's essay does not develop the idea of melancholy past the limit of a frustrated, unwillingly stylized alienation from life. This melancholic condition is a paralysis without relief, a lucidly impotent state which "cannot pass from knowledge to acts. The theater of the world has become, for it, the amphitheater of anatomy." It is a condition which Starobinski the physician has discussed in his *Histoire du traitement de la mélancolie* (1960), a condition amenable to both medical and literary analysis. As a critic, Starobinski later enlarges upon the literary aspects of melancholy, and proposes the idea of a poetic "irony" that surpasses melancholia in order to "act" and create literature.

Starobinski begins by describing melancholy as a human condition, and adapts this idea to literary analysis. Characteristically, this critic uses his knowledge of other disciplines (such as art or medicine) to explain and enrich his literary perspective. Here, he uses his medical observations on melancholy to develop a theory of literature that is independent of medicine, and that progresses beyond his original argument to find a solution for literary melancholy that medical "melancholia" does not have. What Starobinski describes as literary "melancholy" in "L'Encre de la mélancolie" (1963) is far from Romantic languor; it is closer to one of the medieval "humors," or to a state of psychological alienation. This melancholy is an often-described unexplained "profound" sense of alienation from its world. He who suffers from it cannot reconcile himself with space [13] and with time (p. 420). Charles d'Orléans and Du Bellay speak of such a melancholy, traditionally allegorized as a somber female figure under whose influence the poet finds it difficult to write. Melancholy, however, also carries with it a profound sense of existence which enriches poetry, so that it plays a creative role in spite of itself. "If melancholy inspires song, it is not that melancholy itself is creative; it establishes the *lack* (the lack of space, or 'disoriented' space) for which melodious speech becomes both the symbolic compensation and evident translation . . . organizing its own space" (p. 419). Melancholy is then a kind of somber ink, an ink of alienation and difficult experience, which the poet uses to transcribe experience in art.

Melancholy is examined further as alienation in "Ironie et mélancolie" (1966), a study of the melancholic confusion of being and seeing which must finally be transcended by "irony" in order to produce literature. Such irony is a "therapeutic intervention," [14] either of open buffoonery (p. 308) or of an ability to conquer alienation by voluntarily "creating oneself anew" (*"se faire autre"*—Diderot) (p. 299). The theater of Carlo Gozzi, says Starobinski, was taken up by the German Romantics because they saw in it an ironic vision, a vision that kept life at a distance in order to comprehend its larger, even paradoxical meaning (p. 303). E. T. A. Hoffman especially followed Gozzi's example in *Prinzessin Brambilla,* where he taught his hero Giglio Fava to become a new, sovereign personality [15] by quitting his old self. Across the various tests and disguises of hero and heroine in *Prinzessin Brambilla,* there is "a transformation happening inside a consciousness . . . leaving a lower level, acquiring progressively the full possession of aesthetic truth" (p. 439). Now melancholy has become the background for a choice of being, a choice which leads to *commedia dell' arte* in Gozzi, to an "existential transformation" into an authentic character in Hoffmann (p. 456), and to a "moment of becoming-oneself" in art (p. 454). "Melancholy, as the effect of a separation which the soul *undergoes,* is cured by irony,

13. Starobinski, "L'Encre de la mélancolie," *Nouvelle Revue française,* March 1963, p. 418.
14. Starobinski, "Ironie et mélancolie (I): Le Théâtre de Carlo Gozzi," *Critique,* April 1966, p. 304.
15. Starobinski, "Ironie et mélancolie (II): La *Princesse Brambilla* de E. T. A. Hoffmann," *Critique,* May 1966, p. 446.

which is a distance and reversal actively established by the mind, helped by imagination" (p. 451).[16] Such separation and reversal is described in an essay published several months after "Ironie et mélancolie": "La Rochefoucauld et les morales substitutives." According to Starobinski, man in La Rochefoucauld is a "dispossessed" self, empty of all character and controlled by impersonal human passions, who tries to create a new essence and individuality. "From then on, we are in the presence of a new theory of mask and pretense."[17] This second personality "covers without abolishing a first self."[18] It is an "aesthetic transmutation" (p. 225), and an identity chosen in conscious defiance of human weakness. La Rochefoucauld expresses such an identity in the somber elegance of his maxims on human weakness. Unlike Burton, who could only accumulate fragments about melancholia, La Rochefoucauld is able to overcome the paralysis of his alienation to shape a new aesthetic form. His ironic vision encompasses both himself and his disappointment with reality. The use of "irony" in its lesser sense as sarcasm is quite evident in the *Maxims*, and yet Starobinski has not really identified the source and nature of that irony which is the corresponding half of melancholy in his literary theory. His essays are at present heavily weighted toward a description of the author's original state of melancholy. Thus far, the analysis of irony (which in "L'Encre de la mélancolie" he calls a "mysterious increase in power")[19] is little more than the Romantic dictum of "emotion recollected in tranquillity," with some worldly distance added for good measure. In a sense, Starobinski has used the historical idea of melancholy as a humor to describe both psychological alienation (with its metaphysical overtones) and an aesthetic paralysis (whose most familiar example is Mallarmé). Starobinski's original study of medical melancholy thus leads him to a new perspective on literature. This new perspective carries on the theme of vision established in the critic's earlier works, since the melancholic condition implies a double vision of reality and a contrast between what *is* and what *seems to be*.

16. According to Georges Poulet, the essays on melancholy will form part of a larger work. Cf. Poulet, "La Pensée critique de Jean Starobinski (I)," *Critique*, May 1963, p. 387, n. 1.

17. Starobinski, "La Rochefoucauld et les morales substitutives I," *Nouvelle Revue française*, July 1966, p. 33.

18. Starobinski, "La Rochefoucauld et les morales substitutives II," p. 217.

19. Starobinski, "L'Encre de la mélancolie," p. 423.

Starobinski's analysis of vision may embrace various literary attitudes, but it is typically existential in that it concentrates on being and seeming, choice and action, rather than on words or formal structures. Inside existential criticism, Starobinski follows a philosophical, almost biographical approach to literature. He shows more interest in an author's personality than either Poulet or Richard will allow; at the same time, however, he is more concerned with philosophical issues than is J. Hillis Miller. As Starobinski says, his approach "tries to be purely 'existential' (and not sociological or Marxist)." [20] He avoids set views of any kind because he wants to construct a neutral existential mold in which to put literature's subjective visions.

Even though Starobinski wishes to avoid pre-set interpretations, he is a theoretical critic who likes all readings to lead back to a clear methodological basis. In this way, his attitude resembles the general theoretical predisposition of the Geneva School. These critics (especially Poulet and Miller) are willing to accept interrelated "circles" or levels of criticism, but in general they want to connect a world view to each level. Such a position is tolerant of other methods, but it tends to disregard critiques that are not firmly based in an evident theory. For example, Starobinski is openly disappointed that the critical method of Leo Spitzer [21] does not provide "a constant meditation on 'speech,' on

20. Starobinski, *Jean-Jacques Rousseau*, p. 77.
21. Starobinski does not mention Spitzer's criticism of Poulet, although this criticism provides an excellent comparison of formal and existential techniques. Spitzer's article, "A propos de la *Vie de Marianne* (lettre à M. Georges Poulet)," *Romanic Review*, April 1953, pp. 102–126 (reprinted in *Romanische Literaturstudien*, Tübingen, 1959), demonstrates the split between a formal or aesthetic analysis and the existential perspective that characterizes the Geneva School. The essay undermines conclusively any aesthetic interpretations to be drawn from the chapter on Marivaux in *La Distance intérieure*. Spitzer bases his analysis on an assumption that does not comply with the Geneva theory: he says "if you give a complete analysis of the existence in Marivaux that pre-exists his entire work, then it must also take in account this particular work" (p. 104). He shows that Poulet's extrapolation and existential interpretation of certain words and phrases is distorted when applied to Marianne, that similar phrases are taken and distorted from the first and second "Surprise de l'amour," and finally, that Marianne, far from being overwhelmed and subordinated in a perpetual chaos of impressions, navigates securely "through life guided by a compass that is really amazingly stable" (p. 114). Certainly Spitzer's essay gives a closer reading of *Marianne* than does Poulet's chapter, and as a formal interpretation of the novel it is far superior to the study in *La Distance intérieure*. However, the analysis cannot really be compared with Poulet's chapter, which is after all entitled "Marivaux" and not "Marianne." Poulet is not engaged in a search that can be reduced to aesthetic analysis: he seeks rather to understand an under-

culture, and on interpretation," [22] or "an ampler discussion of fundamental problems" (p. 585). Perhaps because he is looking for a method, he also overemphasizes Spitzer's early and latent links with structuralism: "Spitzer, after 1920, merely adapted a structuralism he had already practiced" (p. 590). In general, Starobinski recognizes two critical methods: one that tries to be as exact as science and one that tries to become literature. But both kinds are limited; indeed a "wise criticism" is a method "that constantly encounters the possibility of another way, of a detour, of a changed destination" (p. 581). He would like each critic to demonstrate the limits of his method along with his analysis, and to possess "something like a feeling of default in regard to the work he does not write himself, and the risk he thereby refuses" (p. 580). According to Starobinski, the wise critic must openly "risk" a method to provide one of the possible interpretations of a work; at the same time that he explains the text, however, he must explain his method and its limitations.

Starobinski's tolerance for other methods leads him to experiment with new perspectives, but he never forgets that the work's unique impact exists over and above its separate interpretations. In *L'Invention de la liberté*, he is obviously interested in a sociological structural investigation. The same year, in the article on Spitzer, he speaks of a "sociological or psychological extension of knowledge" (p. 586). His work on melancholy stems, moreover, from medical studies. Starobinski does not so much *adopt* as *adapt* a method to his own uses, however, and insists on retaining all the primary value of an author's individual experience. Even while asserting the social origins of speech, he focuses on this unique experience. If all speech is "inevitably engraved in a socio-historical context . . . it remains nonetheless true that, since Romanticism, we often see at its origin a tormented desire to affirm the *unique* quality of the single experience, what *isolates* it in its truth (or better: in its

---

lying method of perceiving the universe, one that can be found in the various expressions of Marivaux' characters. His chapter describes *l'être marivaudien* (pp. 4, 10, 12, 15, 24, 26, 28, 30), the *personnage marivaudien* (pp. 22, 25, 26, 29), the *étonnement marivaudien* (p. 5) and the *Cogito marivaudien* (p. 5). These observations clearly analyze Marivaux' "literary being" and not any one character in his works.

22. Starobinski, "La Stylistique et ses méthodes: Leo Spitzer," *Critique*, July 1964, p. 584.

authenticity)" (p. 587). At a time when Starobinski is openly interested in sociological analysis, when he writes about the alienation of a "melancholy" poetic mind, he is still able to point up the risks of this very approach. "At the very moment when he tries to decipher the 'alienated speech' of institutions and social relations, the sociological critic risks losing the power to interpret human *speech*: confronted with the difficulty of listening to reality, he often seems to *speak* in its place . . . we risk hearing the solitary voice (the 'metalanguage') of the critic with a method" (p. 596). The "metalanguage" of a critic blinded by his method is the first risk of criticism, according to Starobinski. Like the other members of the Geneva School, he wants to retain the unique impression of the individual author and not to supplant this impression with an objective glance or with false empathy. In order to retain his freedom of perspective, and yet continue to analyze a given literary work, Starobinski frames these various perspectives inside the critical vehicle of a visual metaphor. Complexities of experience are transformed into complexities of vision. Starobinski's sympathy is openly drawn to the vision of a profoundly integrated, organic experience—one which liberates the mind and allows it to create new and personal forms. This preference sets him again in the direct tradition of existential philosophy, and of an existentially "genetic" criticism.

JEAN ROUSSET

Jean Rousset uses the antiformal, humanistic preoccupations of the other critics of consciousness to analyze the formal textual use of extra-literary perspectives. He begins and ends with an individual text, although his path of exploration may lead well beyond it, even beyond the author himself and into his century. Rousset first analyzes textual themes to show how they imply an ideal "utopian" work, but he then returns from this utopian vision to an increased understanding of the real work's aims. This method, he believes, allows him to evaluate the original themes more exactly, and to come closer to the author's creative experience.

Like his predecessor Marcel Raymond, Rousset straddles two worlds of critical thought. Both men combine formal with philosophical insights, but Rousset's formal method is more technical and less traditional than Raymond's. Apart from Raymond, Rousset recognizes the specific influence of Béguin, Du Bos, Bachelard, Spitzer, Picon, Jean-Pierre Richard, and Jean Starobinski.[1] He wants to recognize and use the extra-aesthetic techniques and insights of the more philosophical readers, such as Poulet, Richard, and Bachelard, but wants also to retain an exclusive preoccupation with style, as do Raymond and Spitzer. As he says, his antennae quiver to the work's not the author's intentions (p. xv), and unlike the philosophical analysts, he is content to end with the imperfect, written version of the utopian work. He may resemble Richard in that both examine the evidence of themes to refer to a utopian work, but Rousset calculates his existential data for a different, more formal end.

Rousset has always had a feeling for the existential impact of style and for the interlocking revelations that make up an existential composition. His earliest book, *La Littérature de l'âge baroque en France* (1953), analyzes baroque literature in order to discover its metaphysical position, and then applies this same metaphysical attitude to achieve a greater understanding of separate baroque texts. Rousset's analysis covers the period from 1580 to 1670, which allows him to discuss a series of themes that characterize the creative imagination from Montaigne to Bernini. He distinguishes baroque creation from classical and Romantic creation, and thus isolates and identifies a sixteenth-century *Zeitgeist* of great stylistic and philosophical importance.

The baroque imagination, says Rousset, requires movement, metamorphosis, and expression in material forms. It cannot retire into a series of ingenious introspections, but must work with material reality in a world of sensuous forms. In its concern for the material world it differs from the wholly introspective Romantic effort to "strip bare and isolate the secret roots of individual being." Baroque literature, to be sure, explores the self; but it also tries to bring the self into a relationship with the outside world. The baroque consciousness explores its own metamorphoses as it reflects a changing reality. Baroque art "ends by forcing man out of his orbit, shifting his center of gravity all around him toward the multiple selves that he creates."[2] Artists see the world

1. Jean Rousset, *Forme et signification* (Paris: Corti, 1962), p. xvii.
2. Rousset, *La Littérature de l'âge baroque en France* (Paris: Corti, 1953), p. 252.

as a fleeting reality, "as a successive multiplicity, a series of mutations, a falling away" (p. 121). They are opposed to a static order of composition, to fixed or abstract forms. "The baroque . . . needs tangible forms to translate movement, instability" (p. 200) and baroque artists incarnate the movement of life in a series of concrete images.

These concrete images often serve to cast a number of related reactions into one focal point, which both Rousset and Raymond call a *foyer*. The function of criticism is then to work back from the suggestive image to its theme, to the metaphysical position it implies. *La Littérature de l'âge baroque* uses such a procedure and finds water imagery particularly significant for the baroque mind. The fluid experience represented by water has an immediate appeal for an unstable age: "Nothing is more like man than what moves: a cloud, a bubble—water" (p. 142). Water is an image to man of his own instability; the baroque creator expresses an anguished uncertainty when he describes the play of water "because water nourishes all symbols of fluidity, of inconstancy, of moving plasticity; because it is the privileged place for reflections, plays of light and of waves, for sinuous or spurting forms; finally, because it is metamorphosis itself" (p. 143). Rousset's discussion of water imagery constantly refers to literary ends. As a result, it differs from the discussion of water symbolism in Richard and Bachelard. With Rousset there is no microcosmic "drop," given eternal metaphysical significance for any and all men: he merely identifies a temporal phenomenon, a favorite motif of instability which had importance for certain men at a certain time. In explaining the appeal of this visual motif, he is explaining an element in the mental universe that created it. This mental universe is organized by a series of similar subterranean impulses, which appear embodied in just such concrete images.

After considering the unwritten, metaphysical style of a work, *La Littérature de l'âge baroque* turns to the way in which metaphysical attitudes influence the shape of a composition. The fluidity of the baroque attitude leads to an expansive, unbalanced form: typically (in Andreas Gryphius), to "verses that are too short or too long, unbalanced quatrains; the poem bursts under the violence of an interior impulse which is prolonged outside" (p. 194). This unstable pose both creates and works against its own composition, so that the metaphysical attitude finds its way into the flavor of a text and also undermines its natural move to completion. Rousset's discussion of the baroque experience is evidently indebted to Raymond, and his concern for the relations of physical experience to expression also reflects Poulet and Richard. When he speaks of baroque creation as a self-defeating movement, he is aligning himself as well with a modern disbelief in the possibility of a truly expressive literature. The frustrated certainty of aiming at an "impossible" expression emerges in modern as well as baroque literature, even though the first experience of reality is framed in quite different terms. In both literatures, it wrenches form away from set genres and traditional perspectives.

Rousset is mainly interested in the connection of form with meaning, and it is this theme which guides the essays of his second theoretical book: *Forme et signification* (1962). He intuitively feels the integral structural nature of separate works: he wants to bridge the gap between existential methods and formal entities. Not so germinal a writer as Raymond, Béguin, or Poulet, he concerns himself with making their speculations viable for the discussion of literary works.

The critics of consciousness share one special dilemma with formal critics: that of defining the boundaries between an author and his writing, or between the artist and the man. On first impression, this problem is one of defining spontaneity and sincerity. On a more removed plane, which has special significance for a theory of consciousness, it is the problem of discovering the actual limits and definition of the "work" itself. Because Rousset and his colleagues look for the closest relationship between a man's experience and his expression, they might be expected to value a stream of consciousness, or any method which appeared to offer immediate and spontaneous reactions. But such is not the case. All the critics of consciousness attack this oversimplified idea of self-expression in literature, and Rousset considers at length the odd discrepancy between feeling and utterance. The author may be deceived as to his emotion, he says, and cannot represent well what he does not understand. The emotion itself must be recollected in tranquillity if it is to represent an integrated experience, and thus represent the whole man. Each impression from outside must echo throughout the inner world to find its place in a coordinate whole. If the impression is not assimilated in a total experience, it remains only a superficial expression which appeals to the "heart" but not to the composing "brain." (The distinction comes from

Balzac.) It is the brain which creates and synthesizes everything in a "laboratory saturated with physical experience." [3] A global, pondered experience is the only one which can emerge authentically as literature.

While Rousset is only echoing the general Geneva tradition when he speaks of a comprehensive literary experience, he is alone in distinguishing between the artist's "imaginative sensitivity" and his "empirical emotion." This distinction actually rephrases on an existential plane the formal view of artistic sincerity. To a formal reader, the impression of sincerity must be given by verbal technique and cannot be achieved merely through honest emotions. Rousset agrees that it is not enough merely to experience an emotion; but he would not call any technique competent if it cannot reflect experience. For him, the existential definition of verbal technique includes an ability to synthesize experience.

"Synthesized experience" is what Rousset means by a *foyer*, and it is to this word or idea that he and his colleagues always return. A *foyer*—a *focus*, but also a *source* of themes of experience—is a natural metaphor for the criticism of consciousness, because it expresses an infinite number of themes and impulses collected at one significant core. As a meeting place of connotations, it is inexhaustibly rich and hospitable; but its inexhaustibility makes it a frustrating tool for a critic who wishes to arrive at any set statement about a work. Set statements, however, are not the goal of the existential critic, who wishes to give the reader an example rather than an answer. The critic's example is often a one-way street, for it is easier to follow an impulse to its source than to predict all the results of a *foyer*, but the reader who follows Rousset's route to the core should be able to make his own way out again.

Rousset's use of a series of *foyers* is typical of the criticism of consciousness, which holds that the important organization of any work is found in the substratum by which it mirrors its humanity. For this critic, however, the substratum is not unwritten or nonstylistic. It is an underlying structure which still must wait to appear when the author executes his original plan. It is not a projected formal plan, nor

3. Rousset, *Forme et signification*, p. iv.

is it already plotted in the mind. The real Flaubert, says Rousset, does not appear in the initial plans for *Madame Bovary*, but is given gradual form in the ultimate execution of the book. From Racine to Camus (whom he quotes as saying that one writes to rediscover one's profound attachments), the artist's "secret" individuality emerges only in the fleshing-out of his projected skeleton. This definition of form makes it an "active and unforeseeable principle of revelation and apparition" (p. xi), something which cannot be foreseen either in rules or in intentions. It is, says Rousset, like the fleshly curves and contours which overlie a skeleton and define its living appearance.

Rousset shares with Poulet and Richard a belief in the existential substructure, but in his actual treatment of form he is more concerned than they are with traditional objects of analysis. With Poulet and Richard, all man's utterances reveal his mental universe; one may even read between lines and into poetry that has not been written. Rousset will not go nearly so far. For him the existential personality creates the literary personality, but is not synonymous with it. Flaubert the novelist is separate from Flaubert the letter-writer, and the novelist is more important. Rousset is soon forced to construct some bridge over this gap between his formal and existential perspectives.

To bridge the gap, he thinks of a work as an *organisme vivant*, a living organism with its own boundaries and special nature; but he does not define boundaries in a precise way. Baudelaire may be in "Le Balcon," Flaubert in *Madame Bovary*, and Balzac in the *Comédie Humaine*. Rousset can give only an intuitive definition of a complete form: the work *feels* complete. "In its form," he writes, "it is complete and meaningful as the artist created it . . . the work as such cannot be augmented or diminished; it is, and it radiates through its own being." It is possible to distinguish "variable degrees of presence" with "different levels of fullness and truth" (p. xx), but somehow the work still exists as a structure apart from the author's total production. Rousset is instinctively unwilling to abolish literary works as separate entities, but he needs to discover a nonformal method for proving their existence. As a critic of consciousness, he is unable to accept genres and other formal categories. Indeed, he must find a properly nonobjective method for delimiting the structure of a living work. As a result, he falls back upon another basic element in the criticism of consciousness: the sympathetic intuition of the reader.

Rousset advises the reader to remain alert for the work's "signal," for an "unforeseen and revelatory structural fact" (p. xii) that will indicate the real core and meaning of the work. Until he receives this signal he can permit himself no plan but must try to read with a total adhesion to the movement of the book. The "signal" will point to the "utopian" work of which the real one is but a glimmer, but the critic's route must lead outwards again from the utopian *foyer* to its mundane copy. Here Rousset is careful to make a distinction between Richard's reading and his own. Richard is more interested "in the poet's imaginary world, in his latent work," while Rousset insists on returning to "his morphology and style." Rousset's method, which began with an initial adhesion that allowed him to receive the work's signal, returns to the text in another total adhesion, which now permits him to resurrect the text as a "carnal contact" of reading experience.

Such an open experience leaves a great deal to individual intuition, even while it tries to bring the analysis back to a sense of the written text. At times, Rousset outlines a system of observations that guide intuition, but he invariably returns to an individual appraisal of the separate work. By 1967, he seems to have absorbed some structural attitudes to complement his analysis of the utopian work giving its "signal." In "Don Juan et les métamorphoses d'une structure," he proposes a basic structure for the Don Juan myth: a fickle hero, a plural feminine group as object of this fickleness, and a dead man. Tirso da Molina, Da Ponte and Mozart, and Molière all create different possibilities for this basic structure by stressing or neglecting its various aspects. The basic structure reaches its point of perfection in Mozart, says Rousset, when Donna Anna becomes a figure equal to Don Juan, and when this perfect "mythic" balance is echoed in the perfect musical harmonies at the end of the first act.[4] Such checks and balances openly reflect a contemporary structural thought according to which each "work" is an integral, self-contained part of a larger myth, whose structural equilibrium it must maintain although the individual stresses may be shifted.

4. Rousset, "Don Juan et les métamorphoses d'une structure," *Nouvelle Revue française*, September 1967, p. 488.

"When the component parts are closely interdependent, the displacement of one piece in the system modifies the entire system" (pp. 488–489), says Rousset. Even more: when Goldoni replaces the walking statue with a thunderclap, "the myth is dismantled because the balance of the original triple relationship has been broken" (p. 486). Although Rousset is attracted to structures as a useful means of plotting artistic coordinates, he remains a cautious observer of the individual work. The development of the Don Juan myth, he proposes, indicates "that you cannot pass from Baroque to Romanticism without a profound metamorphosis. Which tends to prove that the differences between them are more important than the analogies" (p. 490). In this rather prudent ending to the essay, Rousset remains true to the tradition of the Geneva School, stressing the individual differences and unique quality of an author's work even against the background of common cultural or "mythic" comparisons.

Rousset's criticism is important because it tries to chart a practical route from the work to the *foyer*, then back to the work again. Although Rousset himself believes in the elusive nature of the reading experience, he tries to map out enough connections between the creative experience and its written form to make an existential reading publicly accessible. Because he moves between the imaginative world and its formal expression, he is the one critic of consciousness, apart from J. Hillis Miller, who clearly connects this criticism with formal analysis of the text.

7

J. HILLIS MILLER

J. Hillis Miller is the only critic in the United States who associates himself with the Geneva School. He is Professor of English at The Johns Hopkins University and the author of three books of criticism: *Charles Dickens: The World of His Novels* (1959), which is dedicated to Georges Poulet; *The Disappearance of God* (1963); and *Poets of Reality* (1965). Miller, who has known Poulet since 1952, when the French critic came to Johns Hopkins for a five-year stay, openly attempts to transfer the methods of the Geneva School to the study of English literature. He combines the formal with the existential approach, as he uses his American training in textual criticism to support the aims and criteria of an adopted criticism of consciousness.

Charles Dickens: The World of His Novels combines a typical Geneva analysis of the artist as creator of a universe with studies of the relationships of characters inside this universe. The world of Dickens' novels contains both the formal pattern of these character relationships, and an underlying metaphysical pattern which is Dickens' own. In his next two books, Miller undertakes a much more ambitious project; he traces a change in literary attitude from one implied universe to another. *The Disappearance of God* revolves around a literary universe in which God is absent, and *Poets of Reality* describes the recovery of a divinely immanent universe that is the basis for a new poetry. The earlier book focuses on five Romantic authors who tried to cope with the absence of God: De Quincey, Browning, Emily Brontë, Arnold, and Hopkins. The later book takes up the problem in more recent authors and describes a contemporary poetic "presence" which fills the "absence" of the nineteenth century. In the twentieth century, says Miller, poets have had to confront not only the absence but the "death" of God. The metaphysical adventure here moves from Conrad's nihilism to the progressive intuitions of Yeats, Eliot, Thomas, Stevens, and William Carlos Williams.

In all three books, Miller moves alternately from an examination of metaphysical qualities to an analysis of the formal qualities that embody them. He uses a "systole and diastole" of concentric readings calculated to reveal the central nature of each author on various interrelated levels. Such an approach, he believes, can hope for a comprehensive, varied, and coordinate reading.

Charles Dickens: The World of His Novels is the first book in English to adopt the Genevan point of view. It attempts to introduce to English readers the existential perspective on literature. Here Miller not only confines his analysis to a single author, but describes in the introduction his personal adaptation of Poulet's theories. "I have attempted," he writes "to assess the specific quality of Dickens' imagination in the totality of his work, to identify what persists throughout all the swarming multiplicity of his novels as a view of the world which is unique and the same." [1] This unique and consistent view of the world guides the author's search for a "true and viable identity"

1. J. Hillis Miller, *Charles Dickens: The World of His Novels* (Cambridge: Harvard University Press, 1959), p. viii.

(p. x) and creates a literary pattern that runs parallel to the metaphysical substructure.

Miller echoes Poulet's doctrine that an author, throughout his works,
takes part in a personal adventure, and that the works themselves represent the author's continual progress toward self-recognition. This
approach "sees a work of literature not as the mere symptom or product
of a pre-existent psychological condition, but as the very means by
which a writer apprehends and, in some measure, creates himself" (p.
viii). An author reveals his existential attitude through the words he
selects and through patterns of literary images and events. Miller's
analysis rests on "data," just as Poulet's rests on extrapolated words
and phrases: there are "unit passages" in an author's work which project an image of his subjective personality. "Taken all together, all the
unit passages form the heart of the imaginative universe of the writer
. . . At the heart . . . is an impalpable organizing form, constantly
presiding over the choice of words . . . For a novel . . . is the embodiment in words of a certain very special way of experiencing the
world" (p. ix). Miller does not lean so far as does Poulet in the direction of supraverbal analysis, but looks to the text for the technical effects of this motivating experience.

Because he writes for an audience trained in the English critical tradition, and is himself educated in this tradition, Miller wants to avoid
a misunderstanding between existential and formal readers. He does
not abandon his primary concern with literary experience, but he is
careful to assert that this experience, if it is to be a valid subject of
analysis, must first appear in words. "A poem or novel is indeed the
world refashioned into conformity with the inner structure of the
writer's spirit, but at the same time it is that spirit given, through
words, a form and substance taken from the shared solidity of the
exterior world. It is in this sense that the words of the work are themselves the primary datum, a self-sufficient reality beyond which the
critic need not go" (p. x). Individual words, however, do not provide
Miller's only data, and his interpretation goes farther than Poulet's
early technique of extrapolation. His analysis is not limited to an author's direct, personal expression, for he discusses sentences, paragraphs,
and even a character's imagining mind as contained within its own
universe. "This study presupposes that each sentence or paragraph of

a novel, whether it is presented from the point of view of the narrator or of some imagined character, defines a certain relationship between an imagining mind and its object . . . the definition of a certain relation between the mind and its world" (p. ix). His emphasis on style, as Miller himself recognizes, brings him closer than other Geneva critics to contemporary American "new criticism." He even goes so far as to call his own work a "discussion of Dickens' novels as autonomous works of art" (p. viii), although he is more concerned with their independence as metaphysical statements than with their separate existence as aesthetic objects. Miller remains the most style-conscious of the Geneva critics, but his definition of style is consistently existential. Style is a "way of living in the world given a verbal form" (p. x).

Dickens, says Miller, uses his characters to project the experiences of his own personal development. He examines himself through his characters, and creates their lives as so many vicarious attempts to achieve ontological integrity. Their grotesqueries, struggles, successes, and rebuffs represent stages in a master plan of existential inquiry that is not resolved until the final books. "The experiences of the characters tend to occur in a single constant succession" (p. 4); their various false conclusions and new beginnings are all a part of their author's personal drama.

The pattern of this drama emerges from the sequence of experiences in the novels. The ending of *Oliver Twist* "is a resolution which is essentially based on self-deception" (p. 84), and it finds a "radical criticism" in *The Old Curiosity Shop* and *Nicholas Nickleby* (pp. 95–96). The "solution" of *David Copperfield* undergoes further examination in *Bleak House* and meets another "radical revaluation" in *Great Expectations* (p. 159). Throughout, the problem facing all characters is one of reaching an authentic self that is related to outer reality but not subjected to it. *Martin Chuzzlewit* embodies a stage in which Dickens investigates the possibility of a human contact "which would guarantee the uniqueness of each person . . . enhancing rather than absorbing and destroying his intrinsic identity" (p. 97). The end of this novel is unsatisfactory, in terms of Dickens' search, for the author "does not yet have the courage to face the real implications of his view of human existence" (p. 142). In *Bleak House* his experience envisages for the first time the "possibility of a truly moral life" in the persistent but unambitious exercise of creative will (pp. 217–219). Finally, Dickens comes to a vision of self-creation which satisfies his needs. "To take responsibility for arranging the world is to take responsibility for making the self, and to escape at last from the grim alternatives of guilty action, passivity, or isolation which are initially the sole possibilities in the imaginative universe of Dickens" (p. 334). This passage, from the chapter on *Our Mutual Friend*, describes a personal "authenticity" stemming from the choice and assertion of character. The vision of such authenticity culminates Dickens' search, throughout his novels, for ontological integrity.

Inside this single world of the author there are a multitude of little worlds and separate characters. Miller, alone among the Geneva critics, describes these secondary characters and their lesser careers. He alone analyzes such characters as they actually function in a novel; he does not merely say that they represent an existence beyond themselves. His analysis of Tulkinghorn's desire for power through knowledge, and of his actual isolation from the world he deciphers, can be seen as a short character study even though it also illustrates a stage in Dickens' concern for human relationships. Miller also writes character studies of Bucket, whose deductive powers are greater than Tulkinghorn's but who is also "cut off from real experience" (p. 176), and of Miss Havisham, who wants "to make her betrayal into the very meaning of her life, and to make her resulting death-in-life a curse on her heartless lover" (p. 257). Each one of these little worlds has its own history, as well as its own niche in a larger universe.

Miller's treatment of these characters as functioning parts of the novel overlaps with his analysis of them as existential clues. Their literary lives are also experimental lives in the world of Dickens' imagination. In *Little Dorrit* the author has a "new way of showing many of his characters altogether aware of their spiritual states and even deliberately choosing them" (p. 235). *Our Mutual Friend* is also an illustrated essay on the best way to achieve selfhood. Miller remarks that *Our Mutual Friend* appears to be a "multi-plotted novel presenting a collection of unrelated lives each fulfilling itself privately" (p. 284), but that it is actually "a kind of slow dance in which all the possibilities of interaction are displayed one by one" (p. 287). His purpose, in *Charles Dickens: The World of His Novels,* is to write a series of revelatory character studies that point toward a portrait of the author.

Here Miller is much more cautious than he will be in his two later books. A number of passages recall the Geneva critics, but these passages are overshadowed by his character studies. He does not yet compare authors' existential experiences; rather, he compares characters, such as Little Dorrit and Dostoevsky's Myshkin. There is a "quality of suffering imagined in each case" (p. 242) which reflects first the characters and only secondarily the author. Even the critic's discussion of reality, which claims such a large part of Geneva criticism, is relegated to a series of comments underlying character observation. Pickwick's adventure is his "gradual discovery of the real nature of the world" (p. 27). Oliver Twist's rose-covered cottage symbolizes the cozy freedom for which he yearns (p. 71). Mr. Mould exists in his household cocoon and the Boffins divide their home into co-existing milieus. The Podsnaps' silverplate injects a note of "sheer, gross, heavy, impenetrable matter . . . altogether resisting man's attempts to assimilate it into his world" (p. 309). It is only toward the end of Dickens' career that matter appears *per se,* an expression of nonhuman reality which is analogous to "the mysterious depth of the human spirit" (p. 318). Consistently this matter is used as a foil to character development. It is a "transcendent otherness which simultaneously denies and gives authenticity to human life" (p. 325). Throughout, Miller is adapting existential perspectives to an analysis that is more humanistic than philosophical. The humanism will remain, but philosophy returns to take the upper hand in guiding the analysis of the next two books.

Charles Dickens concentrates on one man, but Miller's next two books go farther, and place several analyses in the framework of a larger historical context. He is still concerned with an author's metaphysical biography, but he enlarges his scope to write two books that could be chapters for Poulet's "history of the human consciousness." Each author has a separate "structure of consciousness," and reveals an "organizing form which presides over the elaboration" of his works. These structures form mental landscapes, or "inscapes" (Miller adopts Hopkins' term) that can be compared, and the comparison of inscapes among authors is the first step in framing a literary history of the human consciousness.

Miller's history, like Poulet's, is related to a religious perspective.

This perspective is part of the typical Geneva creative theory, but also reflects Miller's particular touchstone for analyzing romantic literary experience. In *The Disappearance of God* Miller chooses to emphasize theological experience because it "is most important and determines everything else" for the writers involved.[2] His procedure is the same in *Poets of Reality*, although the latter writers have various initial experiences and reach more "advanced" conclusions. If the religious experience is "most important" for all these writers, it is also most important for the critic himself. Here is a reciprocal relationship whose boundaries are ill-defined. The recognition of existence (called God or Being) is indeed an important historical theme, but it is also the hallmark of existential philosophy and existential literary theory. Miller uses the Genevan existential approach, with its ideal of a coherent pattern of existence, to reject an age-old philosophy of causation and logical sequence. He dislikes this philosophy because it has fragmented existence into terms of subject, object, and being. Associated with this fragmentation are Aristotle, Protestantism (p. 6), "subjectivism," "urbanization and the failure of medieval symbolism," and modern "historicism" or "perspectivism" (p. 9). All are versions of a subjective, self-amputated perception of reality. Given the hypotheses of the existential approach, it is debatable whether Miller could have chosen any radically different perspective from the one he has selected: a discussion of the existential situation of selected authors in an historical pattern which recognizes first God, then nothingness, and finally immanent Being.

According to Miller, the attempt to have a direct experience of God is rooted in romantic thought (p. 13). This romantic quest had several stages. At first, the writer believed that he could communicate with God by communing with nature, and conceived of God as a Supreme Being incarnate in nature. Later writers no longer believed that they could find God in nature; their God was a transcendental being unavailable to man. This despair of finding God passed through various stages of subjectivism and nihilism, to emerge in a contemporary belief in God as a supreme and immanent Being. This new Being is no longer outside man, but is present in every incarnation of the universe.

2. Miller, *The Disappearance of God* (Cambridge: Harvard University Press, 1963), p. viii.

Early nineteenth-century romantic writers experienced God through nature: as a spiritual force apart from man, but with which man must struggle to be allied. By the middle of the century romantic writers were no longer able to experience God in nature; they could conceive only of a transcendental God above and beyond human experience. The five authors of *The Disappearance of God* begin with such an isolated human experience, and try in their separate ways to reconstruct some avenue of communication with God. Miller defines their careers as "heroic attempts to recover immanence in a world of transcendence" (p. 15). Because their God has vanished, they are left waiting for a new revelation. In the twentieth century, the withdrawal of God turns into the absence or "death" of God, which consequently destroys any belief in man as God's creation. Miller shows that the completely subjective viewpoint, when it refuses to believe in any exterior reality, ends by being unable to believe in itself. Man, as a creature able to conceive permanence or identity, disappears simultaneously with the death of God. Such is the initial tragic situation of the *Poets of Reality*. The poet can no longer believe in God or in himself, and must try to find a new means of attaining ontological integrity. By creating a new vision of reality in the existential structure of his poems, he gradually recovers existential coherence in all things. Finally, he acquires a new belief in divine immanence. This new poetic ontology tends toward [3] a new idea of God: a God who is no longer transcendent or supreme, but immanent and omnipresent throughout reality.

In *The Disappearance of God*, Miller discusses five writers who try to overcome their inability to experience God. The first of these is Thomas De Quincey, the nineteenth century English author best known for his *Confessions of an Opium Eater*. Throughout his life, De Quincey yearns to recover the paradisiacal happiness of his childhood. On the death of his sister, he feels shut out from affection and security; he becomes a wanderer in a strange world. Through opium he glimpses a Godlike perspective which, if re-created in literature, would give him the coherent universe for which he longs. Miller maintains that De Quincey's literary ideals of musical balance and continuity, his "literature of power" with its rhetoric and later structures of logic, are no

---

3. Miller adopts Jean Wahl's phraseology in *Poets of Reality* (Cambridge: Harvard University Press, 1965), p. 283.

more than technical attempts to occupy mental space with a self-sustaining architecture. De Quincey fails because he uncovers only "an infinite abyss which can never be crossed or filled" (p. 58). He is reduced to being "an infinitesimal speck of consciousness an infinite distance from its own inner depths" (p. 71), and he finds himself condemned to relive again and again his first experience of loss. At the very end, he accepts this tragic repetition as the way to God and discovers that man's sense of separation is "his way of holding communion with God." God is perceived after all else is gone, "is present in all negative things: in emptiness, loss, solitude, and grief, in all those experiences which seem to a man to open gulfs in himself into which he might fall forever." God is "the negative image of the creation" (p. 78), a vacuum which is the other face of existence. De Quincey comes to recognize the feeling of loss and absence as his tie with the God beyond reality, into whom he will be resolved at the moment of ultimate loss—death.

Robert Browning's experience is more concrete than De Quincey's: his "negative image of God" is not a vacuum but a "primal chaos . . . potentially anything and everything" (p. 82). This shapeless mass struggles to become individual forms, but is held back by its own weight and bulk. Browning feels that he, like this primal chaos, is "potentially everything . . . actually nothing at all" (p. 95). He attempts to identify himself with God by creating a many-faceted world out of chaos, but fails in this experiment with romantic Prometheanism. This failure leads Browning to what Miller calls an "existential" discovery: "the discovery of his own gratuitousness," and the simultaneous discovery of God's absence from the world and human consciousness (p. 98). Another attempt to experience God, this time through various perspectives on reality, also fails; so that the poet is left in a "precarious equilibrium" between two extremes. This equilibrium functions in an intermediate "realm of imperfection and change" (p. 140), where the poet is as close as possible to God and yet eternally removed. In the final step of his metaphysical career, Browning comes to believe that this intermediate state itself is a form of communion, and that "each momentary form . . . is a new incarnation of God" (p. 156). The many experiments that the poet conducted in an effort to attain God are themselves separate incarnations of reality, and partake (on a small, incomplete scale) of the immanent being who is present in all things.

Helping to authenticate these various poetic expressions of reality is Browning's language, "thick and substantial" with sounds, images, and rhythms expressing an inner vitality weighed down by dense matter. When speaking of Browning's language, Miller moves from the larger "circle" of existential reading to a smaller, more technical circle of formal analysis, and so relates formal methods to existential ends. Browning's poetry has a rough and thick texture; it is "pregnant with things," as the poet himself says, and it reflects the primal matter out of which all shapes emerge. "Grotesque metaphors, ugly words heavy with consonants, stuttering alliteration, strong active verbs, breathless rhythms, onomatopoeia, images of rank smells, rough textures, and of things fleshy, viscous, sticky, nubbly, slimy, shaggy, sharp, crawling, thorny, or prickly—all these work together in Browning's verse to create an effect of unparalleled thickness, harshness, and roughness" (pp. 119–120). Miller's analytical training focuses attention here on the way in which formal effects suggest qualities which are not formal, but physical or emotional. He has moved from a larger to a smaller "circle" of reading, but consistently directs his observations to the larger goal of existential analysis.

Emily Brontë and Matthew Arnold stand in a peculiar position in Miller's book: he does not quite approve of either of them. Because both are heavily influenced by a subjective Protestant tradition, which makes it hard for them to subordinate their own rational personalities to a vision of divine immanence, Miller treats them with an uneasy admiration that is not quite sympathy. In the essay on Emily Brontë, he first uses the Gondal stories as private myths establishing underlying themes, adds to them certain biographical information from Emily's private writings, and ends in a long explication of *Wuthering Heights*. Emily, he believes, suffers from a feeling of "absolute destitution" that stems from her early religious training and leaves her in a world that is "a realm of the unavailability of God" (p. 184). She reaches out of her isolation to become involved with nature, God, or other human beings, and hopes to secure her own identity by seeing it refracted from outside. Her experience is like that of Cathy and Heathcliff in *Wuthering Heights*, where "the existence of each is altogether determined by the other" (p. 175). Miller, like most critics, takes *Wuthering Heights* as the key to Emily Brontë's personality. He is careful to show the correlation in world view between this novel and an early schoolgirl essay on nature. The world of *Wuthering Heights* is a grim, violent world of power, where life is a series of murders and creation depends on a constant exercise of the will. The story of Cathy and Heathcliff shows that neither can reach a full existence independently, but must go together toward fulfilment in Paradise by the "exhaustion of the allotted measure of evil" (p. 202). After the purgative deaths of these two, a peaceful love is made possible between Hareton and the second Cathy. "God has been transformed from the transcendent deity of extreme Protestantism, enforcing in wrath his irrevocable laws, to an immanent God, pervading everything, like the soft wind blowing over the heath" (p. 211). The clue to this interpretation is the peaceful landscape at the end of the novel, which Miller interprets as a symbol of metaphysical reconciliation. At this point his analysis is weak, mainly because he tacks a philosophical happy ending on to the harsh lesson of the text. If this reconciliation does take place between the lines, at the end of *Wuthering Heights,* it is J. Hillis Miller and not Emily Brontë who tells us so.

Matthew Arnold, like Emily Brontë, has an uneasy awareness that falls just short of a vision of immanence. Tormented by the lack of permanence and harmony in all existence, he cannot see the universe as anything but a collection of disparate, self-enclosed elements. He cannot "see nature in the romantic way" (p. 234). He tries to cope with his frustration by following disparate pieces of experience back to a common source, be it unity or nothingness; but he fails. As Miller says, "no way will work, and whichever way Arnold turns he is thrown back on himself, and on his usual state of isolation and fluctuation" (p. 255). Arnold ends by participating in a "direction" rather than in "reality" (p. 264). Like a prophet, he criticizes the world of his time and announces the revelations of the future.

Miller does more than simply appraise Arnold's views or his place in history. Although the critic can pity the poet's state, he cannot sympathize with his position. Arnold's nature poetry is bad: "try as he will Arnold cannot often get depth and resonance in his landscapes . . . In Arnold's hands nature poetry becomes like descriptions in a botanical handbook" (pp. 235–236). Such a lifeless, academic portrayal of nature is to be expected in a man who assumes "that language cannot incarnate God's truth" (p. 247). Above all, Miller dislikes Arnold's lack of moral confidence. "So he remains withdrawn from life . . . [things] present themselves to him never as something he has experienced from the inside, but as a spectacle to be regarded from a distance . . . he seeks rather to understand than to sympathize" (p. 243). "He never has the courage to try that mode of understanding which seeks to comprehend the rationale of an alien way of life by seeing how it would feel to accept it as one's own" (p. 244). "Arnold's conscientiousness is that of the man who never takes the plunge into life because he fears" (p. 246). "The prosodic slackness of the verses, and the singsong of their feminine rhymes match the terrible spiritual slackness and despondency which is their meaning" (p. 259). Arnold's intellectual withdrawal and his unwillingness to submit his personality to any outside element betray an attitude that Miller calls "existentialist" (p. 251), but that he expects modern existentialism to transcend. Because he wants gradually to extend existentialism into immanence, it is easy to understand why his essay on a stubborn intellectual such as Arnold shows a tone of restrained annoyance.

Gerard Manley Hopkins is at the opposite psychological pole from Arnold, although neither achieved the vision of divine immanence. Paradoxically, Hopkins loses this vision of immanence by accepting the very involvement that Arnold refuses. Miller likes Hopkins because, unlike Arnold, he accepts the personal risk involved in seeking immanence, even when he is unable to reach his goal. "Hopkins, like other Catholic converts, is willing to sacrifice everything—family, academic career, even his poetic genius—in order to escape the poetic and personal destiny which paralyzes such men as Matthew Arnold, and leaves them hovering between two worlds, waiting in vain for the spark from heaven to fall" (p. 312). Unhappily, Hopkins ends in about the same position of paralysis and anticipation as Arnold, but his journey there is entirely different.

Hopkins' journey comes to its climax when he accepts the Catholic doctrine of the Real Presence and rejects "three hundred and fifty years which seem to be taking man inexorably toward the nihilism of Nietzsche's 'Gott ist tot'" (p. 312). After his conversion he is able to envisage a Parmenidean unity of subject, object, and word as so many forms of being. This unity crowns his earlier attempts to get a vision of the whole by "gradual ordering of minute details . . . microscopic vision" (p. 276), and fusing reality in "rhyme" (a comparing principle) and "diatonism" (the recognition of stable, abruptly different entities). The proper use of rhyme and diatonism produces an "inscape," or the individual pattern of each writer's universe emerging through repetition. To produce an inscape and its "instress" ("the inner energy which upholds that pattern," p. 287), the writer uses words as "nodes of energy" (p. 280) and as "signs pointing in the direction of their meaning" (p. 285). Poetry creates a large harmony that "makes all things metaphors of all things" and allows the poet to create not just "inscapes of words" but "inscapes of things and their interrelation" (p. 298). Hopkins wants, through inscapes, to connect the poet with reality. At this point in his career he believes in the possibility of such connections through the mediating figure of Christ. Christ, as a link between God and man, lets Hopkins conceive of poetry, the poet, and man as so many different forms of the same Christian reality. According to Miller, "Christ is the model for all inscapes . . . the ultimate guarantee for the validity of metaphor" (p. 313). When Hopkins accepts the vision of a Christian immanence, he succeeds (temporarily) in forging a coherent existential structure for his life and poetry.

Hopkins' concept of language, his vision of man, nature, and art harmonized in one divinely coherent whole, and his willingness to lose himself in the pursuit of these ideals, all appeal to Miller's existential values. However, the poet soon falls back upon the typical romantic notion of the absence of God. The religious experience which allowed him to complete his vision of immanence now forces him to abandon poetry as a devilish, self-assertive "means to damnation" (p. 335). If man and nature change and die, then there is no stable form of rhyme for poetry to celebrate. Hopkins' only hope is to abandon all forms of self-will and to wait for a spark of grace from heaven. The resulting spiritual paralysis is similar to Arnold's, but stems from a different cause. Where Arnold could not abandon himself to a transcendent vision of God, and remained frozen in a posture of reasoned unbelief, Hopkins abandoned himself to this vision but could not work out any formal connections between it and his art. Arnold experiences an absence, or nonexistence of God; Hopkins believes that God exists, but is withdrawn from human affairs; he is thus "left with a blind violence of will toward a God who keeps himself absent" (p. 359). Hopkins, like the other writers Miller examines in *The Disappearance of God*, is "stretched on the rack of a fading transcendentalism" (p. 359) that heralds the recovery of immanence in modern literature.

Miller's third volume marks the climax of his vision of history and literature. The spiritual quest which he analyzed as a "disappearance of God," as a romantic dualism of subject and object, culminates in a new interpenetration, or an "immanence" equally present in all aspects of reality. Two of Miller's most important theories combine at this point: the belief in literature as a form and revelation of human knowledge, and the belief in a progressing history of metaphysical insight. The very form of *Poets of Reality* displays this belief in progress and achievement: all the essays up to the study of William Carlos Williams are balanced in favor of theory and read like a history of literary thought. But the essay on Williams concentrates on elucidating this "new art" of poetry, which is so far beyond its predecessors and in fact represents the latest step "toward the end of ontology." With Williams, Miller discovers the apogee of a movement in contemporary literature and also the appropriate focus of contemporary existential criticism. This third volume is more consciously didactic than the other two, because on it rests the burden of proving and explaining the historical and theoretical bases of his criticism as a whole.

Miller's introduction, "The Poetry of Reality," describes those stages of metaphysical insight that bring the twentieth century past the nineteenth. He still approaches literature through the "particular worlds" of his writers, but he examines through these worlds the hypothesis that "a new kind of poetry has appeared in our day, a poetry which has grown out of romanticism, but goes beyond it." [4] The poets discussed in *The Disappearance of God* lived in a fragmented universe, where God is no longer a power that transcends and unites all existence, where He cannot be seen. In the twentieth century, God does not exist. He is dead, murdered by humanistic egotism. Such is the starting point for the modern "poets of reality," who have to create again a sense of

4. Miller, *Poets of Reality*, p. 1.

coherent existence beyond the nihilism of subjective consciousness. Miller begins with Conrad in order to identify this nihilism, and follows in succeeding chapters a "journey beyond nihilism toward a poetry of reality" (p. 1). This journey toward reality is literary, not historical, and is in fact a "countercurrent moving against the direction of history" (p. 5), but it is nonetheless a central theme in modern literature.

Two qualities in particular distinguish modern "real" poetry from a romantic, fragmented poetry with its tension between subject and object. First, the modern poet learns that to achieve transcendence "the mind must efface itself before reality . . . abandoning the will to power over things . . . When man is willing to let things be then they appear in a space which is no longer that of an objective world opposed to the mind. In this new space the mind is dispersed everywhere within things and forms one with them" (p. 8). When the poet sacrifices his sense of separate identity, he abandons another element in the romantic tradition: its perception of depth. "In the new art these depths tend to disappear" (p. 9). Visual distance, mental distance, human distance, temporal or causal distances—all disappear in a new "copresence" which is simultaneous, immediate reality. Literary vision is likely to be "auditory, tactile, or kinesthetic" as well as visual, for it rejects the sense of distance that a visual approach implies. A poem is "part of the world and not about it" (p. 9), and it tries to restore a sense of immanent presence to the experience it describes.

The God who has disappeared and reappeared as an immanent presence is no longer an objective entity which can be extolled, rejected, or ignored. "The new poets have at the farthest limit of their experience caught a glimpse of a fugitive presence, something shared by all things in the fact that they are" (p. 10). This "God" is total being, glimpsed in the special space of a successful poem. Miller's description of this "God" moves from the traditional nineteenth-century picture of a Supreme Being (Berkeley's bulwark against solipsism) to a "death" and immanent presence that is closer to certain trends in contemporary theology. Whether God, being, nothingness, or immanent presence, this vision of reality controls each author's poetic utterance through the inextricable connections between experience and literature.

The first step in the poetic journey toward reality comes with the abandonment of an earlier road: with Conrad's rejection of civilization and intellect as a lie substituted for reality. Part of the human lie is language itself, which is a fabrication of the intellect. Conrad's means of circumventing this lie, and of revealing the reality it conceals, is to accent the very "lucidity of vision typical of civilized man" (p. 19) until he achieves a dreamlike detachment. In this dream or hallucination, things are "separated from their usual meaning" (p. 19) and the world itself is "put in parentheses, seen as pure phenomenon" (p. 20). Without the usual civilized interpretations—without any interpretation at all—life becomes a pure "qualitative spectacle" (p. 25) in which there are many superficial aspects of reality, but only a universal darkness underneath. Man is an outcast: detached from life by his own lucid vision, he perceives and shares only "the basic stuff of the universe, the uninterrupted. It is what remains, horrifyingly, when every thing or color has disappeared" (p. 28). This dark nothingness is not an absence of being, but the only positive being which exists. Seen as a basic reality, as death and as a futile human consciousness, it finally creates the possibility of communion among men in their very shared lack of knowledge. The main example given is Conrad's *The Secret Agent,* in which "as the characters get closer to death, they approach a condition in which they are the equivalents of one another" (p. 66). It is this despairing view and communication which emerges from Conrad's work, and is the goal towards which he manipulates his literary data and the language of his fiction.

Yeats, Eliot, Thomas, and Stevens move away from Conrad toward the new ontology revealed in Williams. Miller does not assume that these poets duplicate one another or describe the same experience. Each assesses his sense of separation from reality, together with the possibility of reconciliation, in his own way.

Yeats starts from a "desire for a transfiguration of the present world and the present self" (p. 68), and achieves this transfiguration when he "defiantly rejects the way up and celebrates the way down." Both "ways" are ways toward God, by a paradoxical movement which rejects God to choose the human condition. The poet submerges himself in "art and sex . . . the best means of reaching the supernatural" (p. 130), and perceives in this sensual experience a reality whose "concrete moment *is* the infinite" (p. 124). By playing to the full the human role meted out to him, Yeats attunes himself to a superhuman reality.

Eliot has a different way of reaching a sense of superhuman reality, and ends—unlike Yeats—by affirming the pattern of a Christian immanence. This immanence is Eliot's answer to subjectivism, a subjectivism which cuts him off from reality and from other human beings. "His career as a whole may be seen as an heroic effort to free himself from the limitations of nineteenth-century idealism and romanticism" (p. 179). Until its final metamorphosis, Eliot's world is a humanized, subjective world which has no real perception of an exterior object. "Prufrock's paralysis follows naturally from this subjectivizing of everything" (p. 139), and Eliot's early poetry in general is a "structure of fragments" (p. 145). The poet's first response is to establish an order out of these fragments, and to create a unified expression with emotive images or "objective correlatives." Any correlative, however, already admits the isolation of the individual it tries to reach, and Eliot is forced on to a wider conception: the collective consciousness of the "mind of Europe." This consciousness is still subjective, even if on a larger plane. It therefore cannot put the mind in connection with reality, so that Eliot must reject all dependence on the self and assume a "true pattern" of reality which will be objective: "God's order of history." This order is an "abnegation of any humanly imposed pattern in order to recover the divine pattern" (p. 187). Like Yeats, Eliot ends by submerging himself in a concrete moment, by accepting an immanent reality where everything coexists "in the radiant presence of the present" (p. 189).

Thomas starts out with the same feeling of coexistence, but cannot believe in any continuous or permanent form of life. For him "there is no initial separation between subject and object" (p. 190), and the language of poetry fuses them further into a new harmony, but neither subject, object, nor poetry has any permanence. All existence continually rushes toward death and lack of being. Everything changes and dies, so that the reality which Thomas experiences has no anchoring point to give it stable meaning. There is only one point of rest or permanence, and that is death. To reach a feeling of absolute reality, Thomas must take on the perspective of God and see things in the perspective of their inevitable death. Only thus does he bring out the "beautiful and terrible worth of the earth." He reaches an eternal perspective by a "sympathetic identification with the temporal process of the world" (p. 215), and makes his poem a Noah's ark in which "self, world, and deity dwell together" (p. 216) safe from destruction.

Wallace Stevens is the first of these poets to reach the ontological goal represented fully by William Carlos Williams. "This vanishing of the gods . . . is the basis of all Stevens' thought and poetry" (p. 219), and he alternates between subjective and objective techniques to cope with this initial absence. Stevens experiments first with superficial, interacting images, with a "phenomenology of sensation" (p. 228) which is the only means of knowledge left in a world where God is dead. These images catch a perpetually moving reality and lead into a "perspectivism" or technique of "willed metamorphosis." Stevens uses metaphors to multiply perspectives on reality and to attain a momentary conjunction of man and the world. This conjunction is only an empty shell, however, for it does not contain any sense of inner reality. In a different approach, Stevens then effaces his own sense of identity before outside reality impressed on the mind. The images of a specially defined "abstraction" place in the mind the bare, first impression of an object: for example, an abstracted sun becomes a nameless "blazing gold disk in the sky" (p. 248). All abstraction reflects the mind, however, and Stevens' "objective" approach is no more satisfactory than his subjective imagination. Ultimately he goes beyond a simple dualism of subject and object, or his own attempt to reconcile the two. He finds that "the image is inextricably part of the thing . . . There is only one mode of existence: consciousness of some reality" (p. 274). Stevens develops his last poems as expressions of reality; he uses them to hint at an underlying "nothingness" which is the emptying out of opposites and an imageless essence of being. Through the poetry of being, man participates in life. "Speaking belongs to being, and in naming things in their presence poetry brings being into the open." Stevens has come round to a recognition of immanence in poetry which it will be Williams' role to explore, and he marks a transitional point which Miller calls "the next step forward in the spiritual history of man" (p. 283).

This next step is fully developed by William Carlos Williams. "In the work of Yeats, Thomas, and Stevens can be witnessed the difficult struggle to go beyond the old traditions. Williams goes farthest. He begins with the space of immanence and his work is a magnificent uncovering of its riches" (p. 358). Any original experience of romantic dualism is soon transcended, and Williams at the age of twenty suddenly abandons any sense of private consciousness for a feeling which he calls "interpenetration, both ways" (p. 287).

The marks of this interpenetration are a rejection of the old causal relationships and a belief in a simultaneous coexistence of all objects in one realm. Language itself belongs to this realm: words are objects, innately poetic in themselves, and need only to be set off and juxtaposed. Language is a kind of "silence" in that it exists, but does not signify. The poet's manipulation of syntax first "pulverizes" the sentence and then re-creates its words as "fluid energies" with a real life of their own. In Williams' poetry, "words are one thing, trees and flowers are another, but both are possessed within the same inner space" (p. 305). Both are real, but poetry heightens this one reality in words which are "an extension of the processes of the earth" (p. 310). The poem "focuses the world" while obliterating the private sense of both reader and poet, and creates "a new dimension of intimacy" in which mind and world unit (p. 312).

Williams, in order to achieve this poetic immanence, appeals to man's total consciousness. His words "are not primarily visual at all. They are meant to energize the mind in certain ways, and express in their sonority some quality of matter, thickness and weight, or airy delicacy, or any one of the other innumerable textures which our senses may know through words" (p. 313). Words are set apart to give them individual emphasis, juxtaposed to allow structures of interrelated meanings, calculated as a whole to "enter into a natural process and experience it inwardly" (p. 314), forced into puns or oppositions to create "vectors of power" (p. 315) which react upon the reader's consciousness, and made alive to the senses of touch, smell, taste, sound, and sight. Williams calls upon the sound patterns of language as well as on meanings; he creates a mental space with all the dimensions he can describe. After the five familiar senses, a final sense which permits him to communicate and "polarize" the world is the sexual sense. "Close to the kinesthetic way of knowing, but not identical with it, the sexual sense too takes the world into the body and recreates it there" (p. 321). Human beings can be read as easily as "flowers or fish," since their bodies and speech are identical with their inner lives. A strong sexual sense is the best means for realizing the erotic totality of another being. Indeed, Williams' writing, says Miller, "can be defined as an attempt to bring into existence, with silly words, an erotic space inhabited by a woman of the imagination" (p. 327). The poet uses in his poetry all the forms of human reaction: intellectual organization, the five senses, sexual impulses—any human experience he can reproduce in poetry to incarnate a feeling of immanent reality.

The fact that Williams believes in immanence does not mean that he easily achieves it. Three experiences, says Miller, are constantly at work in Williams' writing, and must be balanced off against one another in order to provide the dynamic presence which is required. These experiences reflect "the formless ground, origin of all things; the formed thing, defined and limited; a nameless presence . . . there in every form but hidden by it" (p. 328). It is in the interrelation of formless matter becoming form that Williams' "hidden flame" appears and creates a truly vital and authentic poetry. "Bringing the hidden flame to light is the central motivation of Williams' long career as a writer" (p. 333). This flame lies hidden in reality, and is made to appear when all three experiences coexist in dynamic equilibrium—in a certain "flowering, since things appear before the reader in their words and rise there to a new manifestation" (pp. 351–352). Williams strives to achieve a perpetual radiant balance in which "the poem maintains forever in living poise the moment between birth and death" (p. 358). His goal of metaphysical equilibrium brings with it a new technique, and combines the different aspects of reality to reveal through them a dynamic presence. This presence in things, or this immanence, obliterates and surpasses the earlier tragic distinction of subject and object. In a new and nondoctrinal formulation, it serves to reintroduce the idea of God under a new name: the living presence of reality.

Miller's *Poets of Reality* completes the spiritual history of literature begun in *The Disappearance of God*. The outlines of this history have already been given in Poulet's work, and Miller is evidently heavily indebted to Poulet. His decision to analyze worlds of consciousness, his concept of a progressive history of consciousness, and his technique of selecting indicative passages to reveal a writer's metaphysical position all recall Poulet. References to French sources are more than ever apparent in this book, which is the historical and theoretical apogee of Miller's existential theory applied to literature. Comparisons abound to French and English works, but not to German, Italian, Spanish, Russian, or to any other national literature. Terms familiar from Poulet's criticism reappear here used in Miller's own context: human time and human space, the space of the poem as a mental space, the circle and periphery of a writer's consciousness, a writer's starting point or initial situation, sympathetic instead of exterior or objective criticism, and the ideal of "authentic" writing. Miller's chapters, like Poulet's essays, are broken up into the progressive steps of a writer's spiritual adventure, and his book as a whole is structured on historical and metaphysical progressions. Yeats has "come a long way" (p. 100), Eliot's "career as a whole" (p. 179) is an heroic effort in a certain direction, and Williams "reaches at the age of twenty the place which Wallace Stevens attains only after decades of struggle" (p. 287). This belief in a progress of the Romantic perspective from the nineteenth to twentieth centuries is a special development of Poulet's belief that literary figures incarnate a progression of historical attitudes. Like Poulet again, Miller tends to restrict his references to nineteenth and twentieth-century Romantic literature and its early antecedents, and evolves a criticism which is actually more an explanation of contemporary literary thought than a method of appreciating world literature.

Miller is not merely a disciple of Poulet, however. He combines Poulet's existential approach with its apparent opposite, the formal perspective. As a critic educated in the English tradition, and as one who wishes to adapt the existential view for English literature and English audiences, he naturally tries to synthesize both approaches. He upholds a comprehensive, alternating reading which moves from level to level of interpretation—from circle to concentric circle—in a "systole and diastole of criticism." [5] Miller recognizes that there may be several interrelated manners of reading, and practices a wider, more synthetic analysis than does Poulet, who never abandons his distrust of formal observations. At a point in the analysis where Poulet prefers to read between the lines in order to discover connected themes, Miller usually moves to another circle and attacks the problem from another critical position.

5. Miller, *The Disappearance of God*, p. ix.

Miller, more than Poulet, tends to venture into the formal circle, and to emphasize the effect of a writer's metaphysical position on his poetic technique. Where Poulet collates existential literary perceptions to write a history of consciousness in literature, Miller never abandons the study of style in various circles of interpretation. His criticism always focuses upon the tension between formal and existential impulses in a text. Conrad uses an extremely precise description, with its consequent sense of detachment, to obtain a qualitative spectacle. Yeats uses phrases which suggest transition: "'almost disembodied ecstasy' wavers with characteristic hesitation . . . 'dove-grey' is not quite grey." [6] Eliot's dramatic monologues are completely subjective, whereas Browning's are not: Prufrock speaks to himself, but "Browning's monologuists are usually speaking to someone . . . If both speaker and auditor can see the portrait of the last duchess . . . then these objects have an existence which would continue even if the duke were not there" (p. 137). The essay on Williams is Miller's most consistent effort to link formal qualities with existential effects:

> The simplicity of the sentence structure here, and the emphasis on the tensions between the words makes them stand separate and yet together. Rhythm also works to achieve this end . . . The independence of the words in the poem matches the independence of the things they name. The short lines and brief monosyllables of Williams' verse have exactly the opposite effect from the long rapidly rolling blurred periods of Whitman's line, with its tendency to absorb all particulars into one sonorous whole (p. 298).

Miller's discussion of the manipulation of syntax in Williams makes direct links between formal technique and its existential effect on the reader. On "The Locust Tree in Flower," he comments,

> the verb presupposes a plural subject, so the reader must balance between the possibility that the word "has" may have been left out and the assumption that "come" is to be taken as an imperative. This grammatical uncertainty forces him to hold all the words before his attention at once as he tries various ways to make a sentence of them . . . this is exactly what the poet wants. The

6. Miller, *Poets of Reality*, p. 77.

poem is as much all there at once as the locust tree itself, in its tension of branches, leaves, and flowers (p. 304).

Grammar, the most abstract and unemotional aspect of language, has suddenly become an existential tool with its own ability to formulate reality. Only a critic who still notices and appreciates the intricacies of technical detail will be able to make the link between both aspects of literature.

It is this ability to balance both the formal and the existential perspectives, and to make some sense between them, that makes Miller the most useful of the critics of consciousness in terms of traditional literary interpretation. To be sure, the religious implications of *The Disappearance of God* and *Poets of Reality* restrict his analysis to writers who fall into a particular romantic and neo-romantic pattern. Only future books will show if this restriction is caused by Miller's temporary choice of subject or by his adherence to a humanistic and religious development of the criticism of consciousness.[7] Meanwhile, by discussing grammar, images, rhythm, onomatapoiea, and other technical devices, he has given the uncommitted reader a chance to follow a "reading of consciousness" through techniques that are public and objective.

7. Miller has written an article on "Literature and Religion" in *Relations of Literary Study* (New York: Modern Language Association, 1967), and has at present two books scheduled for publication: *The Form of Victorian Fiction* (four lectures given at Notre Dame in the spring of 1967), and a book on Thomas Hardy.

PART III | THE NEGATIVE CONSCIOUSNESS

MAURICE BLANCHOT

Maurice Blanchot's novels and criticism employ an existential perspective which is complementary to, rather than identical with, the Geneva approach. In any general consideration of the criticism of consciousness, he must be set off as a mirror image of the Geneva critics; the outlines are the same, but the signs are reversed. Blanchot's philosophy refers to a negative rather than to a positive presence; the "presence" or "immanent being" that the Geneva critics see in literature is for Blanchot an "absence," a formless, characterless "antipresence" underlying language and literature. Moreover, where the Geneva critics are subjective, Blanchot is objective; where they emphasize an individual author's experience, he identifies each author with an impersonal or absolute creator. To him, the literary text is not an author's personal,

221

positive expression but an independent entity—a self-sufficient act which uses author and reader only as buttresses of an independent verbalized experience. A novelist as well as a critic, Blanchot combines his critical perspective with his vision as a creative artist and tries to reproduce the same antiexistence in his novels that his criticism finds in all literature. The critical attitudes of the Geneva School and Maurice Blanchot are as polarized as the notions of matter and antimatter. His nihilistic vision counterbalances the positive interpretations the Geneva School gives to existential criticism. Blanchot thus merits an extended treatment in his own right, to restore a balanced view of the whole theory of consciousness in literature.

Blanchot is not an academic critic. His reviews and essays in various journals embrace a far wider scope than the Geneva studies, which usually fall back upon the works of recognized "great" authors. The role of literary journalist leads him to pursue a variable, lively, and truly contemporary criticism, as he considers in turn literary, philosophical, anthropological, political, and linguistic publications. He is not confined to the so-called "great" works, even among present-day authors, and his topics may range as far as the "proper use of science-fiction." However, the wide field of reference which Blanchot manipulates as a reviewer and essayist is limited in import by the extremely circumscribed, metaphysical experience which he brings to bear upon each work.

Blanchot tries to identify, for each text, the absolute existential movement which creates it: an unchanging relationship which exists among author, work, and reader as the work emerges from an indefinable basic existence. This analytical perspective is peculiarly his own, and one which he uses in the plots of his novels and "récits" as well as in literary criticism. It stems from philosophy more than from literary history, and recalls an existential tradition rooted in the works of Kierkegaard and Heidegger.

Emmanuel Levinas points out the relationship between Blanchot and Heidegger's late philosophy, and suggests that the French critic's theory comprises a pessimistic corollary of "non-truth" to the German philosopher's consideration that art founds an existential "truth." [1] The differ-

1. Emmanuel Levinas, "Maurice Blanchot et le regard du poète," *Monde Nouveau Paru*, no. 98 (March 1956), pp. 7–8, 14–19.

ence between Heidegger and Blanchot is that Blanchot's "truth" is interior; he does not believe that external reality may be grasped in any way. Blanchot's refusal to accept external reality, and his concentration upon absolute subjective experience, thus distinguish him both from Heidegger and the Geneva School.

Blanchot never seems to accept the so-called phenomenological reduction by which one assumes an exterior reality, for the only reality which he will admit is language, felt and manipulated by the artist. The universe is not knowledgeable, except as it appears in the "absence" evoked by language. Similarly, the writer explores the human condition in a solipsistic manner; he examines the relationship of language to his own experience, as he expresses it. Although it is usual to speak of Blanchot as a "phenomenological" critic, and of Poulet as "existential," a more accurate use of the two terms might reverse these applications. Blanchot's inwardly turned vision does not examine any facets of reality exterior to the subject, and his theory rejects the idea of a separate, positive existence. Poulet, on the contrary, belongs to a school of thought that recognizes as valid the author's relationships with reality, and builds systems of existence only upon these integrated perceptions. Although Poulet likes to return to a writer's "pure" thought, free of its objects, his original attitude assumes that consciousness has an object and develops itself in relation to external reality. Blanchot's system is more interior than that of the Geneva School, for his method confines itself to the sentient being rather than to that being's impression of an outside universe.

Blanchot differs from the Geneva School in emphasis, not in philosophical position. Like the Geneva critics, he is interested in literature because it best expresses experience; like them, he will not subordinate literature to psychological, sociological, or even surrealist standards. Poulet himself remarks that Blanchot's criticism clearly represents the "criticism of consciousness," and that "there is no purer one." "Literature of literature, consciousness of consciousness," [2] this criticism is distinguished from Geneva criticism not so much by its nature as by its scope: by the fact that Blanchot does not attempt to identify "this something which was the object of thought" (p. 10). Both he and the Geneva

2. Georges Poulet, preface in Jean-Pierre Richard, *Littérature et sensation* (Paris: Le Seuil, 1954), p. 9.

critics define literature as an act, as an experience in which writer and reader move toward self-knowledge. In addition, both emphasize the role of language as a medium of self-creation and communication. Literature for all these critics is an act of awareness in which the writer communicates his sense of reality. They differ in their definition of this reality. The Geneva School analyzes a personal experience while Blanchot concentrates upon an impersonal experience, upon language as the only felt reality. Both, however, are concerned with the same problem: how to define literature itself as an act or experience.

These two approaches are complementary, for they discuss two aspects of the same act. The Geneva critics are concerned with an author's unique experience, but they rarely discuss the *connection* between this experience and the written text. Blanchot, though not a formal critic, does concentrate upon the verbal level of literature, and analyzes the way in which experience becomes form. He does not look at the author as a human being to be recognized for himself, but as a figure who contributes to the creative process. This creative process results in the "act" of literature, in the existential "explosion" of a true reading. Like the Geneva School, Blanchot speaks of an author's "authenticity," which can be tested only by exploring his sense of language. However, where the Geneva critics are often content to assert without analyzing this coincidence of experience and composition, Blanchot examines the metamorphosis of experience into writing.

This metamorphosis, the creative "act" of literature, is the subject of all Blanchot's novels and criticism. This act is impersonal; it derives from the talent of the writer but is completed only by the reader's sympathetic attention. Blanchot's criticism continually focuses on such an act, from his earlier general articles to his later concentrated studies of literary creation. His shorter articles in the 1940's deal with a wide range of literary attitudes, but his concern with metaphorical and magical literature shows that he is already preoccupied with changes of being. He does not include many topical articles in his first collections, *Faux pas* (1943) and *La Part du feu* (1949). Rather, he puts in essays that more openly express his theory of literature. *Faux pas* and *La Part du feu* collect essays that are loosely connected by common subject matter. They all discuss Blanchot's ideas of literature, the writer, and reality. On the other hand, *L'Espace littéraire* (1955) and *Le Livre à venir*

(1959) contain essays that were evidently written to find their place in a book-length exposition. Blanchot organizes his chapters in sequence to reveal progressively a theory of the "space" of literature and of the text that incarnates the literary "act." As he refines this theory in his later articles, he tends to use a more limited frame of reference and a more abstract style. His essays become metaphorical, abstractly lyrical analyses of the literary act. Blanchot's recent work repeatedly evokes an identical experience of literature, which he has gradually reduced to a consistent structure and terminology.

Blanchot writes novels as well as literary criticism, and he uses both genres impartially to express his literary theories. His novels, in fact, are built upon his critical theory of verbal creation. They cannot be understood apart from it. Their style reflects his attempt to explore the connection of language with the ever-changing experience it frames, and their subject is an evocation of the creative experience itself. Blanchot describes his earlier books as "romans," and his later ones as "récits." A récit, according to him, is a tale that evokes the central, inspiring experience of a possible novel. All Blanchot's work explores the experience of conscious creation, either symbolized in novels or analyzed in essays; and this experience acts as a constant referent, providing its own characteristic atmosphere and tone. It is the focus of his criticism as well as of his novels, for Blanchot's essays revolve around the same creative experience clothed in the works of other authors. The reference of his analysis is consequently unique and private, rather than universal and public. Blanchot creates literary works in both essays and evocations. Continually plumbing the depths of artistic experience, knowledge, and creation, he uses his own and others' creations to send back the signals of one basic existential experience. To this aim and critical method he adds the excitement of genuine literary talent. Blanchot's readers find him both an original literary artist and a keen analyst of literature.

Blanchot has not actually changed his literary theory; but he has refined, transformed, and presented it in many different shapes. Its first and simplest form appears in three early essays: "Comment la littérature est-elle possible?" (1941), the preface to *Faux pas* (1943), and "La Littérature et le droit à la mort" (1947–1948). The first deals with the existential "possibility" of literature, the second deals with the position of the writer, and the third with the work's relation to reality. Other essays take up related topics, such as the reader's experience, but in these three Blanchot gives the outlines of his own basic literary perspective.

Blanchot's first discussion of literary theory appears in "Comment la littérature est-elle possible?" (1941), an essay (reprinted with some changes in *Faux pas*) that discusses Jean Paulhan's *Les Fleurs de Tarbes* (1941). Blanchot takes up Paulhan's condemnation of a purist "Terror" in modern thought that will not allow writers to emphasize decorative or formal elements—that keeps them from "picking flowers." The "Terrorists" reject elegant speech and rhetorical convention because they hate anything that obscures meaningful composition. Clichés and elegant turns of speech, they maintain, obscure accurate expression. Blanchot sympathizes with their aims, but says they misunderstand the nature of the problem. There is no pure and absolute meaning that can be reached by peeling off layers of convention; instead, literature must accept and work with all possible accumulated meanings. If literature were to be absolutely unique, a pure personal expression, it would be a perfect silence, unflawed by public language. "At the heart of each writer," says Blanchot, "there is a demon urging him to strike dead all literary forms . . . to interrogate in an inexpressible manner what he is and what he does." [3] But if he gives in to this demon, he must be silent; as a Terrorist in search of perfect expression, he must give up his craft in despair.

Blanchot, then, is not a Terrorist. Although he sympathizes with their goals, he cannot agree with their remedy. On the contrary, he would plunge into more "formal" rhetoric to cope with the same "impossibility" of literature. If literature is truly "impossible," as is perfect communication, then the Terrorists must eliminate the false sense of security that deludes them (and all writers) into thinking that any language describes reality. Once a writer realizes that no language provides a transcription of reality, but only clothes it in "an overlay of impurity and degradation," [4] he is ready to struggle with the real problems of literary expression. He turns away from the objects he thought he could describe, and toward the words he uses to express his own experience. His aim

3. Maurice Blanchot, *Faux pas* (Paris: Gallimard, 1943), p. 102. This essay was first published in three sections in the *Journal des Débats:* "La Terreur dans les lettres," *JdD* October 24, 1941, and "Comment la littérature est-elle possible?" in *JdD*, November 25, 1941, p. 3, and December 2, 1941, p. 3. It was also published as a separate pamphlet, "Comment la littérature est-elle possible?" by Corti in 1942.
4. Blanchot, *Faux pas*, p. 104.

now is to accentuate the closest reality and to examine his language in the light of changing experience. "Thought is to become pure again, a virgin and innocent contact, not by withdrawing itself from words but in the intimacy of speech" (p. 106). Blanchot's "literature" is only "possible" when a deeply experimental rhetoric works to unite public language and private experience.

Existential rhetoric is only one aspect of literature's "possibility," an aspect that depends upon the creative ingenuity of the existential writer. Blanchot's preface to *Faux pas* takes up the situation of the existential writer who realizes that silence is the only "pure" expression, but who is impelled to write in order to give shape to his sense of existence. Such a writer chooses to express his experience rather than merely to feel it; he is a writer and not a mystic. The existential writer consciously distorts what he feels as the basic, colorless, impersonal fact of existence to create against it the written record of his own personality.

Blanchot's writer must seem to communicate in order to recognize himself. Although he cannot really communicate, as each man is inescapably alone, he must describe his solitude to a potential "witness"; otherwise it exists in a vacuum, and has no meaning. "It is not the person who is alone who feels alone; this monster of desolation must have the presence of another for his desolation to have meaning" (p. 10). The use of language itself implies communication and brings another being into perspective. Language also creates a work that can be read by others, one over which the writer, *qua* writer, no longer has unique control.

The writer as creator—even as existential creator—is separate from his work. After it is written he is no longer linked to it, and he cannot be reached (as the Geneva critics would like) through his subordinate role in the new existential text. He has created the work out of his own experience, but it surpasses him. "The author has produced more than himself . . . what he has created is henceforth a source of values whose fecundity surpasses by far the energy dispensed at its birth" (p. 15). The writer is cut off from his work, as the man is cut off from reality. He exists in a peculiar "state of man" (p. 11), a condition of frustrated existential awareness from which there is no issue. He writes to give meaning to his solitude but his work, once written, abandons its source and returns the author to his original isolation.

The author's solitude brings with it a real "anguish," for he cannot create his own identity either with other human beings or without them. This "anguish" is always with him: he is led to it by the act of writing, he expresses it when he tries to write, and through writing he comes to see it as the basic human condition. "Anguish . . . deprives him of the means of being in relationship with another . . . it rejects him out of himself and . . . confuses him with what he is not" (p. 21). Anguish, then, sets the pattern for his work; and he creates in response to its demands.

The existential writer is himself a symbol and "paradox of anguish," for he unites the character of a "mute who has lost his speech" with that of a "master of oratory" (pp. 12–13). He is a mute because he knows that he cannot truly express anything; he is a master of oratory because he masters the unreal craft of language. The writer is always torn between the desire to use his ability and the desire to surpass it—always tempted to sacrifice his identity as an artist to keep the vision of an inexpressible reality. Blanchot's writer is forced to choose between a silence that ignores language (and destroys the writer), and a constant struggle to take language to the brink of silence. If he chooses to explore language—to be an existential writer—then he must reject any kind of "automatic writing." He cannot accept the surrealist theory that the unconscious mind speaks for itself, or that the writer can transcribe reality by a flow of spontaneous, uncontrolled associations. Nor can he accept the kind of "automatic writing" that Blanchot defines as the "habitual form of writing." When an author strings together a series of accepted, unexplored words, then he too is indulging in automatism: the automatism of clichés. Any writing that depends upon language alone, to the detriment of continual mental analysis, falls short of authentic expression. Moreover, there is an automatism already embodied in language, for words have a wealth of public associations that usurp a writer's control. The writer, in "anguish," must test his language for meaning; otherwise he cannot overcome its inertia. Unless he tests each expression, each rule, he cannot achieve an authentic vision of existence. Even this effort, however, is ultimately futile, as language itself is a barrier to communication. Because language must be used, it sets the work apart from an experience that cannot be described, an experience Blanchot calls "non-sense." Because the writer himself touches only a part of the finished work ("as the aesthetic consciousness is only conscious of a part of what it makes"), his effort to grasp existence is also doomed to failure. But within this failure art takes place. The "effort to attain absolute necessity . . . cannot end, and it is this impossibility of succeeding . . . which makes it constantly possible" (p. 26). Literary creation is the possible, positive result of an impossible situation; it is actually a flaw in the very movement it tries to convey.

Blanchot's essay "La Littérature et le droit à la mort" adds another dimension to his theory of literature. First published in 1947 and 1948, in two sections, it has been reprinted as the last chapter of La Part du feu. This essay is more comprehensive than the preceding two. It is more analytical and less assertive. Above all, it focuses on two aspects of literary language: this language's connection with reality, and its relation to the writer.

Blanchot uses two words to describe language's connection with reality: the word "death" used to describe a loss of personal identity in art, and the word "absence" to describe the falsification of reality that exists each time an object is named. "Death" expresses the transformation of personal identity that occurs as part of the literary act. Similarly, objects find a "death" or "absence" when they are named. Blanchot does not originate the idea of an "absence" behind words: it is a familiar existential notion. But he extends it to include a larger "absence" that lies behind all literature and personal experience.

Language here functions in two ways: it appears to communicate, but it actually destroys communication by removing reality from the object it names. "Before I can say: this woman, I must take away from her her flesh and blood reality in one way or another, must render her absent and annihilate her. The word gives me the being, but gives it to me deprived of being." [5] Blanchot discovers, in this deprivation of being, an inherent "dead" aspect of language in all literary creation. "Death," or the annihilation of being, gives language a negative role which the writer must first comprehend and then try to use. In Blanchot's example of the word woman, the "death" or negation of her reality is another indication of her mortality—an indirect reference to a non-being of basic existence in which individual life and literature are both

5. Blanchot, La Part du feu (Paris: Gallimard, 1949), p. 325.

departures from the rule. "Death" both destroys man and makes him aware of his humanity ("man knows [death] only because he is human, and he is human only because he incarnates death") (p. 339). But language's destruction of reality also makes it possible to communicate past reality.

> My speech is the warning that death has been, at this very moment, let loose in the world, that it has abruptly loomed up between me speaking and the being to whom I speak: it is between us like the distance which separates us, but this distance is also what prevents us from being separated, for it contains the condition of all understanding. Death alone permits me to grasp what I wish to attain; it is, for words, the only possibility of their meaning (p. 326).

The double-edged destruction of language forces literature to be impersonal. Just as language destroys reality, it also destroys or transforms the writer. As soon as an existence is named, it becomes inert: the writer implied in the subjective *Je* destroys himself as much as he destroys the object, woman, or cat he describes. Writer, reader, and text find common ground in this state of "death," which eliminates all their personal qualities.

Literature thus destroys all personal traits to become a neutral knowledge of death and absence—of nothingness. In typically paradoxical and metaphorical terms, Blanchot imagines literature as a knowledge-less knowledge, which stands like a conscious, perceiving shadow behind the personification of ignorance. "Literature is that experience through which consciousness discovers its being in its inability to lose consciousness . . . it reconstitutes for itself, beyond unconsciousness . . . a haggard knowledge, which knows nothing, which no one knows, and which ignorance finds always behind itself, like its shadow changed into a look" (pp. 333–334). The play upon knowledge and non-knowledge, being and nonbeing, recurs throughout Blanchot's analyses of language and literature.

In Blanchot's interpretation, language is made up of a series of absences—of nothings. The more successful the communication, the more it piles nothingness upon absence. "Negation is connected to language. In the beginning, I do not speak to say something, but there is a nothing which demands to speak, nothing speaks, nothing finds its being in speech and the being of speech is nothing" (p. 327). Language itself implies a movement toward nothingness. Since "it owes its meaning not to what exists, but to its retreat before existence," language's tendency is to perfect itself by speaking consciously of notions, or absences. "If one speaks of things only by saying about them what makes them nothing, well then, to say nothing is the only hope of saying everything." Blanchot plays with two senses of "saying nothing" in order to impress upon his reader the idea that literature is actually a fictitious arrangement of empty signs, all of which point to an ever absent reality.

The absolute meaninglessness of each word does not make it useless as a tool for communication; the *non-cat* is still not a *non-dog*. A writer may skim across the surface of reality by using language as empty images. Common, public language is content with this skimming, but literary language knows that it skims and is uneasy about doing so. "It sees a difficulty and even a lie there. How can it hope to have accomplished its mission, because it has transposed the irreality of the thing into the reality of language?" (p. 328). Literary language is not satisfied with the partial reality it conveys. It realizes that "speech does not suffice to the truth which it contains," and that this "truth" exists in the very experience which language necessarily misses. "The language of literature is the search after this moment which precedes it. Generally, it calls it existence" (p. 329). Literary language evokes this "moment which precedes it" by examining its own nature as a false—but necessary—representation of reality.

Blanchot's "literary language" accepts as reality the concrete, textual existence of words, and employs them in all their written aspects of "rhythm, weight, mass, shape," plus "the paper on which one writes, the trace of the ink, the book" (p. 330). In a paradoxical development that can only please this lover of paradoxes, Blanchot goes beyond his previous denial that words define reality, and accepts their reality on another plane. Words still communicate, but not because they indicate a shared exterior reality. They are themselves the *reality of human experience,* expressed in the only concrete form available to man. "The name ceases to be the ephemeral passage of nonexistence to become a concrete ball, a clump of existence." "Literature has well triumphed over the meaning of words, but what it has found in words taken out of their meaning is the meaning become thing" (p. 333). Words as incantatory powers give rise to a new presence of objects. "The word acts . . . like an incantation which compels things, makes them *really* present out of themselves . . . Literature . . . is the presence of things, before the *world* is, their perseverance after the world has disappeared" (p. 330). The literary universe is purely mental; therefore it is close to the mind creating it and to the mind reading it. Concrete reality for this universe is the forceful impact of intangible words.

Literature, in this view, contains two perspectives upon the same existential reality. As language, it *represents* the death inherent in humanity and human relationships, and the background of nonbeing into which all apparent being is resolved. As literature, it *evokes* this same hypothesized impersonal existence: "Literature is then the concern with the reality of things, with their unknown, free, and silent existence" (p. 332). Language itself contains the potentiality of these two aspects, for "speech only makes the word a two-faced monster: reality which is material presence and meaning which is ideal absence" (p. 342). However, it is literature that creates the fictional existence communicated to the reader, in which the reader no longer comprehends separate facts (on the level of language) but absorbs a new existence evoked by fictional creation. Blanchot's "literary language" is ambiguous in that it produces, as literature, an existential creation which employs, surpasses, and yet rests upon language's own nature as negative reality. It is this double sense which underlies the phenomenon of literature and which, in Blanchot's theory, comprises the existential importance of the literary act.

The work of art, to Blanchot, is an autonomous, impersonal, and dynamic act. A text has been created and will be read, but its existential reality consists in an intermediate state related to neither writer nor reader. The act of literature is only superficially dependent upon writer and reader: it is an independent "explosion" created between their two existences when the work is read. Both writer and reader may be studied as separate entities with distinct existential patterns: the writer as a creator who must exploit the communicative nature of language even while striving for an uncommunicable existence, and the reader as a re-creator who submits his own individuality to the new life of the work and accepts the reality of language in place of his own subjective experience. However, writer and reader are in fact independent of the work to which both contribute.

In Blanchot's view, the created text is the ultimate independent reality. It reflects and is completed by the personalities of writer and reader, but only in the degree to which each forgets himself in an impersonal existential experience. The poem is "creative speech which forms its objects," [6] and necessarily surpasses the poet. "Poetry does not really belong to the poet, because it is bound to a reality which infinitely surpasses him; it is something which can be made without the creator's having any right over it" (p. 162). Blanchot does not agree with the Geneva critics, who hold that one existential experience runs throughout a series of texts by the same author. Rather, he believes that each individual poem contains its own autonomous act, and that by doing so it represents existence as well as does any personal experience. "There is in each poem an act which sends us back to poetry glimpsed in its essence, essence which, itself, can be glimpsed and exists only in the poem" (p. 167). This essence is a tension aimed at absent reality: "The poem travels toward absence, but to re-create with it total reality; it is tension towards the imaginary." [7] Poetry suggests, mentally and verbally, the nonverbal experience toward which it moves.

This power of evoking essences emerges from a special kind of writing, a newly defined "rhetoric." Blanchot's use of the word "rhetoric," a word normally associated with sterility, shows that he is able to give new and "rethought" meaning to an established notion. By "rhetoric," he still means the artificial manipulation of language for its own sake, but he also means that form of language which removes attention from itself in order to direct the reader's attention to an underlying existence. Existential "rhetoric," as a form of expression, is consciously dull and insipid, mainly because it aims to diminish any strong sense of outside reality. It immolates language in that it negates its own ability to compel attention through striking phrases. Blanchot's "rhetoric" is as neutral and impersonal as the existential act it conveys.

Blanchot's essay "Grève désolée, obscur malaise" (the title itself taken from two clichés) outlines this aspect of style, in which "to write poorly

6. Blanchot, *Faux pas*, p. 159.
7. Blanchot, *La Part du feu*, p. 110.

is to write well." Julien Gracq, he points out, has a "magical" style which reaches a particular effect of *being* through cumbersome, adjectival sentences. The heaviness and length of these sentences destroy literary expression. The style itself "ruins the word by the too-numerous supports which it provides." This ruin allows the author to convey a certain existential feeling, for "a writer can wish to be weighty." [8] "And what if he must, in a certain sense, write poorly? If he should want the impression of awkwardness and disarray to . . . compromise the very form which is to make it tangible?" The world of Gracq's novels is a "qualitative world, that is to say, magic," and its magic consists principally in this new manner of conveying existence. "In magic, things seek to exist in a conscious manner, and consciousness approaches the existence of things" (p. 136). Thus the aim of the modern existential novel (for Blanchot finds Gracq typical of this modern French style) is not at all to create a beautiful book, but to reach for a sense of existence through consciously colorless prose.

In an essay comparing Lautréamont and Henry Miller, Blanchot draws a comparison between existential rhetoric and aesthetic language. Both authors, he maintains, show an inner compulsion, a dominating central force. In Lautréamont's *Maldoror* "we are the prey of a devouring power which drags us into a bewildering series of metamorphoses." In Miller there is "this violent, indefatigable march, this exaltation, which calls up a harassing and crushing sense from the depths of a text where the details are not exceptional nor the ideas very important." [9] Lautréamont's mastery of all the elements of composition (his inclusion, for example, of the ultimate and self-metamorphosing element of humor) creates a more transparent work than Miller's excessively personal use of language. In *Black Spring* Miller is unable to subordinate his individual aesthetic impulse to the independent existence of the work. "The language is always there, the words keep their meaning, the images are beautiful images. The fact is that Miller's world is a too-human world, in which revolt has its limits" (p. 178). As a result, the author is not able to achieve "the movement which a work of perfect rhetoric like *Maldoror* never ceases to bring about

8. Blanchot, "Grève désolée, obscur malaise," *Cahiers de la Pléiade,* no. 2 (April 1947), p. 134.
9. Blanchot, *La Part du feu,* p. 171.

. . . the passage from metaphor to metamorphosis" (p. 179). In perfect rhetoric an author's thought cannot be distinguished from his
work, which creates its own overriding personality.

Among the critics of consciousness, Blanchot is most concerned with
the independence of the created work; and for this reason he has been
called a "formal" rather than an existential critic. Only a very slipshod
use of "formal" could associate him with English and American "formalists," but he does maintain a sense of separate works which distinguishes him from the Geneva critics. Blanchot is concerned with the
separate, self-contained form of each work, rather than with a personal
document extending through several works. Like the Geneva critics,
he speaks of a novel's "core, the interior pole which is the vision of
the novelist, the feeling (explicit or not) whose command he follows,"
but he accents the fact that this core is "inseparable from the concrete
organization in which it is developed." [10] For Blanchot, what is apparently author, model, or subject in a work is actually a particular
aspect of the completed independent act. To identify aspects of the
novel from the outside alone is to neglect their "authentic relationships" inside the "universe of forms and words." [11] *Maldoror,* the example of perfect rhetoric, is also the ultimate achievement of style
working to exist independently. It is a work which has become a veritable *thing* because its various qualities are assimilated into one driving
overall impression. Here language is truly transparent: the work is
comprehended as a series of metamorphoses, of existential tensions for
which the author, the language, and the apparent subject matter exist
only as effaced and contributing parts.

Blanchot's conscious use of language cannot be called reactionary
or "classical," as some would have it.[12] He is not a strict formalist; he
merely wants to apply existential perspectives to formal problems. In
other words, he combines the novelist's care for language with the
theorist's belief in existence. For Blanchot, the language of literature
evokes a chaotic fundamental existence through a conscious rhetoric,
and so achieves effects that are "magical" and "marvelous."

10. Blanchot, "Le Roman pur," *Journal des Débats,* December 4–5, 1943, p. 2.
11. Blanchot, *Faux pas,* pp. 225–226.
12. Alexandre Astruc, "A Propos de 'Fax-pas,'" *Poésie 44,* no. 19 (May-June 1944), p. 90.

This existential rhetoric, or magical expression in which "the unlikely is the truth of the real," [13] cannot be overemphasized. It describes the style of all Blanchot's novels. In an essay of 1948, "Du Merveilleux," he again outlines his literary theory while ostensibly discussing current novels that contain fantastic themes. The "marvelous" world (like Gracq's "magical" world) is a realm in which the author, by suspending exterior reality, can use purely subjective observations to create an interior world. Marvelous vision (like the "act" of literature) is independent: "the marvelous presupposes a reader and author who are themselves imaginary, consequently rather removed from the regions of our habitual geography" (p. 125). All Blanchot's novels exist in such a magical realm, where the experience of literature is discussed in allegorical or symbolic terms.

Thomas l'obscur, published in 1941 and revised in 1950, is the first of Blanchot's existential novels. It describes the struggle of the author (as a personified absolute) to lose himself in a kind of death by which he comes into contact with the absolute work. This work is personified as Anne, and she, like the author, will "die" in order to be expressed: "to give nothingness a body." [14] Certain themes of existential or personal importance to Blanchot find themselves symbolized as part of the narrative: Thomas' look destroys the reality of the people he meets ("each man died as he met him") only to resuscitate them "shapeless and mute" (pp. 56–57). The writer "betrays" the work, but in ambiguous terms which could apply to existential theory or to an ordinary misunderstanding: "He was not deceiving her, and yet she was deceived by him" (p. 69). At certain points ordinary realistic description sets the tone, such as in the landscape descriptions at the beginning and end, or when Anne is discovered "sleeping" on a garden bench. However, in addition to these scenes Blanchot injects into the work strange metamorphoses, futile searches, and bizarre events which jerk the narrative out of familiar surroundings and compel a "marvelous" interpretation. Thomas fights with a giant rat; he listens to an oracular cat in a tunnel ("O superior cat that I have become for an instant to attest to my death," p. 46); he digs his own tomb for the seventh time

13. Blanchot, "Du Merveilleux," *L'Arche*, nos. 27–28 (August-September 1948), p. 123.
14. Blanchot, *Thomas l'obscur* (Paris: Gallimard, 1950), p. 130.

and tries to climb inside it; and when he meets Anne she continually changes shape. At one point she appears as a gigantic, ferocious black spider with eight legs. The book, for the most part, is written in the third person, although the point of view alternates from Anne to Thomas: only in chapter eleven does Thomas use the subjective *Je*.

All the events in *Thomas l'obscur* may be interpreted according to Blanchot's literary theory. The same theoretical correspondence holds true for later novels, in which the style itself comes closer to Blanchot's description of neutral, colorless speech; but the earlier novels are marked by a taste for the bizarre which the author tones down in his later tales.

Amindanab, published a year after *Thomas*, is clearly bizarre, but includes a plot symbolic of the literary experience. An ambiguous signal seems to summon its hero, Thomas, into a roadside building. He tries to answer the summons by making his way to the fourth floor; and when he finally discovers Lucie, she denies having called him. The scene, which ends in a night of oblivion, immediately recalls death motifs in *Thomas l'obscur*. Symbolic descriptions abound: Thomas is asked first to rent an underground, lightless room from which he must try to work his way out to the light. (The image of the writer's isolated cell of human existence also appears in *L'Arrêt de mort* and *Le Dernier Homme*.) There is an obvious symbolism in the names: Thomas (Doubting Thomas?) digs his way into the ground (probes the depths) in his search for a way out. His nails split, and heliotropes grow out to show him the way to the light. This "light" is Lucie. Such symbolic acts pervade Blanchot's entire work, but they become less fantastic and more ordinary as time goes on.

Blanchot's last novel of fantastic rhetoric is *L'Arrêt de mort* (1948). Its narrative form, and occasionally its manner of vision, strongly recall Poe's *Ligeia;* the comparison is not improbable, as Blanchot, the same year, mentions *Ligeia* in "Du Merveilleux." The hero of *L'Arrêt de mort* is closely associated with J., whose horoscope predicts that she will not die. J. dies, revives at the author's return, and dies once more. It is only then that what is "extraordinary" and "important" happens. The author lives with a "thought" which "is not entirely a person, even if it acts and lives like one." [15] He meets Nathalie, who is also com-

15. Blanchot, *L'Arrêt de mort* (Paris: Gallimard, 1948), p. 62.

pared to a thought. In a series of gradual approaches to a truth obliquely implied, he "recognizes" her and accepts her companionship as an eternal part of his life. *L'Arrêt de mort* begins this transformation of fantastic stories into colorless existential situations: although the characters are still generally recognizable, their outlines are blurred. Nathalie may be introduced as "on," so that the pronoun referring to her becomes "il"; then again a new schema of references begins with "la personne," and the pronoun becomes the feminine "elle." Blanchot systematically removes the accustomed clues to recognition so that the reader is left merely with an existential situation repeated in various contexts. After *L'Arrêt de mort*, Blanchot's tales omit the more melodramatic aspects of fantastic tales, and strive towards a purely transparent form as he has described it: one in which the striking effects of language and description are subordinated to a pale, colorless expression conveying an extraordinary series of existential tensions.

Blanchot's novels are all subjective, and his subject is an impersonal experience. In other words, he describes the perceptive universe of this subject, but withdraws from the figure itself any characterizing qualities. The artist-subject emerges in the text as an impersonal subject conceived by an absolute creator.

This impersonal subject and creator is only a theoretical possibility, which each writer approaches in his own way. Blanchot as a novelist has his own manner of writing, and as a critic he identifies different aspects of creation in the works of other authors. Certain authors always stand for the same creative roles: Mallarmé, for his cult of the word and the re-creation of an idealized, fictitious universe in a consummate work; Rimbaud, for a renunciation which symbolizes the relationship of possible and impossible in literary creation; Kafka, for a sense of *métier* in art and for the technique of third-person impersonal composition; Hölderlin and Artaud, for their literary communication of the intuition or aberration called madness; Lautréamont, for his self-creation as a new and purely literary existence in *Maldoror*, and Sade, the "writer par excellence," for his isolated composition and attitude of negation. The last two writers become almost mythical examples for the existential theory of literature: Lautréamont as a being taking shape in his work, and Sade as the "absolutely free," absolutely subjective, creator.

Such partial images of the absolute writer are completed by a short parable in *Le Dernier Mot* (1947), where the writer is said to be related to his work as a living man is related to a statue of himself. The parable begins with an image of the writer entering school as a teacher: presumably, the schoolchildren are the work's readers. "Suddenly, they asked me the traditional question in schools: 'Are you the teacher or really God?' I looked at them sadly; there were so many ways to answer, but first they had to be brought back to common discipline." He writes on the board: "But it is only with your throat choked by fear that you will learn to speak"; then he tries to introduce them to the involvement or "anguish" necessary for literary creation. Finally, he is asked "What are your connections with the statue?" to which he answers "But first you must recognize my sadness." The children (or readers) do not want to look for the metaphysical roots of his communication; after banging on the plaster statue "as if, being brass or bronze, it could have answered to their blows," [16] they become tired, leap on the writer, and set about pulling him to pieces.

Such is the situation of the writer, who creates and is apparently responsible for an existential "explosion" which, in fact, far surpasses him. Blanchot's theory does not go past this early description of the writer's predicament, but he gradually refines its expression and style in later novels and essays. Both genres seem to work toward the same end, and occasionally exchange techniques. Dialogue and symbolic narrative invade Blanchot's essays, and a muted, thoughtful, essay-like style permeates his later tales. There is no one genre specially suited for his aims, but all contribute to make literature the "only translation of the obsession of existence." [17]

The volumes published in the 1950's as *L'Espace littéraire* and *Le Livre à venir* develop two aspects of Blanchot's literary theory: the impersonal space of literary creation and the incarnate text. Although these two books are collections of essays, as are *Faux pas* and *La Part du feu*, they are more centrally organized than the earlier volumes. (The essays are arranged in such a way as to develop a single argument throughout.) Moreover, they complement each other in that one considers the space of the work while the other considers the work

16. Blanchot, *Le Dernier Mot* (Paris: Fontaine, 1947), pp. 21–24.
17. Blanchot, *La Part du feu,* p. 334.

itself. In *L'Espace littéraire*, Blanchot concentrates on a space in which writer, reader, and fundamental existence coincide. He defines and "approaches" this space, relates it to the incarnate work, and compares it to the existential space of absence and death. The critic illustrates the "space of literature" by reinterpreting the myth of Orpheus, and concludes with an analysis of space's relationship to written expression and original experience. *Le Livre à venir* shifts its emphasis from literary space to the literary text, and its chapters refer more often to specific books. Under the headings "Le Chant des Sirènes," "La Question littéraire," "D'Un Art sans avenir," and "Où va la littérature?" Blanchot discusses language and symbolic creation in the works of various authors. Here, as in *L'Espace littéraire*, he explores the vital point of creation, the extreme experience in which the writer and his work verge upon extinction.

In *L'Espace littéraire* he maintains that this extinction takes place because the work is "absent" from all its component parts: "It is . . . and nothing more." [18] The work is a solitary entity that communicates its own isolation to writer and reader. "Whoever reads it enters into this affirmation of the work's solitude, just as whoever writes it belongs to the risk of this solitude." Solitude fills the "literary space" in which the work actually, or mentally, exists. Whoever has any relationship with it runs the risk of experiencing the absolute, or disappearing in an absolute situation.

Only a "work" exists in literary space: what exists on an ordinary, tangible level is a book. The book begets the work, which is created in the violence of an existential act. "The writer writes a book, but the book is not yet the work. The work is only a work when there is pronounced by it, in the violence of a beginning which is all its own, the word *being*, an event which happens when the work is the intimacy of someone who writes it and someone who reads it" (p. 13). This "work" which Blanchot discusses is purely mental and purely alive: it is a web of impulses organized according to the text, but fully alive only in the mind.

Blanchot's view of the work undoubtedly distorts the formal struc-

18. Blanchot, *L'Espace littéraire* (Paris: Gallimard, 1955), p. 12.

ture of any given text, for the "book" is removed from the category of aesthetic technique and rechristened a "work" in the category of existence. On the other hand, this same book gains a new structural dimension when regarded as an act of reading as well as an act of composition. As an act and not an object, it is endowed with life. "What is a book which nobody reads? Something which is not yet written. Reading, then, is not rewriting the book, but causing the book to write itself or *to be* written—this time without the writer as intermediary, without anyone who writes it" (p. 201). Reading, for Blanchot, is more than an acquiescence with the work. It is the creative faculty quickening a work from its inert materiality. The act of reading creates in an even more positive way than the act of writing, for it creates the final act of literature. Writing, on the other hand, is a compromised, imperfect creation with its roots in absence. Surpassing both writing and reading is the work's total vision, in which both reader and writer are complementary subordinate aspects.

When the writer writes a book, his work exists also as a network of impulses in mental space. This "space" is both the space opened by the tension of reading and writing ("the space violently deployed by the mutual struggle of the power of speech and the power of hearing" p. 29) and the abstract space in which the work is related to absence and death ("the central point of the work . . . the work as origin" p. 49). "The space where everything returns to profound being . . . is the space of the poem, the orphic space to which the poet has no access, where he penetrates only to disappear . . . the work as origin" (p. 146). The work at its origin is not confined by language, and the inner space of absence and fundamental being is a space in which all art finds its source.

Blanchot is fascinated by the way in which the language of literature symbolizes creation, but he knows that the act of creation involves more than literature. He assumes an orphic experience for which all media are but various expressions of the same profundity. Any artistic object "is turned toward elementary depth, toward that element which is elemental profundity and shadow and of which we know this: that objects make no allusion to it, but that all the arts, in the appearance of *being* which they give to the *matter* of which, afterwards, it is said that their works are *made*, cause to rise up among us in the unique event of the work" (p. 234). Art is the expression of profundity, and is related primarily to the elementary forces.

Art's source in the basic, unformed elements of existence indicates a risk of absorption and extinction for both being and language. Art approaches the "space" of neutral existence when it seeks its authentic source. It verges upon an impersonal, undifferentiated affirmation in which any separate, formal creation threatens to dissolve. "This experience is that of art. Art, as image, word, and rhythm, indicates the threatening proximity of a vague and empty outside, neuter, nul, limitless existence, sordid absence, stifling condensation where being ceaselessly perpetuates itself under the genus of nothingness" (p. 255). Such a dangerous element is also then the "space of death," and art itself, "as origin or further, the experience of the Open," is "the search after a true death" (p. 159).

Blanchot attributes to Heidegger the notion of death as that which brings man to the extreme point of possible action, and makes him aware of his human nature. He hastens to add that Heidegger does not apply the notion to literature or art. The "possibility" of death is important for Blanchot because it is symbolic of the artistic experience. If the central yet impossible point of literary creation is the movement in which the *Je* moves to an *Il,* a loss of personal consciousness before a larger impersonal existence, then there is an open parallel between the literary loss of consciousness and the same loss found in death.

Such a movement is analyzed in Dostoevsky's Kirilov, in Mallarmé's *Igitur,* in Rilke's Malte, and in Kafka. Because human nature examines itself in this movement toward unconsciousness, it is a proper subject for existential literature. The existential artist tries to grasp and communicate this ultimate experience: to know "death" without losing consciousness. Kirilov personifies this decision to experience and examine unconsciousness when he contemplates his own death: "If he succeeds in making of death a possibility all his own and purely human . . . he will have been consciousness of disappearing and not disappearing consciousness, he will have entirely annexed to his consciousness its own disappearance, he will thus be realized totality, the realization of everything, the absolute" (p. 98). Kirilov's suicide is in fact self-defeating; once dead he cannot be aware of his loss of con-

sciousness. He shows only that the search for ultimate awareness must remain in the living mind. This purely mental experience of death belongs to Mallarmé's *Igitur,* or to Rilke's Malte. In *Igitur* the hero presages and enacts his own death: "He dies by the mind: by the very development of the mind, by its presence in himself" (p. 112). In Rilke "the discovery of Malte is that of this force, too great for us, which is *impersonal* death" (p. 133). Death for Rilke becomes "the empty depth of impossibility" after having been an absolute chance (p. 134). Both authors attempt to portray the ultimate point of human consciousness, but end by symbolizing the impossible relationship of being and consciousness which characterizes human existence and literature.

Blanchot frequently chooses specific figures to represent aspects of his literary theory. Among authors, Rilke, Dostoevsky, and Mallarmé are especially important, while Orpheus, Ulysses, and Oedipus are significant figures of myth. This technique of personification indicates a metaphorical or *allusive* approach, and suggests more levels of experience than pure scientific language can include. For example, Blanchot takes abstract existential notions and gives them emotional impact as "death," "absence," or "space." In *L'Espace littéraire,* Blanchot develops the personification of literary ideas beyond a simple one-to-one relationship. He adds a new dimension of time to this symbolism when his personification extends throughout the plot of a myth. The central personification of *L'Espace littéraire* is the myth of Orpheus, which Blanchot interprets in "Le Regard d'Orphée."

For Blanchot, Orpheus is the absolute writer, and Eurydice is the core of existence which inspires, dominates, and is lost in his work. Orpheus' descent to Hades symbolizes the existential movement which draws a writer toward fundamental being. His return to the world, without Eurydice, represents the opposite movement, in which the writer creates a text. Orpheus returns to the light of day but fails to bring with him more than a remembrance of lost existence. And yet, Orpheus must look at Eurydice. The poet's movement is not complete without a continued fascination for the "night," and his act, which originally seemed a failure, is actually necessary for his role as poet.

Eurydice, in this interpretation, can never be reached. She is "the utmost limit that art can reach, she is, under a name which dissembles

and a veil which covers her, the profoundly obscure point toward which art, desire, death, and night seem to tend." Eurydice represents the point at which personal experience and basic existence are joined. "She is the instant in which the essence of night draws near like the *other* night." Orpheus, in order to produce the creation which is required of him in his role as artist, must not look directly at Eurydice. He may descend toward her, but only if he turns away his face: "Orpheus can do anything except confront this 'point,' except look at the center of the night in the night." His work as a writer is to bring this point as close as possible to actual communication with the upper world, "to bring it back to the light of day and to give it, in daylight, form, shape, and reality." The myth now touches upon that element of impossibility which Blanchot has always found in existential literature. A writer whose attention is always turned toward the surface, and away from essences, misses the vital core of creation and writes only empty sentences. In order to maintain true contact with inspiration, Orpheus must forget his concrete work and try to see its essence. "Orpheus . . . forgets the work which he must accomplish, and he necessarily forgets it, for the ultimate exigency of his movement is not that there be a work, but that someone confront this 'point.'" There is a certain amount of failure in either act.

In turning toward Eurydice, Orpheus seems to bring about complete destruction. He destroys the work by ignoring its completion, he sends Eurydice back into Hades and oblivion, and he himself will be condemned and destroyed on his return to the upper world. Such destruction, however, completes the integral movement of his search. It is this *movement* which is important, "which does not want Eurydice in her daylight truth and with her everyday graces, which wants her in her nocturnal obscurity . . . not to make her live, but to have living in her the fullness of death" (pp. 179–180). If she were closer to the light, she would be a shell hollow of meaning. Left unrecognized in the dark, she could never inspire artistic creation.

Orpheus' impatient look embodies the very movement of inspiration, and thus is necessary even though "we feel only the defeat of inspiration, we recognize only misdirected violence" (p. 182). He has broken the ritual procedure which compelled Eurydice to follow him into the

superficial light of the upper world. His look releases her, "shatters the law which contained, retained her essence" (p. 184). In this sense, it is a successful look. Up to the moment of inspiration, composition is a mechanical, laborious and inessential task; when the artist briefly ignores the technical, "successful" aspect of his search, he is able to return to the world with a new work inspired by lost Eurydice.

This look, and the movement it implies, is an expression of complete liberty: liberty for Eurydice, liberation from the technical concern of the work, and liberty in which the artist loses himself by contemplating the essence of the night. The look is a moment of inspiration which consecrates his work by embodying in it the experience of existential discovery and loss. Orpheus, thus interpreted, symbolizes the exigency of art, and the necessary failure which consecrates literary creation.

Blanchot continues to use his allegorical method with figures such as Sisyphus and Heraclitus. Like Camus, he is fascinated by the image of Sisyphus, this "absurd" or essential being who consistently appears as a modern symbol of human experience. Blanchot's interpretation of Sisyphus does not resemble Camus', however, for he denies that the existential Sisyphus can know happiness. (Elsewhere, Blanchot comments that he finds Camus' experience more valuable than Camus' interpretation.) [19] In turning to Heraclitus, the pre-Socratic philosopher, Blanchot compares his "indicative" speech with Socrates' "denotative" language: one is literary and the other public. Socratic language communicates immediately and directly. It is a speech "that one can exchange and made for exchange . . . never a beginning speech. And thence . . . it renounces any language turned toward origin." [20] Heraclitean language, however, is original and existential. It is oracular, creative, and "prophetic." "The language in which origin speaks is essentially prophetic . . . it does not draw support from anything which already is, nor from a current truth, nor from language alone, already spoken and verified. It announces, because it begins." This tense, spare writing (compared to Char's poetry) evolves from a concentration upon separate phrases: it "invents simplicity, discovers the richness

19. Blanchot, "Le Détour vers la simplicité," *Nouvelle Revue française*, May 1960, p. 929.
20. Blanchot, *La Bête de Lascaux* (Paris: Ed. G.L.M., 1958), p. 16.

of poor words and the illuminating power of a speech which is brief, deprived of images, and as if ascetic." [21] The figure of Heraclitus, representing prophetic speech, complements the figure of Sisyphus, who represents the existential situation of man.

As Blanchot develops his theory of existential writing, his myths become more complex. He uses Heraclitus and Sisyphus solely for their allegorical significance. The larger myths, such as that of Orpheus, do more than interpret single figures: they describe an active relationship between these figures that expresses the all-important *movement* of literature. In Blanchot's chapter "Le Chant des Sirènes," from *Le Livre à venir* (1959), he describes literature's relation to reality as Ulysses sailing unscathed past the Sirens. The Siren song of reality is "betrayed" when Ulysses listens and escapes, and the Sirens plunge to their death in despair. Ulysses' safe return after hearing their song now seems a cowardly escape from real involvement, and his tale of hearing the Sirens is only a pale evocation of their fatal reality. The theory of literature behind this myth is the same as that in "Le Regard d'Orphée," but "Le Chant des Sirènes" carries the plot farther. The Sirens disappear as did Eurydice, but they reappear when Homer describes them in the *Odyssey*. Blanchot thus equates the figures of Ulysses, the adventurer or seeker after reality, with Homer, the writer or craftsman describing "reality." These two figures combine in a larger myth symbolizing the creation of literature.

The Sirens' song draws navigators toward the space of destruction, "toward this space where singing would truly begin." [22] The origin of the song is obscure and inhuman, as the Sirens are neither beasts nor women; but the music itself appeals to hardy, adventurous navigators, to writers who have chosen to voyage beyond the safe havens of accustomed reality. "This song . . . was a distance, and what it revealed was the possibility of traversing this distance, of making of the song the movement toward the song, and of this movement, the expression of the greatest desire" (p. 10). Ulysses causes the death of the Sirens when he hears their song and escapes. The Sirens reappear as elements of his tale, transformed and "conquered by the power of technique which will always claim to play safely with unreal (inspired) powers"

21. Blanchot, "Héraclite," *Nouvelle Revue française,* January 1960, p. 96.
22. Blanchot, *Le Livre à venir* (Paris: Gallimard, 1959), p. 9.

(p. 11). The story of their encounter becomes, in microcosm, the allegory of the writer and his work: of Homer and the *Odyssey*.

Blanchot calls this difference of experience and literature the difference between *récit* and *roman*. "The tale begins where the novel does not go and nonetheless leads by its refusals and its rich negligence" (p. 12). In the *Odyssey*, the writer's experience appears on a double plane and surpasses the tale of Orpheus and Eurydice: it symbolizes the writer's communication with essence and inspiration, but it also illustrates the ultimate, "absent" incarnation of this experience in the final work of art. Ulysses and Homer share the same experience on different levels and, from the perspective of the Sirens, they share the same nature—they are "a single and same presence" (p. 13).

Even this double interpretation of the Sirens' song does not complete Blanchot's myth of literature, and the critic finds a further parallel sea myth in Melville's *Moby Dick*. "Between Ahab and the whale, a drama is acted out which could be called metaphysical . . . the same struggle that is acted out between the Sirens and Ulysses" (p. 14). Ahab personifies the danger of self-destruction within the writer, while Ulysses surrounds himself with the restraints of technique, maintains the interval between himself and destruction, and escapes. "It is undeniable that Ulysses understood a small part of what Ahab saw, but he held firm in the midst of this understanding, while Ahab was lost in the image. That means that the one rejected the metamorphosis into which the other penetrated and disappeared" (p. 15). The two seafarers represent the dangers of metamorphosis for the writer, a metamorphosis in which one succumbs while the other escapes.

Blanchot's larger myth of literature contains two metamorphoses, each successful in its own way. Each takes place in a special view or "time" of experience. In the "time" of the tale, or of the essential experience, it is Ahab who culminates his search by complete involvement with the whale; in the "time" of the writer, who must return to earth remembering a now-absent experience, it is Ulysses who triumphs by retaining his own identity. For the experience to be written, and the "récit" to become a "roman," Ulysses must escape from the Sirens. Before there can be literature, the writer's pure experience must lose itself in the impure but concrete forms of language.

Blanchot calls these two levels of literature two categories of reality.

"If . . . you say that what makes the novel advance is everyday, collective or personal time, or more precisely, the wish to give speech to time, the tale has this *other* time in which to progress, this other navigation which is the passing from the real song to the imaginary one." The myth of literature itself symbolizes two aspects of creation that Blanchot wants to emphasize in *Le Livre à venir*: the existence of the book as an incarnate reality using symbolic language, and the journey of the author to an extreme point of danger and of experience.

In *Le Livre à venir* Blanchot examines a symbolic language already introduced as Gracq's "magical" expression and Heraclitus' "prophetic" speech. This language is heavy and "authentic"; it communicates a sense of being. "Its weight is the sign of its authenticity . . . Prophetic speech is imposed from the outside, it is the Outside itself" (p. 102). Such is the voice of existence, an undifferentiated, neutral experience expressed in ordinary, colorless speech. "If prophetic words were to reach us, what they would make us feel is that they contain neither allegory nor symbol, but that, by the concrete force of the word, they strip things bare" (p. 105). A "symbol" in this speech is an *act*: not the mere parallel transcription of a real object, but an experience suggested by the movement of language. "Any symbol is an experience, a radical change which must be lived, a leap which must be made. There is therefore no symbol, but a symbolic experience" (p. 110). To grasp a symbol as experience, one must go past its simple form as an image.

Blanchot gives this interpretation of symbolic language on the grounds that a symbol is "symbolic" only to the reader. To the writer, it is the form of life his experience takes. If he wants to preserve the existential vitality of his book, he must experience as reality whatever seems "symbolic" to the reader. "The symbol exists for the reader alone; it is he who feels bound to the book by the movement of a symbolic search." If a writer actually transfers his experience, he does not do so by depending on symbols as striking, colorful images, which catch attention for themselves, but by using language itself to symbolize his experience. Blanchot uses Hermann Broch as an example. "Broch's ideal," he points out, "would be to express all opposed movement simultaneously and as if in a single sentence . . . [Each sentence] would like to exhaust the world, pass through all the levels of experience, and each time unite everything which clashes" (p. 149). This speech is preartistic, or "artistic" only in an existential sense—where craft appears in its ability to disguise itself as experience.

Blanchot's concern with existential experience leads him to put the artist closer to the genesis of a work than most critics would allow. An artist's extreme involvement leads him to risk "failure" or "error," and to be accused of this failure by well-adjusted objective critics. Blanchot retorts that the so-called "errors" and "failures" of Mallarmé and Baudelaire account for their unique creations. "Each artist is bound to an error with which he has a particular connection of intimacy" (p. 131). The artist's "error" is not, of course, a mistake, but a chosen side path—a "wandering." To Blanchot, Sade's "wandering" symbolizes "l'écrivain *par excellence*"; all writers, however, have their characteristic routes or "errors."

In *Le Livre à venir,* Blanchot (like the surrealists before him) is interested in the relationship of madness to the creative experience. A chapter on Antonin Artaud, whose conscious experimenting with "surreal" feelings led to suicide in an asylum, describes Artaud's experience of a negative reality, a reality that resembles Blanchot's own "night." "What is first is not plenitude of being, but crack and fissure . . . corroding deprivation: being is not being, it is this lack of being, living lack which makes life feeble, intangible, and inexpressible, except by the cry of a ferocious abstinence" (pp. 49–50). Artaud is perhaps another Ahab, an existential experimenter who has not returned to the surface with words. In "La Folie par excellence" a preface to the translated *Strindberg et Van Gogh, Hölderlin et Swedenborg* of Karl Jaspers, Blanchot agrees with Jaspers that madness as possible knowledge must be distinguished from madness as psychological illness. Jaspers has emphasized the certitude and freedom of creation in Hölderlin's last, "mad" works, and Blanchot describes in them a "trajectory in which the truth of total existence, become pure poetic affirmation, sacrifices the normal conditions of possibility . . . pure speech . . . established on the abyss." [23] What seems to be madness is always an extreme experience, but an artist's existential situation is also extreme. It carries

23. Blanchot, preface in Karl Jaspers, *Strindberg et Van Gogh, Hölderlin et Swedenborg* (Paris: Ed. de Minuit, 1953), p. 25. See also "La Folie par excellence," *Critique,* February 1951, pp. 99–118.

the creator toward a point of self-destruction which may have all the marks of insanity. In terms of literary creation, however, it is associated with a special kind of knowledge and may not be assimilated to the categories of illness adopted by psychology.

Although Blanchot dismisses psychological judgments as irrelevant to literature, he discovers a movement of immense future importance for him in the psychological technique of question and answer. An article on Freud is the first sign of this interest in psychology's "human" discovery—which is, he says, parallel to the "discovery" embodied in literature. Freud's system of interrogation has a definite existential value in that it is "an extraordinary effort of discovery and of language invention which permits him to retrace, in an evocative and persuasive manner, the movement of human experience, its conflicts, its moments." [24] It is valuable for the literary critic because its analysis of themes and impulses implies a valuable method for existential criticism.

The most important lesson of the Freudian approach is its use of a tense, impersonal dialectic relationship to reveal human impulses. "The principal merit of Freud is to have enriched human culture with a surprising form of dialogue" (p. 490). Blanchot's description of the dialectic relationship precedes his own use of dialogue in several articles and a book. He speaks of "this relationship . . . this stark dialogue where, in a space separated and cut off from the world, two people invisible to each other are drawn little by little to confuse themselves with the power of speech and the power of hearing, to have no other relationship than the impersonal intimacy of the two aspects of discourse" (p. 489). This dialogue is a series of questions and answers which attempt to probe being: as such, it continues Blanchot's previous image of a dialogue between an author and the work he seeks to create. Such a setting, with the coming-to-terms and mutual interrogation of two beings, has long been apparent in Blanchot's novels. It may equally be applied to the existential quest described in his literary theory.

An article published in 1960–1961, "La Question la plus profonde," considers this dialectic of question and answer, or of question embodying an empty answer, as a third "movement" of literature after *L'Espace littéraire* and *Le Livre à venir*. This third movement has its own myth

24. Blanchot, "Freud," *Nouvelle Revue française*, September 1956, p. 486.

of literature, for Blanchot reinterprets the story of Oedipus and the Sphinx to describe the dialectic process. "La Question la plus profonde" discusses a general attitude of questioning that becomes the human gesture *par excellence,* a questioning which refers always to a same basic existence. All questions are "directed toward one, the central question or the question of everything." [25] Each separate question moves toward one answer, but refers to an indeterminate horizon of possibility. "Questioning is advancing or retreating toward the horizon of every question" (p. 1083). To question anything is to question the framework in which it resides: to question everything.

For Blanchot, a question embodies a perfect movement because it is still open to both positive and negative answers. In the question "Is the sky blue?" there exists both the immediate possibility of such a fact, and its questioning, its eternal openness as a yet unsettled condition. The question is more desirable than the answer, for it contains aspects of an existence that will never be fully known. "Yes" (the sky is blue) withdraws the possibility of speculation and interpretation. "We lose the straightforward, immediate datum, and we lose the opening, the richness of possibility. The answer is the misfortune of the question" (p. 1084). In this sense, the movement of the question is the only comprehensive, perfect movement, retaining both the essential facts and their mobile existence. Speech is completed by its possible negation: "It is not incomplete inasmuch as it is question; it is, to the contrary, speech which is accomplished by the fact of declaring itself incomplete. The question replaces full affirmation in emptiness, it enriches it with this emptiness." Just as Orpheus' journey is completed by his loss of Eurydice, so the question remains complete only when it is unanswered. In addition, the question's emptiness and absolute potentiality make it a perfect symbol for the existential condition. It embraces a tension of various movements, and catches the subject in motion. The dynamic tension embodied in a question is simultaneously close to all the faces of existence, for "interrogation is the movement in which being turns and appears as the turning of being" (p. 1085).

The "turning of being" is inherent in the movement of dialectics, through which (but not in which) the "most profound question" ap-

25. Blanchot, "La Question la plus profonde (I)," *Nouvelle Revue française,* December 1960, pp. 1082–1083.

pears. This deepest question is not asked, but implied by all the other questions and answers. There are two kinds of questions, in Blanchot's view. There is a "question of relationship, question of everything" which is pursued through dialectic interrogation, and a "profound question" which appears only in the background of dialectic futility. (This distinction recalls that of "public" and "literary" language.) The interminable movement of dialectics, an eternal series of questions and answers engendered one upon another, represents one basic movement of interrogation. As such it symbolizes "the most profound question," whose movement contains both negation and proposed reality. "When dialectics reign, collecting everything into the unique question of relationship; when, by its action, everything has become question, then the question which is not asked is asked." [26] Separate, insignificant questions evoke a general frame of analysis in which everything is put to question; everything acquires an unfulfilled but potential quality as it is resolved into one implied Question.

In the myth epitomizing this essay, it is the Sphinx who voices the most profound question, which Oedipus answers as though it were a mere "question of relationship" (*question d'ensemble*). Man confronts the nonhuman, and a positive element confronts the negative aspect of its own reality. "Oedipus before the Sphinx is man before nonman. The whole task of the question is to bring man to the recognition that before the Sphinx, the nonman, he is already before himself." [27] The Sphinx exists as an inhuman interrogation confronting man, and "when the Sphinx speaks, in the language of lightness and danger which belongs to her, it is to give voice to the most profound question." The apparently playful, valueless enigma which she poses for Oedipus is in fact a question involving his very being: "He must answer with his life" (p. 283). When Oedipus responds, in the same uninvolved gesture of technical knowledge which preserved Ulysses from the Sirens, the Sphinx dies and "disappears in the very language which comprehends her." Oedipus' temporary triumph stems only from a misinterpretation

26. Blanchot, "La Question la plus profonde (II)," *Nouvelle Revue française*, January 1961, p. 89.
27. Blanchot, "La Question la plus profonde (III)," *Nouvelle Revue française*, February 1961, p. 282.

of the question and of his knowledge. "Later he will put out his eyes to try to reconcile light and obscurity, knowledge and ignorance, the two adverse regions of the question." It is the question of man which underlies the Sphinx' riddle, and which now disappears to become incarnate in the "answer" provided by Oedipus. "The most profound question has disappeared, but it has disappeared in the man who bears it and in this word—man—with which the answer was given. Oedipus . . . *knew how* to answer, but this knowledge only confirmed his ignorance and was even possible only because of this profound ignorance. Oedipus knows man as a question of relationship, because he is ignorant of him—and ignorant that he is ignorant—of man as profound question." The Sphinx represents another aspect of literature in Blanchot's personal myth, in that she seems to incarnate fundamental being much as did Eurydice and the Sirens. The role in each myth is different: Eurydice is that which is sought, the Sirens are an appeal from beyond, and the Sphinx is a questioning element placed before man. In each case the figure represents an overwhelming and unfamiliar existence. In the latest myth "the question . . . puts us in relationship with what has no end. Something in the question necessarily exceeds the power of questioning" (p. 286). The Sphinx embodies a more profound question than she can ask, and yet Oedipus must respond to both interrogations.

The Sphinx represents two aspects of reality, just as literature had two levels or "times" in "Le Chant des Sirènes." The Sphinx speaks one question, but she herself *is* the most profound question. Questions which can be phrased and conveyed by language (like the riddle) are examples of a superficial "question of relationship" in which language seems to be denoting something particular, but actually conceals and avoids the basic question of existence.

Blanchot's theory of creation refers now to a theory of language, as so often happens in his critical essays. It is the nature of speech to seem to seize what it can only grasp as absent, and "questioning is this detour which speaks as detour of speech" (p. 287). The flight of graspable reality which Blanchot finds in existence is represented, still unattainable, by language. Language exists on the same level as the Sphinx, for in its own nature it represents the unposable question of existence. "Language is the understanding of the movement of hiding and of turning away, it watches over it, it preserves it, it is lost in it" (p. 290). Both the Sphinx and language voice apparently "real" questions and answers which compose questions of relationship.

At this point Blanchot is evidently distinguishing between "question" as we know it, and the unknowable, positive-negative tension which he chooses to define as "question" in existence. The first question, that conveyed by language, has its logical extreme in dialectic interrogation. The second question, symbolized by language, appears through the first; for when the interminable movement of dialectics reveals an eternal question, it makes manifest "the most profound question."

Blanchot's profound question proposes, then, another statement of his views on literature and literary language. Oedipus represents rational man; he attempts to deal with exterior reality in terms of a scientific and logical thought that perceives rational connections, but he succeeds only in forcing the profound question to embody itself in his own being. Oedipus also represents the writer, in the same sense as does Ulysses. For Blanchot, the writer is a human figure who delves into his own existence in order to express some essence of reality. Oedipus meets this essence in the Sphinx, and he "captures" it (retains its memory, its "absence") through technical knowledge. The writer retains only a part of the original experience, but he does render this part available in the language of literature.

Blanchot tries to reproduce in his novels this sense of existence that he examines in his criticism. At various times throughout his essays, he has declared that novels are particularly well suited to convey experience. Blanchot composes his novels as structures of interrelated impulses, as a *jeu de forces* organized to reveal the tensions of existence.

Such a novel is far removed from the contemporary *roman nouveau*, which is often taken as the sole representative of modern existential writing. Blanchot's novel tends to subordinate the actual objects of reality, and the emotions they arouse, to the inner, vital tension they imply. It is scarcely a novel at all, in the usual sense of the term, for it tends to reduce all narration and description to a series of colorless, apparently unrelated attitudes. Blanchot's style was not always so abstract, and it has developed from his early weird and marvelous tales to a spare evocation of ordinary surroundings. Even the stress upon these surroundings has diminished, so that the last real use of a setting occurs in *Le Dernier Homme* (1957), where an isolated community recalls the sanitorium in *Der Zauberberg*.[28]

In *Le Dernier Homme* the "purity" of these surroundings allows the author to concentrate on the three main characters: the author, a woman, and a sick, aging man. The novel's action consists in their various interrogations, tensions, misunderstandings, and their gradual coming to terms. Symbolically, the movement is similar to that of the myths of literature and to Blanchot's other novels, especially *Au Moment voulu*. The woman is the work itself; she disappears toward the end when the author goes to question the "being" who is the ultimate, "the last man." The second part of the tale evokes the existential event, when the author finally meets "the last man." In the final pages the person of the narration shifts from *Je* to *Il*, according to the movement which Blanchot has discovered in literature from his early studies of Kafka to those on Mallarmé.

In such a work of fiction, there are few references to the reality that is so important in *Der Zauberberg*, or in *Le Voyeur*: characters take a walk, sit by a piano, speak of leaving the house, or sit in the snow; but the main body of the writing is always taken up with observation, interrogation, and interpretation of attitudes. Thus Blanchot arrives at his play of forces, at the transparent communication of effects which is his aim. He wants both to convey existence and to symbolize creation. In the technique of this novel "the most profound question" is already represented, for that question exists and is not asked.

This "most profound question" has always been, in one form or another, the central burden of Blanchot's novels and essays. The form of its communication, however, varies. The latest movement of the essays suggests a new form of interrogating existence. A series of questions and answers existing in the mind, without any attachment to outside reality, evokes Blanchot's "profound" sense of neutral existence. This dialectic examination of reality brings literary style closest to the structure of human experience.

Blanchot first experimented with such an existential style in an article called "Entretien sur un changement d'époque," published in *La*

---

28. Cf. especially page 98 of *Le Dernier Homme* (Paris: Gallimard, 1957). Blanchot mentions *Der Zauberberg* in several studies, and considers Mann one of the great contemporary writers.

Nouvelle Revue française for April 1960. The article's title seems to anticipate a passage from "La Question la plus profonde," where Blanchot states that the "question" is "held in reserve until this turn in time when the epoch falls and the discourse ends. At each change of epoch, it appears to emerge for an instant." [29] The "Entretien" is written in conversational dialogue form and recounts the discussion of two disembodied interlocutors. There is no environmental setting and no description of the people involved, so that the literary movement itself proceeds in a veritable, interior *jeu de forces*. The essay itself does not resemble those Blanchot usually writes for *La Nouvelle Revue française;* it appears to be his first published experiment with dialogue, a style he uses in his latest tale, *L'Attente l'oubli.*

L'Attente l'oubli contains the same basic plot structure as *Le Dernier Homme,* or indeed, as all of Blanchot's *récits* when existentially understood. It begins as the writer sets down his notes on a meeting with "her." No one is given a name, and the third person singular is used almost exclusively—even where normal usage would require a first-person form. Only "she" (the Absolute Work) uses a subjective manner of speech, and this use gives way to the third-person form as both writer and work approach oblivion (*l'oubli*). Throughout the book the writer puts down what he thinks she says and means, listening as he writes, and checking what he has written against her speech. He finds that there is a perpetual gap between their understandings of each other and also between their changing concepts of themselves. As they speak, a new relationship arises between the "presences" projected by their words: the presence of "her" sister-work, which is concrete if not absolute or true, and the author's presence as creator of this concrete work. There are then two pairs of existence: the author and his envisaged ideal, and the projected author and his created work.

This double pair of existences is created in *L'Attente l'oubli* by a patient attention and expectation (*attente*); the author waits for the other being to reveal itself at the end of a series of mutual interrogations. The oblivion (*oubli*) of the title is the elementary silent being into which all knowledge resolves. While "she" persistently tells the writer "Act so that I can speak to you," he realizes that he possesses

---

29. Blanchot, "La Question la plus profonde (II)," p. 89.

nothing but the power of speech. "It is the voice which is entrusted to you, and not what it [or *she*] says." As long as he writes, all the separate parts of knowledge and discourse remain apart. When he attains knowledge of "her," and they merge in perfect understanding, writing ceases. In the end, both the absolute work and the writer are carried along by the movement of discovery which their dialogue has established. They fall into oblivion, silence, and "the reserve of things in their latent state." [30]

This latest tale of Blanchot states once more the familiar literary "plot" where the same aspects of existential knowledge act out the same roles. There is always a writer who tries to capture essences, and who is directly confronted by a woman: the ideal work, or the absolute being he hopes to grasp. He confronts her in a series of scenes or dialogues, described so as to suggest a love affair. Blanchot's earlier books still describe the outside world, but these descriptions have no metaphysical importance and tend to disappear. The absolute work has many aspects, and may have a sister-work, which is the face she shows to the world; but the latter only obscures the original relationship between author and work. There is one more side to this theory: the idea of nothingness, or absolute being, in which the ideal work ideally exists. This absolute being may be personified as a man, in which case the "plot" takes on overtones of a lovers' triangle, or it may be only tacitly understood. If the author attempts to reach knowledge of "her," he is concurrently drawn towards the silent, elementary existence in which "she" is found. If he is successful in finding "her," both "she" and he (now impersonal) merge in a basic, voiceless existence.

Although Blanchot's plot remains approximately the same, his style changes over the years to reflect his gradually formulated idea of existential language. He has often spoken of a magical speech: "heavy," "prophetic," nonevocative, and perpetually self-examining. It is the opposite of glib, "automatic" writing; it does not exist for an effect, but tries to disappear before the truth it conveys. In *L'Attente l'oubli* Blanchot has developed this style to an extreme degree. He uses a "neutral, colorless speech" which eliminates almost all references to plot and environment. Occasionally he mentions a chair, table, door, window,

30. Blanchot, *L'Attente l'oubli* (Paris: Gallimard, 1962), p. 162.

couch, light, corridor, or balcony, but nothing more. Instead, there is a perpetual dialogue and a series of unending interrogations which leaves the reader with nothing to grasp except an intangible movement of impulses toward knowledge.

Blanchot does not excuse himself either for this repetitive theme in his criticism or for the repetition of plot in his narrative. In *L'Attente l'oubli* he even seems to justify it. The artist "is at this moment engaged in an error from which he does not want to be shut out, and which is only the repetition of his oldest errors. He does not even recognize it, and when they tell him: 'But this thought is always the same thought!', he contents himself with reflecting, and finally answers: 'Not entirely the same, and I would like to think it through again a little'" (p. 27). Blanchot's thought is indeed "not entirely the same," for he gives it a series of transformations in his novels and essays. However, the structure of this thought is the same, and offers again and again the same relationship between writer and work, seeker and sought, creator, creation, and the existence into which both are absorbed. This structure governs the search and the style of all Blanchot's works as he tries to reproduce, in both criticism and novel, man's shifting understanding of his own nature and of the world in which he lives and creates.

This close connection between essays and novels, between style and theory, shows that Blanchot's work is based upon a unique existential experience. Because the experience itself dominates his theory and writings, his work cannot be called conventional literary criticism. Instead of distinguishing separate texts, Blanchot discerns in all literature an absolute "movement" of creation. In *Lautréamont et Sade* (1949) he says that practical criticism is a necessary evil. It exists only because the reader wants to communicate his feelings about a given work. Criticism is always at fault, says Blanchot, because the reader reads himself into the work. He tends "to substitute himself for what he admires, to believe himself secretly a little wiser than the work, a little more real than the author, because the work is finished in him and depends on his reasons for admiring it." [31] The reader does not inflict his personality on a work by choice, or by imposing outside rules and standards. The modern critic rejects such open evaluation, and would like to disappear

31. Blanchot, *Lautréamont et Sade* (Paris: Ed. de Minuit, 1949), p. 9.

behind his reading. He wants to become "not the foreign eye which judges, gauges, defines and suppresses what it sees, but the thing itself, augmented by a look" (p. 10). However, the very fact that he *looks* at the work distinguishes him from it: the critic who thinks he explains a text to potential readers finds that, in fact, he superimposes his own mental structure on "the always moving power of the work" (p. 11).

Two paths are open to the critic: he can explain the work in terms of his own critical vision, or he can try to send the reader into the work by pointing out the difficulties of its analysis. In either approach, the immediate effect of the work is lost (and the existential *effect* is the quality most prized by Blanchot) "because there has been substituted, for the work's own power of uprooting and carrying away, a perfected system of dams and filters which obstructs . . . the reader" (p. 13). Thus the critic must prepare himself to lose, perhaps to destroy, the integral impression of the work which first attracted him. When he realizes that he must substitute himself for the work if he is to "criticize," he chooses one element to emphasize at the expense of the others; and Blanchot chooses not the formal elements, but his own existential understanding of the work at its most vital point. He singles out an impersonal "truth" and tries to see the work "in its most important light, to seek the point where it is greatest, truest, richest."

The critic, in order to carry out such an analysis, must have great sympathy for the author, a sympathy which precludes any exterior judgments of value. Therefore Blanchot, like the Geneva critics, rejects evaluation. He is concerned solely with "great" books. "Bad works are not worth all the ill said of them, nor all the trouble taken to say it. Even speaking of them is too much" (p. 14). In practice, Blanchot has already made his judgment when he chooses to speak of a book. For him (and the Geneva critics as well) an aesthetic choice precedes and is hidden in the main existential analysis. This analysis itself, however, contains no judgment. Blanchot emphasizes that a critic must fully accept a work in order to find the proper sympathetic vision. "Neither critic nor reader is ever completely mistaken when overestimating a work, on condition that . . . it is by an effort, even exaggerated, to recognize in it a 'new' sense, the working of an important truth." The overestimation of a work implies a willingness to see some truly new element in its composition, to free oneself from limiting traditional interpretations or personal prejudice. Sympathy—even too much of it—is a positive step towards comprehension.

The reader's sympathetic or "submissive" attitude lets him enter the author's mind and accept the work's peculiar rhythm. The most impressive example of such a rhythm is Lautréamont's *Maldoror*, which forces its reader to submit himself to its literary discipline and "furious lucidity" (p. 15). "In these conditions how could he want to regain his equilibrium, to see where he is falling? . . . He goes and he plunges in. There is his commentary" (p. 16). This reader is drawn up into *Maldoror*'s "existential explosion": when he tries to explain his experience, however, he loses part of his sympathetic identification.

The reader who "submits" to a text may carry unconscious prejudices, however. He may try (like Gaston Bachelard) to recognize his own prejudices and to correct his analysis, but he can never be aware of all his prejudices. Always "in excess or default in reference to the work" (p. 33), the critic's reading ends in a compromise much like the existential compromise of literature. The description of an "impossible" creation now applies as much to criticism as it did to literature: the critic can do without his "look" as little as the writer can do without language. Blanchot has shown that the writer cannot really communicate with the being inspiring his work, and now he shows that the reader cannot really communicate with the text.

A critic, like a writer, must nonetheless arrive at some form of compromise in order to maintain his role and not relapse into silence. Blanchot suggests that the most valid approach is a kind of thematic criticism, an analysis of symbols expressing an underlying existential movement. In this respect, his approach resembles the Geneva methods. He does not accord the same importance to perceptions of the environment, but he sees themes of perception as keys to the comprehension of existence.

When Blanchot analyzes a text, he isolates its dominant themes. The text of *Maldoror* organizes itself around a series of symbols developing in time, with more or less intense reference to a central theme. Here it is not the image itself which is important, but the existential reality it symbolizes. "It is already poetically more important to recognize, between the praise of the hermaphrodite and the praise of mathematics, full of grace and modesty, a curiously similar light and a slow rise in level from one world to the other" (p. 106). *Maldoror* moves gradually from level to level of related images—images related not only to each other, but also to the underlying movement in which they find their significance. There are frequent descriptions of flaming comets, billowing hair, whirlwinds, fire, and streaking meteors, in which the critic must learn to recognize "not only the persistence of such an image, but its transformations, which are not arbitrary, but always oriented in a sense forever more extended and more dramatic" (p. 109). A movement of creation and transformation emerges through these progressively heightened images.

Blanchot does not give a static, formal analysis of images describing a symmetric pattern. Instead, he discusses these images as part of a developing awareness in the book. To Blanchot, images are the means by which one approaches "a creative progression, the irreversible movement of a becoming order." He decries a lifeless and exhaustive explication which ignores the sense of time, and treats the book as "a thing which has always been made, whose significance, sought independently of the meaning of its movement, particularly neglects the movement by which it was made" (p. 54).

There are two particular contexts in which the movement in time is important to Blanchot's theory. First, since he assumes that a text presents a given existence revealing itself in time, he understands that the reader's sympathetic comprehension of this existence must also include a temporal dimension. Second, the movement of the text's existence is also the movement by which the writer, using and exploring language, creates his work. The sense of creation itself, which is an inescapable part of the process of writing and of reading, is lost by the synthetic over-all view of static criticism: it is this movement which Blanchot wishes to restore.

It is not often that Blanchot discusses criticism *per se*, for his interest is first of all in the creation of literature, and only incidentally in the approach to a finished work. Apart from the early section in *Lautréamont et Sade*, his critical theorizing is confined to certain topical remarks. He even questions the possibility of an adequate criticism: "First of all, it is not certain that criticism exists." [32] Two proponents of a

32. Blanchot, "Le Mystère de la critique," *Journal des Débats*, January 6, 1944, p. 2.

"sympathetic" criticism, however, receive his approbation: Charles Du Bos and Albert Béguin.

Du Bos, says Blanchot, endowed criticism with an aspect of personal experience. "He helped give a value of creation to critical activity. He made of it . . . a vital experience, a personal means of search and discovery." [33] This creative reading evokes a hidden, secret book behind the actual text. "Any book, even a modest one, has its secret, which flees and can only be approached by superimposing on the real book the ideal book which could not be written. If we want to understand a work profoundly, we must see the work less than find the one to which it brings us, which is like its truth, its rule, and of which it represents only the—often admirable—absence." The theme of the implied book is one which Blanchot proposed in "Comment la littérature est-elle possible?" and "La Littérature et le droit à la mort." Such a "book" is the ideal, "experienced" text which a critic tries to approach.

Blanchot attributes a similar attitude of personal involvement to Albert Béguin, when he reviews the latter's *Léon Bloy l'impatient.* "We owe him also a deepening of criticism, considered no longer as an exercise in judgment, but as a witness upon oneself, as a means of seeking and contesting oneself." [34] Béguin's approach is a personal one and tries to use the experience of a work of art in its own development. It presupposes a certain empathy which is, on a subjective plane, the equivalent of the absolute reader's experience for Blanchot. Blanchot describes this procedure as reading a work "while trying to penetrate its meaning, accepting it entirely, without any reservations and by a completely interior adherence." Although he has pointed out the difficulties inherent in this method, it is still the only one compatible with his view of literature.

One of the most surprising assertions in Blanchot's criticism, which seems to come from literary hypotheses rather than from critical observation, is an assumption of sincerity as a measurable quantity in literature. It is Baudelaire's experience which enables him to use language authentically: "It is this experience which authenticates the word *atrocious* . . . and which gives all its importance to the actually banal

33. Blanchot, "La Critique de Charles du Bos," *Paysage-Dimanche,* December 2, 1945, p. 3.
34. Blanchot, "Léon Bloy," *Journal des Débats,* July 20, 1944, p. 2.

image of the abyss." [35] In an article on Montherlant's "La Reine morte," Blanchot distinguishes between scenes of a "profound truth" and scenes in which "you feel that the author wrote them with all his talent, but did not believe in their necessity." [36] Blanchot shows that he is not at all willing to assume a dichotomy between experience and expression, and opposes Béguin's theory that Pascal wrote the *Pensées* for calculated effect and not from "anguish": "it seems that we feel deceived, if a book moves us which wants to move us." He declares that "for the language of the *Pensées* to be read as the language of worry and anxiety, the *Pensées* must have sprung from an anxious heart that only anxiety made speak." [37] Here the critic is openly reduced to arguing from emotion.

Blanchot does not leave the argument upon the plane of emotion, but justifies the same approach upon the grounds of existential necessity. Effective use of language, he claims, must rest upon the actual experience whose impression is conveyed in the work. "In a work made of words, language, to be accomplished even imperfectly, needs existence to lend it support, to come lift it out of a sort of bankruptcy, and to try to guarantee its invincible bad faith" (p. 264). He adds that "all the different manifestations of language require, according to infinitely variable connections, the participation of existence with speech." If Blanchot gives himself the loophole of "infinitely variable connections," it is still evident that he is attempting to judge a work's sincerity without having any measure. He is also subordinating the role of discipline in literary creation in quite uncharacteristic fashion. Blanchot has departed from his standard of textual independence, for he implies that the reader's impression of a work is actual proof of its sincere introspection. This disturbing air of literary naiveté (of which Blanchot is rarely guilty) seems to come from the fact that he is applying a theory of absolute composition to a particular concrete expression. As an explanation of literary creation, his theory is consistent and unimpeachable. As a standard of criticism, it is not always sufficient to evaluate a written text.

35. Blanchot, *La Part du feu*, p. 153.
36. Blanchot, "Sur la pièce de M. de Montherlant," *Journal des Débats*, March 31, 1943, p. 3.
37. Blanchot, *La Part du feu*, p. 261.

Among the few critics Blanchot has considered, Du Bos and Béguin seem closest to his own sympathies. He discusses Albert Thibaudet briefly in *Faux pas*, but views him simply as an historical, comparatist critic: and Blanchot does not really find such criticism interesting. In later articles he virtually ignores the question of criticism. There is a brief attack on aesthetic criticism in *L'Espace littéraire*.[38] In 1953, he discusses Dionys Mascolo's *Le Communisme*, and comments that real art is not *engagé*. "The poetic work, the artistic work, if it speaks to us about something, speaks of what is apart from any value, rejects any evaluation, tells the force of the beginning which becomes lost and obscured, as soon as it becomes value."[39] In answer to an "Enquête sur la méthode critique" in 1959, he restates briefly his attitude towards a personal subjective criticism. As proposed in *Lautréamont et Sade*, it is by a personal experience (necessarily "prejudiced" but properly self-analytical) that the reader approaches the existence of a work of art. "We all start with prejudices, and it is from them (even if they are unfounded) that understanding can progress. The task then remains to interrogate one's own point of departure in regard to the text (or event) to be interpreted, and thanks to this very text. To put it another way: there is no understanding without prejudging, and it would be contradicting the very meaning of comprehension to make it artificially free of all 'prejudice.' Thence, however, the necessity of watching oneself constantly and, while interrogating the text, the obligation to let oneself be interrogated by the text."[40] In June, 1961, he points to an example of criticism which he thinks successful: Michel Butor's essay on Baudelaire. What satisfies him in this essay, he says, is the fact that Butor "does not interpret it, so to speak, but responds to it by a slow circling movement, dreaming in his turn . . . beside this dream, and letting the latter arouse him to a more vivid understanding of Baudelairean truth."[41] Although he occasionally speaks about the proper way to read a book, Blanchot concentrates upon the creation of a work rather than upon its criticism. In the decade after 1950, both essays and

38. Blanchot, *L'Espace littéraire*, pp. 210–211, 238–240.
39. Blanchot, "Le Communisme, par Dionys Mascolo," *Nouvelle Revue française*, December 1953, p. 1099.
40. Blanchot, "Réponse" to an "Enquête sur la méthode critique," *Les Lettres nouvelles*, June 24, 1959, pp. 9–10.
41. Blanchot, "Rêver, écrire," *Nouvelle Revue française*, June 1961, p. 1096, n. 2.

novels restrict his former wide scope to a more integrated preoccupation with central experience: with the existential marvel which is, for Blanchot, the creation of literature.

Blanchot's experience as an author experimenting with forms brings him to analyze a movement of creation, or the internal unfolding of a work, in many other writers. When he speaks of works close to his own theory of literature, his sympathetic understanding gives him a unique insight into their special nature. In Lautréamont, for example, he identifies different techniques as so many attacks upon the reader's comprehension, and is the first to speak of Lautréamont's literary rhythm: a rhythm that comes into being in the course of the work and which the reader must try to assimilate. Blanchot's experience as both author and critic, and his obsession with the existential "knowledge" of literary creation, give him a peculiar insight into just that part of modern literature that other less adventurous critics fear to approach.

Blanchot does not erect a system of interpretation, but illustrates a manner of reading. He reinterprets literature as a creative act, and carries through this interpretation in his novels and criticism. Each analysis is calculated to grasp the text as a creative process, and tries to reproduce a moment of creation defined as the literary moment *par excellence*. This critic does not offer an objective method of observation to be adopted by the general public; instead, he stresses a manner of reading that espouses the work's structure of consciousness. Each text, he says, has a unique structure of consciousness, although this unique structure represents an existential awareness that all great texts have in common. Blanchot, then, shares the Geneva critics' view that literature is an act of consciousness, and that true criticism must be a "criticism of consciousness." He is not a "critic," if the term implies using a public method that can be imitated, but he is an *analyst* of literature who probes, in criticism and novel, the many forms taken by literature as consciousness.

CONCLUSION

The Geneva School and Maurice Blanchot act as two poles of a theory of consciousness in literature. This theory is still developing, and thus cannot belong exclusively to a fixed group of men. However, the critics discussed here represent the beginnings and present development of the criticism of consciousness and illustrate a wide range of its possible interpretations. They all analyze literature as an act of awareness: awareness of the self, of external reality, and of the linguistic structures that express such awareness. Although each critic develops his own view of consciousness in literature, they all analyze the way in which literature incarnates conscious experience.

The word "incarnate" may seem too strong, and yet it is a key word in this theory. For these critics, the "author" is not the man who wrote the book but the implied being who gradually assumes form as the work is created. The text itself depicts this "author," just as a photograph would depict the historical author. The historical author gives birth to the text, but only by lending his skill in writing so that the book may take form. Once the book has been written, it is independent of its writer; it has become an "object" of analysis, but a "living object" that expresses a new life. The "author" is incarnate in the book because he does not exist outside it.

The goal of the critics of consciousness is to make the acquaintance of this incarnate author—or better, to reproduce his experience in themselves. As the "author" begins to take form and reconcile his separate visions of reality, the critic tries to duplicate this awakening by accepting all the forms of its experience, by espousing the themes and stylistic rhythm of the work. Any other manner of reading would be useless for a critic of consciousness, and he is especially opposed to an objective analysis that paralyzes the living act of literary creation.

When the "author" takes form in the book, he is conscious of several kinds of experience. He is aware of his own subjective nature, of the physical world that surrounds him, and of a conflict between the inner and outer worlds that he must reconcile into a coherent structure of experience. Each critic may stress a different aspect of literary experience, but he will fit his chosen aspect into a comprehensive description of the "author's" total experience.

All the critics discussed here hold to this general approach of analyzing literary consciousness, but they differ in the interpretation they give to literary experience. Such differences reflect personal value systems, however, and do not affect the approach itself. The Geneva School tends to see literary experience as a positive, individual creation that reflects a fixed (perhaps divine) universe. Blanchot, on the other hand, sees no positive creation in literature, but only a repeated evocation of a basic, formless sense of existence into which all things resolve. Both interpretations still refer to the same view of literature as an act of consciousness; but one is the positive consciousness of an approachable reality, and the other is a negative consciousness that denies all possibility of real knowledge.

Blanchot and the Geneva School share one further belief: their assumption that literature specially reflects man's knowledge of reality.

This assumption is not shared by the "structural" critics, who see literature as only one source of data for human consciousness. For the critics of consciousness, however, literature has a privileged position in that it is the only real transcription of existence available to man. Their belief that literature incarnates reality is based on a theory of language, a theory that man's ability to create and use language defines him and sets him apart from the rest of creation. Language is used to its fullest potential in literature for two reasons: the author is specially endowed with the power to understand and use speech, and he manipulates whole structures of language in his work. Because of the writer's special relationship to language, then, and because the critics of consciousness believe in language as the definitive human expression of experience, literature emerges for these critics as the supreme incarnation of human consciousness.

The critics of consciousness represent first of all the development of a literary attitude, and only indirectly a philosophical theory. A familiarity with their works provides a fairly accurate picture of the existential perspective as it is now applied to literary criticism, and is useful for readers who wish to move outside their own historical and educational perspective. Ultimately, however, the appropriate question for a reader is not "Are these men good existential philosophers?" but rather "Do they make a convincing case for the application of an existential perspective to literary analysis?" If the answer to this question is a tentative *yes*, it is a *yes* that calculates the amount of enrichment the existential view can bring to the reader's experience, and not an exclusive adoption of the whole existential theory.

There is, of course, no one "existential theory." These "existential" critics already differ and are even now still developing their separate procedures. They do have in common a distinct area of reference, whose scope and illumination is different from that of other critiques. Although eclecticism is frowned upon by formalists and critics of consciousness alike, it is only reasonable to ask how each reading can enlarge (and yet keep exclusively literary) the definition of literature and of literary work. Formal criticism has already defined its realm of analysis, and has proved its relevance to the text's formal aspect: the critics of consciousness do not dispute this achievement, but focus on another realm entirely. It is for them to prove the relevance of that realm to the commonly recognized works of literature which they discuss, and to show that their definition does not contradict (however much it may ignore) the other aspects of literature. These critics are not at a loss, however, for examples of the historical importance and theoretical relevance of the existential view.

This criticism's most obvious claim to our attention is that it reflects a broad stream of contemporary thought, a humanistic revival which is only part of a larger social transformation. This revival draws many contemporary writers, artists, philosophers, and theologians to erect a humanistic system of values outside the old disciplines of religion or the state, and to establish each person's spiritual fulfilment as a human being as the ultimate standard of value. In aesthetic terms, this revival provides for a re-evaluation of previous standards and limitations, and broadens the references of all art by multiplying its paths into the human consciousness. Such an historical comparison is not, of course, a theoretical justification of the criticism of consciousness. It does indicate that this criticism is validly modern; and as such it illuminates similar contemporary ways of thought and expression.

Whether this movement is called a criticism of consciousness, existentialism, neo-romanticism, neo-humanism, geneticism, or something else, it reflects a general pattern of inquiry into human consciousness and human identity. It is no news that the impressionists, Dadaists, surrealists, cubists, and neo-realists experiment with various human perspectives. Composers of atonal and electronic music also manipulate sound to find new paths into the human consciousness, and new responses from audiences forced to react outside the sphere of their previous experience. Modern dance and ballet build upon previous choreographic techniques to evolve new manners of framing and revealing the human personality. In literature itself there is a dissolution of old genres which reflects their inability to formulate a new perspective. From the "stream of consciousness" technique to the "new novel," old concepts of plot and character dissolve to follow man's shifting perceptions before human and material reality. Modern theater mocks the artificial separation of actor and audience, and destroys old concepts of theatrical reality to place man at the center of the stage. Movies experiment with oblique and eccentric photographic effects, with spontaneous lines and gestures, to recover a sense of immediacy from the paralyzing stereotypes of cinematic habit. If the techniques are different, the aim is one and the same: to recapture a sense of human consciousness in art, and to focus and communicate human experience beyond (or transparently through) the devices of form.

Many contemporary artists experiment with forms to incarnate their examination of man in the universe. Here there is a definite split between "modern" writers using familiar "realistic" techniques and modern writers trying to find a modern perspective for their expression. Just as Sarraute and Robbe-Grillet have thrown the concept of the novel into question by rejecting Balzacian plot forms and biographical characterizations, so certain playwrights have also rejected familiar dramatic realism for a more experimental perspective—and in doing so have questioned the limited scope of the "new novel's" rebellion. *Le Voyeur* and *Le Planétarium* reject the old historical, biographical, rationalizing and comprehensive approach to plot and character; and so do *En Attendant Godot, Who's Afraid of Virginia Woolf,* and *The Caretaker.* In varying degrees, this new theater creates consciously flat characters who reject the very orthodox reality they seem to present. All three plays hint at a different perspective and projection of human reality in which the characters live out their lives. This new technique is all the more obvious as an "existential" method of presentation if one sees that it directly contraverts the realistic staging and "rounded" characterizations of Sartre—who conveys a contemporary philosophy through familiar nineteenth-century stage techniques rather than through inventions and experiments in genre. Sartre, from "Les Mouches" to "Les Séquestrés d'Altona," permits his characters to remain real psychological entities with approachable problems and philosophies. He never disturbs his audience by presenting what would indeed be the concrete statement of existential "anguish": characters amputated from a reality which they strive to grasp and create before our eyes. Whatever the formal elements which our traditional criticism will rightly single out in these more experimental works, there still remains a new technique of presentation which has more direct relevance to the existential perspective than to the biographical and realistic forms of nineteenth-century novel and drama. There is, in the case of Sarraute, Robbe-Grillet, Beckett, Albee, Pinter (and perhaps René Char opposed to St.-John Perse, Antonioni as opposed to Fellini) a conscious rejection of the picture of a rounded, integral human being as subject of art. Here is a desire to present not merely characters in search of a soul, but parts of human beings struggling to create themselves as larger beings, as parts of a coherent universe.

To assert that the criticism of consciousness illuminates similar trends in contemporary art and literature is not to prove its relevance as literary criticism. If this criticism is to be more than a mere expression of modern taste, it must shed new light on old literature from an angle not hitherto explored. It must offer new insight to readers who are not committed to existential values, and offer this insight in a way that does not depend upon any extra-literary definitions. The criticism of consciousness is not extra-literary in the sense that it ever goes outside its own definition of literature, or bases its arguments on information not represented in the text. It often shocks readers brought up in the formal tradition, nonetheless, and many of these readers dub it "extra-literary" as soon as they find that this criticism simply does not bother discussing the purely formal characteristics of the work as object. The criticism of consciousness does have a potential niche alongside formal criticism, however, in a realm at which formal criticism hints but refuses to explore.

This proper realm of the criticism of consciousness is the same realm that formal critics skirt, but try to imply, when they use words such as "flavor," "uniqueness," "quality," "impact," and the much-misused "greatness." No good formal critic, of course, neglects trying to bring out such qualities through his objective analysis, and in practice he often succeeds. G. W. Knight has already recognized a difference in level between "good" and "great" literature, and the prevailing formal assumption is that one will reach an idea of "greatness" by a thoroughgoing analysis of what is "good." Evidently, an approved moral content does not make a work either "good" or "great," and the need remains for a cogent analysis of the human qualities made formal in literature. Whatever the separate successes of formal criticism, there remains a wide gap between formal standards of measurement and the analysis of human qualities in literary terms. Objective criticism recognizes problems of "sincerity," "authenticity," "greatness," "flavor," "maturity," and "humanity," as well as a host of allied impressions, but is forced to conclude that these are mere subjective impressions and as such are either deceptive or impossible to analyze. It is precisely these impressions that form the material for a criticism of human consciousness, which provides an example and a systematic means of attacking these heretofore untouchable problems.

If such terms as "sincerity" and "greatness" are to be considered at all (and one reaction of formal criticism is to reject them altogether), they imply a relationship of the text with human experience. This relationship in the criticism of consciousness is very different from anything envisaged in formal theory. When formal criticism considers human undercurrents, it sees them as subjective elements influencing (but separate from) the final work. Small wonder that such a criticism is unable to trust its evocation of a human experience which it keeps always at a distance. The criticism of consciousness tries to combine the given words of the text with the subjective, latent state of this same text, and then measures the coordination of these two poles. When Poulet remarks that Lebrun Pindare's lines on the topos of the sphere whose center is nowhere are cold, wordy, and unfelt, he gives as a reason that Lebrun cannot believe in the world view he expresses. Although the critic does not carry his argument any farther at this point, what he has suggested is a form of coordination between expression and experience which can be analyzed textually—using his own criteria. If Poulet's work (taken as representative of much that is best in this criticism) undertakes to reproduce the actual patterns of a man's perception and development, then a correlation of the deduced pattern and that asserted by Lebrun should either coincide or fail. It is their lack of coordination which causes these lines to be flat and inauthentic, in Poulet's terms. The criticism of consciousness examines primarily the coordination of experience and expression, and its method of analysis and stress in evaluation will be quite different from the formal criteria with which we are familiar.

Most of the critics discussed here emphasize the pole of experience rather than that of expression. This emphasis is only to be expected in a theory which is just now beginning to be accepted as a valid way of looking at literature. Poulet himself begins with the rudiments of his later method; with categories of time and space in which to collect human data for further processing. Before him, Raymond and Béguin struggle to winnow out what is new in their own perspective from a multitude of traditional ways of looking at literature. These theories are all in the process of developing and making their way in the world, and they naturally tend to overemphasize the novelty of their view and its difference from prevailing schools of thought. Only Miller (perhaps for geographical reasons) reaches a compromise between formal and existential techniques in a system of alternate reading: a system which is approved, if not always practiced, by his fellow critics.

Is there a function for such criticism, beyond what it does with terms like "authenticity," "maturity," and "humanity"? From the example of its practice, it appears that the specific interpretations given to matter (more exactly, the phenomenological interpretations) involve observations which are duplicated nowhere else. The shifting perceptions of matter in either traditional or modern authors are a subject peculiarly adapted to this criticism. When Miller speaks of the Podsnaps' ugly, massive, impersonal, and impenetrable silverplate, he identifies a literary expression of a manner of seeing the world: he implies the Podsnaps' relations with the world in which they live, and the vision in Dickens which allowed him to create such a picture. This same silverplate can be interpreted as a simple setting (photographic realism), as historical color, as a psychological symptom or a sociological phenomenon, and as a formal recall of similar descriptions. A political existentialism, such as Sartre's, would not pause long before condemning the antisocial meaninglessness of this display of shiny matter. All these interpretations are possible separate analyses, but they are all also linked into the image of a way of life which none alone suggests. This over-all image is the interpretation provided by the criticism of consciousness in a reading which does not depend on exterior standards but adopts the universe of the author momentarily in order to understand it. With this sympathetic identification comes the ability to feel a new coordination of subject and object, and a subsequent desire to emerge from this experience and report its order of perception. This ambitious project is duplicated by no other literary theory or practice, and remains the peculiar province of the criticism of consciousness.

Not all critics will be able to pursue both the formal and the existential approach at once, nor will they choose to. These are indeed two separate critiques, each with its own frame of reference, and they may well not be compatible for the same critic at the same time. Whether or not one accepts the validity of this literary perspective is a matter of personal choice and evaluation. On the other hand, the criticism of consciousness is distinctly able to broaden the horizons of readers educated in the objective tradition of criticism. These critics offer the glimpse of a new dimension in literary perception, and their example uncovers substructures of the objective work which point to hitherto unseen or unappreciated formal echoes. Blanchot's description of Lautréamont manipulating the reader's response, and of the narrow vision in Henry Miller's images, Poulet's analysis of Proust's panoramic vision, Miller's demonstration of interrelated patterns of discovery between Dickens' novels, Richard's utopian work which governs the real one, Starobinski's analysis of the invention of forms in the eighteenth century, and many other such observations are sufficient in their own field but can easily lay the groundwork for a separate formal analysis. These two approaches are interrelated even if they cannot be superimposed, and it is possible to move from one level to the other without losing sight of the same literary work. A comprehensive view of this work is always dependent on the breadth of the definition of literature applied to it, which depends in turn on the individual reader's imagination and ingenuity. The place of the criticism of consciousness in an ideally comprehensive view is assured by its discovery of literature as a tracery of human perceptions, present in the creating mind, latent in the work, and given a new and final genesis by the act of reading.

INDEX

INDEX

"Allemagne *1926–28*," *see* Raymond
Ame romantique et le rêve, L', *see* Béguin
Amiel, H. Fr., 98, 99, 104
Amindanab, *see* Blanchot
Anticlassical tradition, 22, 23, 31, 35, 37, 38, 47, 62
Arnold, Matthew, 205–206, 207
Arrêt de mort, L', *see* Blanchot
Artaud, Antonin, 69, 238, 249
Attente l'oubli, L', *see* Blanchot
Aubigné, Agrippa, d', 23, 27–28
Authentic expression: style representing experience, 6, 44, 63, 64, 248; "whole" expression, 24; automatic writing, 228
Author: incarnate in text (as literary being or *moi*), 7, 28, 29 87, 139n, 171; as *cogito,* 13, 43, 77, 86–90 *passim,* 94–99 *passim,* 114–116 *passim,* 123, 124, 135; as creator, 25, 65, 170–171; representing humanity, 27, 39; foyer, 61, 102, 191; existential writer, 228, 254
Automatic writing, 228

Bachelard, Gaston, 13–14, 29, 37, 70–76 *passim,* 79, 123–124, 126, 131, 141, 143, 144, 161, 188, 189, 260
Balzac, Honoré de, 93–94, 100–102
Barthes, Roland, 70
Baudelaire, Charles, 23, 32, 37, 86, 97, 98, 102–103, 113, 114, 116, 120, 143, 146–148 *passim,* 152, 154, 155, 249, 262–264 *passim*
Béguin, Albert, 11, 27, 40, 49–73, 74, 75, 79, 81, 82, 84, 102, 112, 121n, 124–125, 126, 141, 188, 262; *L'Ame romantique et le rêve,* 52–55; *Cahiers du Rhône,* 58–59; *La Prière de Péguy,* 60–61; *L'Eve de Péguy,* 61; *Pascal*

Béguin, Albert (*Cont.*)
par lui-même, 62; *Bernanos par lui-même,* 63; *Balzac visionnaire,* 63–66
Bergson, Henri, 37, 59, 76, 110
Bernanos, Georges, 57, 63, 114, 116, 117
Bernanos par lui-même, *see* Béguin
Blanchot, Maurice, 4–8 *passim,* 70, 79, 98, 99, 104, 120n, 126–127, 131, 166, 221–265; "Comment la littérature est-elle possible?" 226; "La Littérature et le droit à la mort," 229–232; *Faux pas,* 227–229, 233–235 *passim; La Part du feu,* 229–235; "Du Merveilleux," 236; *Thomas l'obscur,* 236–237; *Amindanab,* 237; *L'Arrêt de mort,* 237–238; *Le Dernier Mot,* 239; *L'Espace Littéraire,* 240–245; *Le Livre à venir,* 240, 246–249; "Freud," 250; "La Question la plus profonde," 250–254, 256; *Le Dernier Homme,* 255; *L'Attente l'oubli,* 256–258; *Lautréamont et Sade,* 258–261
Bloy, Léon, 57
Boehme, Jacob, 98
Bonnefoy, Yves, 2, 156, 162
Breton, André, 114
Broch Hermann, 248
Brontë, Emily, 204–205
Browning, Robert, 203–204, 216
Burton, Robert, 180–181
Butor, Michel, 264
Byron, George Gordon, lord, 119

Cahiers du Rhône, *see* Béguin; Raymond
Camus, Albert, 3, 115, 192, 245
Céline, Louis Ferdinand, 155–156
Char, René, 114, 117, 156, 161–163
Chardin, Jean-Baptiste, 179
Charles Dickens: The World of His Novels, *see* Miller
Chateaubriand, René, 114

277